Special Sound

THE OXFORD MUSIC / MEDIA SERIES

DANIEL GOLDMARK, SERIES EDITOR

oxford
music/media series

Tuning In: American Narrative Television Music
RON RODMAN

Special Sound: The Creation and Legacy of the BBC Radiophonic Workshop
LOUIS NIEBUR

Special Sound

The Creation and Legacy of the BBC Radiophonic Workshop

LOUIS NIEBUR

OXFORD
UNIVERSITY PRESS
2010

OXFORD
UNIVERSITY PRESS

Oxford University Press, Inc., publishes works that further
Oxford University's objective of excellence
in research, scholarship, and education.

Oxford   New York
Auckland   Cape Town   Dar es Salaam   Hong Kong   Karachi
Kuala Lumpur   Madrid   Melbourne   Mexico City   Nairobi
New Delhi   Shanghai   Taipei   Toronto

With offices in
Argentina   Austria   Brazil   Chile   Czech Republic   France   Greece
Guatemala   Hungary   Italy   Japan   Poland   Portugal   Singapore
South Korea   Switzerland   Thailand   Turkey   Ukraine   Vietnam

Published by Oxford University Press, Inc.
198 Madison Avenue, New York, New York 10016

www.oup.com

Oxford is a registered trademark of Oxford University Press

Library of Congress Cataloging-in-Publication Data
Niebur, Louis, 1971–
Special sound: the creation and legacy of the BBC Radiophonic Workshop / Louis Niebur.
p. cm. — (The Oxford music/media series)
Includes bibliographical references and index.
ISBN 978-0-19-536840-6; 978-0-19-536841-3 (pbk.)
1. BBC Radiophonic Workshop—History.   2. Electronic music—Great Britain—
History and criticism.   3. Radio music—Great Britain—History and criticism.
4. Television music—Great Britain—History and criticism.
5. Sound—Psychological aspects.
I. Title.
ML32.G7N54 2010
786.706'041—dc22   2009045761

Recorded audio tracks (marked in text with 🔊) are available online at www.oup.com/us/specialsound
Access with username Music2 and password Book4416
For more information on Oxford Web Music, visit www.oxfordwebmusic.com

3 5 7 9 8 4 6 2
Printed in the United States of America

To my parents, Stephen and Linda, for their love and support

Acknowledgments

I would like to thank the BBC Written Archives Centre, Caversham, Reading, for permission to quote from archive documents, and Julie Snelling and Rachel Bowles in particular for indispensable research assistance. All transcriptions are by the author.

Thank you to the University of Nevada, Reno, College of Liberal Arts and the Department of Music and Dance, who generously funded my research. I would also like to thank the Barry S. Brook Publication Endowment Fund of the AMS for their generous support. David Gilbert and Bridget Risemberg and the staff of the UCLA Music Library. Lucy Stoy at the UNR Multimedia Center. The British Library, the BBC Windmill Road Archive, Tim Day and the National Sound Archive. I couldn't have written this book without the clerical assistance of Katherine Goodyear, Courtney Klipp, Erika Chau, at UCLA, and Julia Bledsoe and Cynthia Prescott at UNR. Nina Mackey, who got me thinking. Mark Ayres, Gary Gillett, Clayton Hickman, Gary Russell, Ed Salt, Mike Ivy, Tristram Cary, UKNova, Jay Dennis, James Kenneway, Chris Kenneway, Byron Adams, Christina Baade, Jennifer Doctor, Christopher Scheer, Aaron Cain, Sue Ellen Case, Philip Brett, Claudia Gorbman, Andrew Dell'Antonio. Mitchell Morris, Julianne Lindberg, Chris Montandon, Drew Davies, Adam Burton, Damon Stevens, David Ake and Mikel Alvarez. Extra special thanks to Paul Condon and Jim Sangster. A very special thank-you to the composers and engineers of the Radiophonic Workshop, especially Richard Attree, Desmond Briscoe, David Cain, Maddalena Fagandini, Jonathan Gibbs, Brian Hodgson, Peter Howell, Paddy Kingsland, Roger Limb, Dick Mills, Elizabeth Parker, Ray White, and Richard Yeoman-Clark. Natalie, Mike and Violet Lukich, K-9, and Oscar for keeping me smiling, and, of course, Scott Evans, always supportive in the face of overwhelming nerdiness.

Contents

About the Companion Web Site   xi

1   Radio Drama and the Birth of Electronic Music   3

2   Ideological Struggles and Pragmatic Realities   35

3   The Golden Age of Special Sound   64

4   The Coming of the Synthesizers   120

5   The Second Golden Age   157

6   The Price of Success   182

Notes   219

Selected Bibliography   239

Index   247

About the Companion Web Site

www.oup.com/us/specialsound

Oxford has created a password-protected Web site to accompany *Special Sound*, containing many musical and video examples from throughout the Radiophonic Workshop's long history. Readers are encouraged to watch and listen as they read. A book like this, concerned as it is with discussing unique and strange timbres, is aided immensely by the ability to direct the reader to the Workshop's actual sounds, tunes, and harmonies.

Examples available online are found throughout the text and are signaled with Oxford's symbol ◑.

Special Sound

1

Radio Drama and the Birth of Electronic Music

Origins

We in the twenty-first century are surrounded by electronic music. And the British Broadcasting Corporation's (BBC) electronic music studio, the Radiophonic Workshop, which operated from 1958 to 1998 had a significant role in creating this state of affairs. Most musicologists would probably balk at this statement, but the simple fact remains that to unravel a narrative of the past century's music that leads to its ubiquity in this one requires us to reexamine the story of the creation and development of electronic music as it has traditionally been told. One soon realizes that the standard story cannot begin to account for this music's presence in nearly all aspects of contemporary media, at every level of musical production, from the most esoteric art music to the humblest radio advertising jingle. Part of the problem until now has been the limited scope of inquiry by scholars. The narrative created by music historians does not usually begin until after the Second World War, so it predictably finds itself poised firmly between two academic centers of the postwar musical avant-garde: Paris and Cologne. Musicologists' tendency to describe the origins of electronic music as the near-exclusive domain of these two locations is borne out in those few pieces that have made it into the tentative canon of postwar "classical" musical works. This is not to devalue the innovations created through the musical experimentation at Paris and Cologne (as well as a few other sites, like the Columbia-Princeton studio); these innovations were invaluable. On the contrary, most of the world's electronic studios that later emerged depended on this groundwork to establish their initial techniques of production. I offer the possibility, however, that the development of the electronic music that surrounds us today was influenced as much or more by other factors, in particular a specifically English brand of music originating outside the sanctioned musical establishment.

Francis Bacon's prescient theorizing of "Sound-houses" in his *New Atlantis* of 1627 might be the first exploration of the notion that music could be created from sound sources other than traditional musical "instruments." But it would be several hundred more years before this theory was expanded upon by the early-twentieth-century Italian Futurist movement, the history of which has been recounted several times.[1] In Paris in the 1940s the experiments of Pierre Schaeffer (1910–95) unveiled the true potential of a music composed by the alteration of previously existing sounds. Initially he attempted to manipulate sounds recorded from his environment by rerecording them in a controlled way onto shellac discs. With the development and availability of the more versatile magnetic tape after the war, Schaeffer created a body of work posited on these principles of *musique concrète*. These experiments influenced an entire generation of French composers, including his greatest ally and collaborator, Pierre Henry (b. 1927).[2] Around the same time in Germany, composers such as Herbert Eimert (1897–1972) were exploring the use of electronic sound sources in contemporary music. The principles behind this *elektronische Musik* were closely associated with politically powerful serial techniques in vogue at the time in academic circles in Europe and America. Eimert and others, such as Karlheinz Stockhausen (1928–2007), saw in electronic composition a completely new way of constructing timbre from scratch. Stockhausen's disenchantment with traditional instruments was articulated in his statement that "any attempt to subordinate the different structures of the different instrumental tones to a general rational principle of proportions is bound to fail."[3] Inherent in such a comment is the root of a profound difference between the two camps of the burgeoning electronic music culture. The Germans believed that by using preexisting sounds as the concretists did, always retaining some hint of associative baggage, it was impossible to create something entirely new.

In a historical interpretation that ultimately favors German techniques it is invariably Stockhausen who, after studying *concrète* techniques with Schaeffer before moving on to "pure" electronic sound, is credited with converging the two styles into what would become electro-acoustic music. The work that demonstrates this convergence most prominently is his 1956 work *Gesang der Jünglinge*. This interpretation, however, ignores French works that essentially do the same thing by taking advantage of the developments in electronics at Cologne (Henry's 1956 *Haut voltage*, for example). It also downplays Schaeffer's sympathy for serial composition. His disapproval was mostly directed at those using the method, and their stubbornness in limiting themselves to such a small number of notes, rather than at the principles behind the method.

But there was one aspect of the philosophical foundation of electronic music both sides agreed on and ultimately positioned themselves against. This principle was the suitability of electronic music for television, film, or radio. They considered this use an insult to the music, reducing its importance by ultimately turning it into a servant of the words or images it was meant to "support." In a manifesto on the principles behind *elektronische Musik*, H. H. Stuckenschmidt dismissed this usage outright, declaring that "as spokesman for the group, Eimert has disassociated himself from . . . any incidental manipulations or distortions haphazardly put together for radio, film or theater music."[4]

The basis for this initial disagreement was that Parisian *musique concrète* was thought to convey the original character of its original sounds too greatly, but the two sides agreed that to highlight or accent this "flaw" was a fundamental error of aesthetic judgment. They both knew that film and radio would latch onto this supposed flaw as an advantage. The musical culture out of which both *musique concrète* and *elektronische Musik* grew was inextricably bound up in nineteenth-century Romantic notions of musical autonomy and the idea that each composition should be functional—that is, oriented toward an internal integrity. Audiences (and composers) of modernist concert music by the middle of the twentieth century had been carefully indoctrinated to regard the value in music as residing primarily in its foundational structures, its building blocks, and they listened for these organizing principles with what Theodor Adorno called "structural listening." Academic music—that is, music worth listening to—was meant to have developed along a purely artistic path from the end of the eighteenth century toward greater and greater dissonance until the needs of composers could be met only by the creation of artificial sounds.

Luckily, the observation that electronic music was suitable for a specific kind of dramatic situation was noticed early on by a group of British enthusiasts, who followed in the footsteps of French radio drama and German *Hörspiele* producers. It was, of course, exactly the kinds of sounds produced by this supposed detachment from the outside world, from culturally contingent concerns, that most appealed to these producers. The outlandishly dissonant language of electronic music, as inherited from Schoenbergian expressionism, was, as Susan McClary noted, "one derived ultimately from a condensation of traditional signs of madness, rage, suffering."[5] If one were to add to this list signs of paranoia, alienation, and fear of the unknown, it is a short leap to a representation of the unknown itself—space, aliens. This music, supposedly free from any kind of signification, in fact contains a rich vocabulary of stereotyped associations, ready to be drawn upon at will. It should come as no surprise, then, that the original drive to create an electronic studio at the BBC would come not from their Music Department, but rather from the Drama and Features Departments.

The BBC

The BBC started life as the British Broadcasting Company from 1922 to 1926. It was incorporated in 1927 as a monopoly with exclusive rights to broadcast free from commercial interests. In considering the issue of advertising, the leaders in government and within the BBC were concerned by their perceptions of American radio; the free-market, sponsor-based broadcasting there seemed to represent a lack of standards, stemming from the need to satisfy sponsors. From its very beginning, the BBC controlled most of the professional music making in Great Britain. As the largest producer and distributor of music in the United Kingdom, the BBC was continually faced with the challenge of satisfying all musical tastes from within one centralized location. Historians Paddy Scannell and David Cardiff accurately describe two conflicting policies at work within the organization: On the one hand, the BBC vowed to maintain a high standard of excellence for the performance of what was deemed "great music." On the other, the Corporation carried with it the mandate of its first director general, John Reith, who believed above all else in the cultural education of the population at large.[6] This "democratizing of music" manifested itself through aggressive music appreciation campaigns. In practical terms, during the early to mid-1920s the central administration was governed by the belief that "new" signified "great," choosing Music Department programming staff on that basis and exposing listening audiences, most of whom were not experts or experienced music listeners, to challenging works by modernist composers, such as Schoenberg, Stravinsky, and Bartók. By the 1930s, the administration had shifted its music policy, aiming instead to preserve and disseminate the standard "greats" of the classical repertoire (Bach, Mozart, Beethoven, Schubert, Brahms, etc.), opening a schism with the Music Department, which continued to program new music with enthusiasm.

As early as 1924, there had been talk of creating a separate network to offer "highbrow education and better class material."[7] Although the notion was dropped then, it was revived in 1930, when J. C. Stobart, the director of the BBC's Education Department, recommended the creation of what he called the "Minerva Programme," which would cater to an older audience and feature gardening tips, nature programs, and religion.[8] Alongside this, Stobart envisioned the "Venus Programme" as the home of more avant-garde music. One of the original intentions of the second proposed service was that it would offer rather than impose culture. These proposals weren't pursued immediately, but the idea of a cultural service arose again during the early years of the Second World War, when the BBC began to seriously consider how to deliver the ideals of cultural programming within a public service environment. Ultimately, the BBC divided its postwar radio output into three distinct networks polarized around musical and cultural/class difference: the Home Service, the Light Programme, and the Third Programme. This third network would offer the kinds of highbrow programming the advocates of music craved, as well as productions of "challenging" dramatic works.

The Third Programme's musical output, however, largely maintained the entrenched attitudes of the administration rather than the more progressive elements within the Music Department. By the mid-1950s, many within the Music Department itself had been largely converted to the more modest aims of the "music appreciation" attitude that dominated the midcentury BBC. There *was*, however, a small public for difficult, contemporary music. This audience craved examples of Germanic *elektronische Musik* based on serial principles, and the more abstract French *musique concrète*, and their voices weren't entirely unheard. By the end of the 1950s, and into the 1960s, these audiences in favor of a more challenging music reacted to the paucity of contemporary music on the Third. One listener with the pseudonym "D. Reihe" wrote to the *Radio Times*, "I am heartily tired of seeing so many letters from people without the patience or intellectual capacity to appreciate modern music. I suggest we might have one week every year during which, in the Third Programme at least, all tonal music was completely banned."[9] This suggestion was not taken up, but the opinion was not unique: "I had thought that we had now reached in our musically backward country a point where even those who do not regard atonality as inevitable and dodecaphony as logical are at least willing to admit that it is a legitimate genre."[10] This reflects the challenge Third Programme administrators faced: balancing the desire to expose audiences to contemporary music and the need to satisfy larger, more conservative audiences with "easier" music. This challenge would only intensify with the increasing presence of electronic music throughout the 1960s, which for many defied the very definition of "music."

Radio Drama

There is a stunning disparity between producers, audiences, and critics interested in difficult new music and equally difficult new drama. After the war, drama on the Third Programme encouraged both the technical innovations made possible by tape recordings and the fundamentally different and original theatrical works emerging from France (as exemplified by Jean-Paul Sartre, Samuel Beckett, Jean Anouilh, and others). This postwar development in the Drama Department was far from new. In fact, it was the BBC's successful struggle to develop experimental theater through the use of radical techniques *before* the war that determined the Corporation's significant influence in this sphere in the decades following. For example, the battles in the 1920s and 1930s between experimental producer Lance Sieveking and his nemesis, Val Gielgud, head of the Drama Department, encouraged a consistently cutting-edge output. With ideas from other important innovators as well, there emerged in the 1930s a new kind of broadcasting: BBC "Features," a uniquely British combination of documentary reporting and dramatic storytelling that embraced revolutionary sound techniques.

Almost all of the postwar broadcasts of plays and music containing electronic and concrete sound were on the Third Programme, but as an editorial branch, it produced no original content. Rather, it was the supply departments (Features, Drama, etc.) that produced programs and offered them to the editorial departments. These departments then arranged their schedules according to the material with which they were presented. The editorial branches were nevertheless empowered to commission works, and frequently did so. The Third Programme was exceedingly confident in its dramatic and poetic broadcasts, and during its first ten years, as it settled into its role as "cultural provider" for Britain, commissioned some of the most important radio plays ever to emerge from that genre. These included Dylan Thomas's *Under Milk Wood* and Beckett's *All That Fall*. Cutting-edge stage drama, especially those works associated with the revolutionary Theatre of the Absurd movement, exerted a profound influence on BBC radio drama producers. Douglas Cleverdon and Donald McWhinnie (from Drama Department and Features), in particular, pushed sound design to its limit. Martin Esslin, in his essential book *The Theatre of the Absurd*, described the movement, which contained authors as different in style as Eugène Ionesco, Arthur Adamov, Jean Genet, and Harold Pinter, as coalescing around the idea of "a world deprived of a generally accepted integrating principle, which has become disjointed, purposeless—absurd."[11] Having their basis in nineteenth-century nonsense poetry, music hall traditions, and early-twentieth-century surrealism, Theatre of the Absurd plays, according to Esslin, "express [the] sense of the senselessness of the human condition and the inadequacy of the rational approach by the open abandonment of rational devices and discursive thought."[12] Although the absurdist authors were not part of any organized "movement," their works nevertheless make manifest the disjointed senselessness and irrationality of the universe, depicting it through senselessness and irrationality. The radio plays conceived under its influence then were unified by an insistence on an anti-realist aesthetic, embracing sound techniques geared toward the odd, surreal, and distorted, and existing as a bridge between poetry or music and reality. Alienating their audience through the removal of the sounds of a familiar reality, the radio works used electronics and words in a way unique to Britain. It

is from within this system that the first use of electronic sound in Britain reso-
nated as a result of an effort to integrate what had been purely musical concep-
tions of electronic music into established dramatic movements.

Radio Comedy

Perhaps the most exciting thing about the creation of the BBC's own electronic
studio at the end of the 1950s is the way so many factors played a part in its
development. Yes, the early works to emerge from the studio incorporated
Continental academic electronic techniques into an already-experimental corporate radio drama culture. But almost from the beginning, much lower-brow,
populist programming had played with sound in interesting ways, particularly in
radio comedy and science fiction on the Home and Light Programmes. Radio
comedy's early and modest use of electronic sound effects belies the profound
influence these sounds had on later dramatic productions. The ephemeral, top-
ical nature of comedy and variety programming makes it particularly vulnerable
to scholarly neglect, but, as one would imagine, in a genre so often dependent
on the selection of the right sound for the right gag, comedy formed a vital
location for experimentation in sound production.

Influenced by earlier rapid-fire sketch comedy programs such as *It's That Man
Again*, *The Goon Show* exploited sound to depict impossible scenarios and ridiculous situations. But unlike earlier series, *The Goon Show* exploited the surreal to
a degree theretofore unheard in comedy. In this program, comic sequences didn't
have to connect in any logical or rational progression; rather, something as simple
as a random sound effect could bridge scenes, or entire sequences could consist
of nothing but a collection of sound effects. The long-running radio series began
in 1951, with Spike Milligan, Harry Secombe, Peter Sellers, and, in the first two
series, Michael Bentine. By 1953 the remaining trio had evolved into *The Goon
Show*, with an established set of recurring characters as the loose framework for
each week's Light Programme entertainment. It ran continuously until 1959.
From the beginning, the trio made full use of the range of traditional sound
effects (car sounds, explosions, crowd noises, etc.), but by the fourth or fifth
series they really began to move outside traditional boundaries. As the show's
style evolved, they began to alter and distort standard effects, becoming more
willing to push audience's abilities to understand what (if anything) these distortions were meant to represent (and this on the supposedly "easy" Light
Programme!).

One of the earliest and most basic tricks used on *The Goon Show* was the
speed-altered turntable or tape. In episode 19 of series 4, after a reference to

Scotland Yard, a chorus of bagpipes is heard to gradually speed up until they are stopped by Peter Sellers's character, Major Bloodnok. In what was already established by this time as a running gag, Bloodnok had a notoriously sour stomach, represented throughout the run of the program by a series of more and more outrageous sound effects. He calls the pipers to halt with an "Ooohhhh! That's enough, lads! Oooh! The wind in the pipes, oh dear!!!" The sped-up effect, either tape or disc, would have been inserted by what was known as a "grams operator" (another name for turntable was "gram," short for gramophone). In episode 2 of series 5, Harry Secombe's maniacal laugh is heard to speed up, and in episode 26 of that same series, a random sequence of Hawaiian music is sped up to a fever pitch before dropping out, functioning purely as a link between two scenes.

Probably the most virtuosic use of sound effects (and the most surreal) in the early *Goon Show* episodes occurs in episode 12 of series 6, broadcast December 6, 1955. The episode contains literally hundreds of effects during its thirty-minute running time, but some highlights include a sped-up funeral march, backward sped-up speech, and variable-speed-adjusted horse clip-clops. The episode opens with a subtle acknowledgment to the debt a complex program like this owes to sound technology—often with three grams operators armed with five or six turntables each, ready to insert the correct sound effect at the precise moment required. It also draws attention to the previously unproblematized presence of sound effects and grams itself. The announcer Wallace Greenslade begins, "This is the BBC Light Programme. Now here is a record. [Insert grams recording, 'This is the BBC Light Programme.'] Thank you." The audible pop and crackle of the grams sound effect recording, so often unintentionally apparent, here is highlighted as the gag. These surreal broadcasts, and the effects that drive them, are, by the late 1950s, simply begging for electronic methods to push them into even more extreme territory. As sound effects moved further and further from "realistic" versions of themselves, comedy radio moved into territory traditionally associated more with science fiction.[13] While the two genres approached these sounds from different directions, they ultimately arrived at the same place.

Radio Science Fiction

The first program on British radio that utilized electronic sound effects was *Journey into Space: A Tale of the Future*, an eighteen-part science fiction serial for children initially broadcast on the Light Programme from September 21, 1953, through January 19, 1954. Written by Charles Chilton, the series depicted Space

Captain Jet Morgan and his crew in their various attempts to explore space in the futuristic year 1965. The original series spawned two further serials, *Red Planet Mars* and *The World in Peril*, in 1954 and 1956. Although the first *Journey into Space* serial exists only in a version recorded in 1958 for the BBC's overseas transcription service (and renamed *Operation Luna*), the sound effects throughout all three serials, and this rerecording, were produced in the same way.

The two primary electronic sound effects for the program highlight the potential for confusion that such new noises could engender. The first sound, a rising electronic sine tone, is initially heard over the voice of the announcer bellowing "Journey! Into! Space!" The second sound effect is much more enigmatic. Heard after the rocket has been launched, and after the crew has lost contact with Earth, it is a more musical, more "alien" sound. It has no connection to any traditional sound, although it appears to be constructed of the same basic sine wave, with reverb added.

How are we meant to understand the significance of these new sounds? In particular, how would contemporary audiences have been expected to understand them? Film sound theory can provide an entry for constructing one possible explanation. When a character in a film picks up a violin and begins to play it in front of the camera, audiences understand both what the sound is and where it is coming from. They see the source of the sound and recognize the sound itself as belonging to that visualized object. There is synchronization between the image and the soundtrack. What happens if the violinist walks off camera *before* beginning to play? How does the audience know whether the sound is meant to be interpreted as diegetic or nondiegetic? Why should audiences believe in a sound emerging from a source invisible to them? Theorist Michel Chion has labeled this, a sound one hears without seeing the originating cause, *acousmatic*, and the object, the source of the sound, becomes an *acousmêtre*, a specter-like phenomenon that evokes an inherently mysterious unknowableness. Consequently, the *acousmêtre* has been a staple of the horror film: the all-knowing, all-seeing killer's voice on the telephone; a voice echoing out in a dark seemingly empty theater, calling to his frightened victim, who frantically looks around in search of the invisible voice.

The same acousmatic situation is potentially present when a transistor radio is shown in a film and music is meant to be playing from it. However, as Chion also notes, since a radio (unlike, say, a violin) has no one characteristic sound associated with it, the audience must think a bit harder about the source of the music or voices emerging from it. If the sound is music, is there any way for an audience to know whether the director intends for this to be diegetic music, emerging from the radio, or from some other diegetic source, or nondiegetic music, emerging from outside the film's diegesis? In this particular case,

11

filmmakers have developed certain stereotyped conventions involving timbre: filters and reduced volume levels, to reproduce in an exaggerated way the high- and low-frequency clipping present in a small radio with a cheap speaker. Audiences have learned to interpret these audio signs: although we recognize the visual object as a radio, we must accept on faith that the sound is emerging from this object.[14]

Science fiction film or television presents a different kind of problem, but one for which Chion's concept of acousmatic sound can be useful, albeit in a more focused sense. When, in a science fiction film, the audience is shown a piece of "advanced technology" making noise, they make the assumption that the artificial noise is emerging from the piece of fictional machinery. This is a kind of *synchresis*, Chion's term for a sound with a synchronized visual and auditory component.[15] Synchresis does not rely on an absolutely literal representation of a sound; rather, it is the combination of synthesis and synchronization that tends to make the listener believe an image and sound are related. Again, the sound and image do not necessarily need to be exact analogues: Chion uses the example of an axe chopping a log at the precise moment the visuals show a baseball player hitting the ball. It is "the forging of an immediate and necessary relationship between something one sees and something one hears at the same time."[16] But in the case of science fiction technology, is this really what is going on? It seems instead a mysterious kind of acousmatic sound, since the audience has no idea what kind of sound that particular piece of equipment should make; like the radio, the new equipment is not associated with a characteristic sound. In the case of a ray gun, or spaceship, the sounds are largely part of the imaginary—combining as they do the expectation of traditional sounds associated with the generic "type" of equipment, and an ignorance of the specific object—and are therefore impossible to truly understand in the sonic literalness of their representation. This problem is different again from the true *acousmêtre* of the robot in science fiction, who embodies mystery, wonder, and fear through the presence of a voice without the comforting image of a human face. Chion's terms as they stand do not account for this eventuality, and it is necessary to expand upon them. For those situations where created sounds exist as representations of a fictional technology, I will refer to "synchretic *acousmêtre*," since they embody elements of both terms at the same time.

How does one transfer the concepts of synchretic and acousmatic sound to broadcast radio, where there is ostensibly no visual component? I would argue that the conventional nature of most sound effects renders them, in radio, *virtually* synchretic in that an audience's assumptions of the source of sounds are generally proved correct. If a character in a radio play announces, "Hark! A horse approaches!" and the sound of galloping hooves (be they real horses or coconut shells) follows and gets louder, listeners do not need a visual picture of a horse to believe that a character has just ridden up on a horse. Here synchretic sound combines synthesis—the actual sound effect—with synchronization (a function of the dialogue, other sound effects, and context). Both of these elements are essential for a pure synchretic sound, and in this book I will refer to instances of synchresis in radio as "virtual synchresis," to indicate those moments when radio simulates such simultaneities. Likewise, although technically all sounds in radio are acousmatic, those particular moments that simulate the filmic technique of the *acousmêtre* in radio will be referred to as "virtually acousmatic." As Chion demonstrated, there can be degrees of synchresis, as embodied, for example, by badly dubbed films: one learns the customs and codes of filmic conventions at an early age, and the viewer judges whether or not both synthesis and synchronization have been totally successful. A sound can become acousmatic only when it loses that safety net of both synthesis and synchronization, a phenomenon familiar in science fiction, and as we have seen, such a sound can often venture into the territory of the synchretic acousmatic.

One potential problem with this reading of the original term *synchretic* is that Chion originally intended for synchretic sound to refer exclusively to an instantaneous coincidence of sound and image (as in his example of the chopping axe) rather than a continuously occurring sound. While I would like to acknowledge my expansion and (perhaps) exaggeration of his definition to include sounds that are not limited to a specific discrete sound, I think it is a potentially useful term to describe a sonic event that is obviously meant to emerge from an object in visual—or contextual—synchronization.

In the first example from *Journey into Space*, one is immediately led to believe the rising tone is meant to be some element of a rocket launching, since to the sound has been added a traditional sound effect of a rocket blast. Our suspicions are confirmed later in the broadcast when the same combined sound effect is heard at Jet's rocket launch. The inclusion of the sine wave is then obviously meant to imply some sort of "advance" on contemporary rocket technology—that extra boost that will enable Jet and his crew to travel to the Moon and beyond. The ability to combine the synchretic nature of a rocket launch with the mysterious acousmatic "unknowableness" of the futuristic technology renders the rocket a virtual synchretic *acousmêtre*.

The second sound effect is more complex and requires the audience to interpret more speculatively the sine wave they hear. Over the ship's radio, the crew of Jet's ship hears this mysterious sound, electronic, with reverb. "Hey, listen, what's that?" a character asks. "Don't know! Gives you the creeps, don't it?" "Haven't you any idea what it is?" "Sounds like music, but like music I've never heard before." This virtual acousmatic sound works to create suspense and fear precisely because the audience has no way of connecting this bizarre sound with any earthly one. In addition, it is not obviously attached to anything. The source of the sound is completely obscured and exists outside radio's frame, while at the same time it is obviously meant to imply some kind of "alien menace." Both sound effects were created by using recordings of oscillator tones passed through the National Physical Laboratory's reverberation chamber, and in 1953, the BBC's audience would have had limited contact with this kind of electronic sound, making the impression all the more mysterious. The ineffable quality of music is being drawn upon here to add to the enigmatic nature of the sound. Unlike the bizarre sounds in radio comedy, however, the science fiction sound effects encourage the audience to attempt some sort of interpretation, to form some kind of understanding of the place of these sounds in a rational universe. We can now outline two positions for electronic sound effects by the 1950s: sound as representation of "unknowableness," whether surreal, comic, threatening, or acousmatic (or any combination of these), and sound as coherent representation of a rational, logical, but unknown technology, a synchretic *acousmêtre*. These are the positions taken up by radio drama when these techniques were incorporated into radio drama and features in the 1950s.

Electronic Sound in Drama

Beginning in the early 1950s, radio audiences began to tire of the relentless barrage of "realistic" sound effects in radio drama and suggested that perhaps using sound effects more selectively—only when they were immediately relevant—would suit drama better. This letter from 1953 is typical of audience responses: "Surely one of the curses of the age is noise. The other night in *The Lady Vanishes* the background effects were almost continuous and so loud that it was almost impossible to hear the words. Must realism be carried so far and can nothing be left to the imagination?"[17]

In his influential (and still unsurpassed) guide to the philosophy and production of radio drama, Donald McWhinnie noted the frequent unsuitability of constant realistic sound effects for radio, preferring the role that the occasional but well-placed effects can have in furthering a story. He noted that "in radio, as in poetry, we attain definition by concentrated intuitive short cuts, not by a mass of elaboration and detail."[18] Famed poet and playwright Louis MacNeice's 1952 play, *One Eye Wild*, was hailed by critics as a play that reflected the new spirit of the day in its concision; one critic remarked that "*One Eye Wild* is equally experimental [as his earlier *The Careerist* and *The Queen of Air and Darkness*] but much less pretentious; the action is confined to one day, there is no special music (though lots of significant effects)."[19]

A combination of the state-sanctioned "difficult" Third Programme and the emergence of television as a polarizing factor in audience attentions was cited during the 1950s by critic Michael Hardwick as another reason for the burst of creative energy within radio drama at the time.[20] With the new network, plays that explored more controversial ideas or less accessible storytelling techniques finally had an outlet. Just as the pressure to remove the gratuitous use of realistic sound effects was growing, there was a strong and increasing desire for sound effects that were much less literal than had been the vogue in the past. Even productions that weren't directly related to the Theatre of the Absurd movement began to feel its influence. The Drama Department script editor noted in 1958 that "we now receive much more essentially radio material than the sort of scripts that are written with no particular medium in mind."[21] Alongside this was a willingness to expand the role of sound effects, letting them act in some respects as music. Following McWhinnie's idea that sound effect can act as storyteller, these new, more abstract sound effects worked in combination with dialogue to forge a rich atmospheric texture. Rayner Heppenstall's 1952 feature, *Dear Sensibility*, was one of the first productions to demonstrate this attitude. The work, an impressionistic sketch based on Laurence Sterne's autobiographical memoir, *A Sentimental Journey*, concerned itself with the minute details of Sterne's trip through France and Italy. Heppenstall described the production as "essentially a concerto for solo voice and sound effects."[22]

A key figure in this new movement was author Giles Cooper. Cooper's style served as a more accessible link to the often inaccessible approach of Theatre of the Absurd authors. His radio adaptations of contemporary fiction offered opportunities for ambitious producers to utilize progressive sound ideas. In March 1955, Archie Campbell produced Cooper's adaptation of *Lord of the Flies*. Campbell strongly believed in the power of evocative sound effects serving as music. In a memo to McWhinnie in his capacity as assistant head of Drama, he wrote, "My intention was not to use music as such but rather to introduce various rhythmic sound effects, composed in musical terms and arranged for a small section of wind and percussion instruments."[23] He offered as possible examples a brush on the drums to represent a "Desert Island Theme."

The first of Cooper's plays that called for the use of sound effects as an integral, indeed motivating, force behind the drama was *Mathry Beacon*, produced by McWhinnie in 1956. To describe the plot briefly: A military outfit during World War II, consisting of four men and two women, is stationed to guard a mysterious new anti-German weapon known as the Deflector. The crew have no idea how the machine works or even whether it works at all (it doesn't). Years pass, the war ends, a new war starts, they have children, and still they guard the useless Deflector until, twenty years later, one of the crew smashes it and its sound stops. They realize they have lived most of their lives under the hypnotic authority of the Deflector, which ultimately served no purpose at all.

The Deflector itself is never described. The script indicates only that "the sound made by the Deflector is a high, rhythmic humming. While musical in its effect it must not appear to be instrumental in origin."[24] Like the "alien" sound in the *Journey into Space* plays, the Deflector is described musically, to act in the same way as electronic sounds were seen to behave. The Deflector was to be a constant presence in the play, a character watching over the others in a gradually overpowering way, shifting from benign synchretic *acousmêtre* to threatening *acousmêtre*. Technology is also meant to be a metaphor for the stifling status quo, a consistent theme in Cooper's writing. Pieces of machinery frequently stand in for middle-class capitalistic security, accompanied by all kinds of culturally deter-mined baggage: masculinity, sexuality, industry, the expectation to "work hard." Here, in *Mathry Beacon*, the direct possibility of a technological, electronic solu-tion to the requirements of drama is immediately apparent. The reason this kind of solution wasn't immediately seized upon was that by 1956, there still didn't exist a thorough understanding in England of exactly what the French and German electronic and concrete experimenters had been working on, or similar radio drama productions in those countries.

It had only been a year since the first broadcast of *musique concrète* on the BBC and since the first electronic music had been written for an English feature— Tristram Cary's *Japanese Fishermen*. The musical community generally reacted with hostility to such efforts, and the few broadcasts that had been aired had been largely dismissed as novelties. This attitude was to change, however, if not among musicians and the Music Department, then among the producers and writers of radio drama. In March 1955, a commentator in the *Score* wrote, after asking when the BBC was going to give England a proper electronic music studio, that "it is perhaps too much to expect the Music Department to be inter-ested. But if producers of radio plays and sound engineers only knew what fas-cinating never dreamed of noises they could also get from it, they might easily start a lively campaign in favor of its creation."[25]

This seems to capture the spirit of the critical and creative mood of the time. The year 1955 was a watershed period for the BBC and electronic sound. June 1955 saw two significant electronic/*concrète* broadcasts on the Third Programme, both organized by Douglas Cleverdon from European originals. On June 7, the opera *Nadja Etoilée*, with traditional music composed by Maurice Jarre and *musique concrète* by Parisian concretist André Almuro, was broadcast. This was the start of an ongoing collaboration between Almuro and Cleverdon (and, for

Almuro, the beginning of a personal campaign to encourage the use of *musique concrète* in England), but for the broadcast of this initial work, originally recorded at the RTF in 1954, Cleverdon only wrote a brief introduction outlining the methods used by Almuro. "It cannot," he wrote, "strictly be described as 'musique concrete' [*sic*] in as much as it is not derived from non-musical sounds, but takes as its basic material music performed by an orchestra."[26]

Cleverdon also wrote an introduction for the June 29 broadcast of Henk Badings's Italia Prize–winning *musique concrète* opera *Orestes*. In trying to prepare audience members for what they were about to hear, he adapted Badings's own notes to his opera: "Listeners may like to know that the preparation of the opera involved a number of technical devices, including the use of frequency filters, ... the montage of fragmentary extracts from earlier scenes, and the raising of the vocal pitch of the chorus of the Furies by doubling the speed of tape recordings."[27]

This exposure to the techniques of *musique concrète* was to have a profound effect and influence on Cleverdon. Because he was attached to the Features Department rather than Music, he was able to escape the ideological baggage attached to the tradition of avant-garde music in Britain. *Orestes* received a positive response from the press. The independent music critic for the *Radio Times* called it a "highly successful experiment," but insisted on a distinction between this work and *musique concrète*, which he noted "is an assemblage of noises, bearing no relation apart from its rhythm to music, as we normally understand the term."[28] On the other hand, it was generous praise for a British music critic of the time to acknowledge that "Henk Badings uses these devices for genuinely musical ends."

One of the biggest stumbling blocks for composers interested in tape techniques was quite simply the lack of tape. Magnetic tape wasn't immediately available in England in a practical and durable format until the early 1950s. As mentioned above, the first original electronic music composed for BBC radio was Tristram Cary's *Japanese Fishermen*, broadcast on October 5, 1955.[29] Cary (1925–2008) is important in the history of British electronic music not only because he was one of the first to compose using the cut-and-paste techniques of *musique concrète*, often in combination with traditional instruments, but also because with no institutional support he built up his own studio far from the centers of electronic music. If he has been excluded from traditional histories, it is because his music at the time was mostly for radio, television, and film, all traditionally critically disparaged genres. He is probably now best known as the composer for "The Dead Planet" (1964), the first *Doctor Who* story to feature the Daleks.

While serving in the Royal Navy during the war, Cary specialized in radar, receiving an education in electronics. This education, combined with his compositional experience—he had been composing since he was fourteen—led to the possibility of "realizing music as a recording rather than a performance," using the technology of magnetic tape and turntables (much the same realization Schaeffer had made at roughly the same time).[30] Without Schaeffer's resources, though, and without access to contemporary writings on the subject, he was only able to theorize his ideas.[31]

After the war, Cary continued his interrupted college education and studied composition in London, incorporating the electronic techniques he had experimented with since the war using a lathe purchased in 1946 for £50. He bought his first tape recorder in 1952. Cary made his living composing traditional incidental scores for the BBC (including, in 1954, *The Saint and the Sinner, The Trickster of Seville*, and *Belshazzar's Feast*, all produced by Frederick Bradnum), which brought him to the attention of Terence Tiller, who produced *The Japanese Fishermen* for Features Department to be broadcast on the Third. The music was created on Cary's equipment in his Earl's Court studio and used sine oscillator pitches recorded onto 78rpm discs, since tape was still quite difficult to come by, and Cary, like Pierre Schaeffer, had perfected his techniques on shellac discs. The electronic sounds he recorded were used in combination with traditional percussion instruments, also treated, such as pitch-altered drumbeats and reversed xylophone melodies.[32]

Cary's production was followed, in December 1955, by Douglas Cleverdon's first *musique concrète* project: *Night Thoughts*, a "radiophonic poem" by David Gascoyne, with music (both concrete and traditional) by Humphrey Searle, portrayed London by night. Cleverdon and Searle worked together, composer Searle learning as he went, unfamiliar with the techniques of *musique concrète*. He recalls:

> To accompany the long dream sequence in the centre of the feature,
> we asked the famous percussionist James Blades to record all possible
> kinds of percussion sounds. We then played these backwards at various
> speeds; we could only make the speed either twice or four times as fast
> or slow; the BBC had no variable-speed controls in those days. In spite
> of these technical handicaps, we produced some very interesting
> sounds and were later congratulated by a French composer of
> electronic music on what we had been able to achieve with such
> meager resources.[33]

Cleverdon produced the third in Henry Reed's popular *Hilda Tablet* series of satirical plays, *A Hedge, Backwards*, broadcast February 29, 1956. Mary O'Farrell starred as a domineering amalgam of Elisabeth Lutyens, Ethyl Smyth, and

Benjamin Britten (both Lutyens and Britten thought Reed was poking fun at them in the character of Tablet, and were furious). Always desperate to try new compositional things, and usually failing dramatically, Tablet attempts her own special brand of *musique concrète* for her new production of *Anthony and Cleopatra*, which she labels "*musique concrète renforcée*." To realize this, Cleverdon used his knowledge and experience of *musique concrète*, now increasingly known in Britain as "radiophonic techniques," to collaborate with composer Donald Swann to create "some examples...based on comb and paper, Marjorie Westbury's zip fastener, etc."[34] This very "Third" kind of humor counts at the very least on the audience's familiarity with the ideas behind *musique concrète*, an example of its growing presence on the Third, the techniques being used for the first time in comedy there. The influence of *The Goon Show* is clear, albeit in a more high-brow context, with undeniably lowbrow results.

All That Fall

Of all the early productions to take advantage of these new techniques, Samuel Beckett's *All That Fall* was the first to incorporate them wholeheartedly as a fundamental component of the drama. More than anything before it, Beckett's first English-language radio play, which premiered on January 17, 1957, on the Third Programme, brought the potential for tape effects in drama to the attention of the wider public. In the relatively experienced hands of Donald McWhinnie as producer, it also proved to the BBC's administration the importance of setting up their own facilities for the production of such effects.

Beckett's original radio work continued the trajectory of his earlier plays, such as *Waiting for Godot* (1952), which had explored issues of isolation and existential angst against a backdrop of a world in half-focus. *All That Fall* forced him to come to terms with the supposed limitations of the medium and deal with a central tradition in radio drama: the primacy of language. One of the foundational tenets of Absurdist theater is the devaluation of language, and in this play Beckett returns self-consciously to the subject of language and speech. The central character, Mrs. Rooney, repeatedly draws attention to her own use of language:

> *Mrs. Rooney:* Do you find anything...bizarre about my way of speaking? (*Pause.*) I do not mean the voice. (*Pause.*) No, I mean the words. (*Pause. More to herself.*) I use none but the simplest words, I hope, and yet I sometimes find my way of speaking very...bizarre.

19

Reducing the sensorial spectrum to pure sound, Beckett is able to move beyond language—indeed, revel in the "bizarre"-ness of it—to explore the way other kinds of sound impact the total experience of the play. As Martin Esslin notes, "The Theatre of the Absurd has regained the freedom of using language as merely one—sometimes dominant, sometimes submerged—component of its multidimensional imagery."[35] Language can be just another sound effect, one of several elements in the larger sound picture that combine to convey the impression of "a universe freed from the shackles of logic."[36] McWhinnie believed that in the face of television, and reviving a thread of earlier producers, "if Sound Drama is ultimately to survive it must be on its own terms—that is to say, with specially scripted work which makes full use of radio's unique flexibility, intimacy, and capacity for imaginative and evocative story-telling."[37] From the beginning, Beckett and McWhinnie were convinced they did not want "realistic" sound effects. Instead, they were after sounds that could create, through *acousmêtre*, a dreamlike feeling never too far from nightmare.

The story of how Beckett's play came to be written for the BBC has been recounted expertly by both Clas Zilliacus and Martin Esslin, and I won't repeat the process in detail here.[38] Suffice it to say, in June 1956 Beckett had been approached in Paris by John Morris, the controller of the Third, who offered him the opportunity of contributing something without the pressure of a definite commission. Beckett responded by sending Morris the manuscript for *All That Fall* on September 26 that same year, and after revisions in collaboration with producer McWhinnie, submitted the final version on October 15. McWhinnie met with Beckett several times in Paris to discuss the production and was encouraged by Beckett's enthusiasm for sonic experimentation. As McWhinnie noted in an article written for the BBC staff magazine, *Ariel*, "Beckett may have had no technical expertise, but he did have...an imaginative awareness of sounds and silence."[39] Realizing the scope of the effects required, McWhinnie recruited Desmond Briscoe, a drama studio manager experienced in sound effects, to help him devise the unique sounds they would be looking for.

Desmond Briscoe was born in Birkenhead but moved to Manchester as a boy. He began his music career as a drummer, then as a conductor of "Harry Desmond and His Band," before he joined the BBC in Manchester at the age of sixteen as a program engineer. After beginning the war first in India, then in the Education Corps in London, he returned to the BBC in 1946 as a program operations assistant for radio drama. His job was to control the balance of instruments in musical performances and drop recordings of sound effects into productions by such producers and writers as D. G. Bridson, Louis MacNeice, Lawrence Gilliam, and Joan Littlewood. Although he had never been to Paris specifically to hear *musique concrète* (as McWhinnie had), he had heard recordings of works by Schaeffer and Stockhausen and was fascinated by them. He had worked closely with McWhinnie on a number of productions, and McWhinnie approached Briscoe with the script for *All That Fall*, explaining what he and Beckett had in mind. Briscoe, in turn, recruited engineer Norman Bain to act as his assistant and grams operator on the play. It was to be recorded in the Piccadilly Two studio, a popular location for experimental programs because it contained its own control booth for the importation and playback of effects.

Beckett's play concerns the journey of the elderly Maddy (Ma) Rooney to the train station to meet her blind husband, Dan, who has arrived late due to an unexplained delay. Most of the play's dialogue is delivered by Ma Rooney alone, and those she does meet with during the course of her long walk are presented as though in a dream. By the end of the play, it is revealed that the delay was the result of the death of a child who fell out of the train carriage. Her dialogue, however, foreshadows this revelation throughout, and the inevitability of the discovery is echoed in the passivity and non-emotion of Rooney at the play's conclusion as she continues on her weary journey.

The primary issue the production team had to address concerning the sound effects was the question of their realism. The principal effects required were the sounds of approaching people and vehicles, the train station, the rain, and the sound of Ma and Dan Rooney's footsteps. It is never made clear whether what the audience hears is "reality" in fact, or reality heard through the filter of Rooney's mind, and from the first line of the play McWhinnie skews the listener's perception by re-creating the animals' sounds with human actors imitating the sound of animals:

> *Rural sounds. Sheep, bird, cow, cock, severally, then together.*
> *Silence.*

The use of human voices lets the listener know right away not to necessarily trust at face value any of the sounds they are about to hear. Everything is, like Rooney, just slightly "off." McWhinnie acknowledged that this decision to skew sound in the direction of the surreal (as Esslin had intimated) is, in fact, a mirror of the philosophical tenets of the play itself: "It is a stylized form of scene-setting, containing within itself a pointer to the convention of the play: a mixture of realism and poetry, frustration and farce."[40] Tape effects, although important to the production, were actually used only a few times here; most of the effects came from simple treatments of standard sound effects, or from specially made recordings Briscoe created himself using an echo chamber. He recalls, "I was responsible for making, personally, many of the sounds, and for the sound treatment and mixing of the whole production; many of the sounds were, in fact, made in the studio with the actors, and it was virtually a one-take session."[41]

As new characters approach Rooney, their arrival is signaled by a sound effect that has been treated to distort or echo it. As they get closer, the sound gradually comes into focus, losing the treatment, until at their arrival next to her the sound is natural and realistic. For example, a few minutes into the play, when Ma Rooney's reverie is interrupted by Mr. Tyler on his bicycle, the stage directions indicate: "*Tyler coming up behind her on his bicycle, on his way to the station. Squeak of brakes. He slows down and rides abreast of her.*" The requirements for the effect were twofold: Briscoe and McWhinnie had to both realize the desired effect, that of a blurred object slowly coming into focus, and devise an effect that could be played live in the studio as the actors delivered their lines. As McWhinnie noted, "It is often more rewarding to use real sounds unrealistically—that is to say, distorted, with some of its original characteristics removed, in order to convey a special kind of auditory effect which cannot be achieved so easily by musical means."[42] In this case, Briscoe used a recording of a bicycle bell and treated it with a thick echo. This echo is gradually removed as the volume is raised, to indicate its closer position to Rooney. This is also done with an approaching car later in the play, and an approaching horse cart.

Probably the most extended effect in the play was the arrival of the up-mail and down-mail trains, as Ma Rooney waits for her husband's arrival, as can be heard in music example 1.1.◐ The stage directions are thus:

> *Immediately exaggerated station sounds. Falling signals. Bells. Whistles. Crescendo of train whistle approaching. Sound of train rushing through station.*
>
> Mrs. Rooney: (*above rush of train*). The up mail! The up mail! (*The up mail recedes, the down train approaches, enters the station, pulls up with great hissing of steam and clashing of couplings. Noise of passengers descending, doors banging, Mr. Barrel shouting "Boghill! Boghill!," etc. piercingly.*) Dan!...Are you all right?...Where is he?...Dan!...Did you see my husband?...Dan!...(*Noise of station emptying. Guard's whistle. Train departing, receding. Silence.*)[43]

McWhinnie wrote of this scene: "In production it is impossible to exaggerate this moment. The sound-complex in its grotesque fantasy must fulfill the wildest expectations and fears of the people who have been biting their nails on the platform; we should hear it as the nightmare realization of their own heightened anxiety."[44] Briscoe and Bain approached this effect, the treatment of the sound of the up-mail train as it arrives, by replaying the recorded sound of a train, and the accompanying whistles, back on itself, creating what is known as a "flutter-echo" effect. This in turn is recorded, resulting in a blurry, confusing, echolike sound. As the train is meant to be coming closer, the volume is brought up on the main playback head while simultaneously the signal to the recording head is reduced, gradually resulting in a simple untreated sound effect. Briscoe recalls the process: "We had heard the sound before on records of *musique concrète*—it wasn't our invention—but it was the first time that we had used it on radio drama. It was particularly good for suggesting that slightly 'fantasy feeling' of things happening in a larger-than-life way."[45] As the down-mail train arrives and the passengers depart, human voices that had been sped up (as heard in *The Goon Show*) are heard, opening and closing doors, creating a cacophonous rattle of slamming doors and muttering, distorted high-pitched voices. After the train leaves the station, both the flutter-echo and the frequency/speed acceleration are used as it fades into the distance, gradually rising in pitch, moving faster and faster, and getting quieter and quieter until finally disappearing altogether.

Creating the sound of the rain presented another big challenge for the production team. Again, McWhinnie wanted a stylized sound to replace a realistic one, and Briscoe came up with quite a unique solution, and one that highlights the interest experimental techniques were garnering among the more ambitious young producers within the BBC:

> I got various people who happened to be around for one reason or another, and when we started doing these sorts of things, when we were working in the studio all sorts of people used to turn up just to watch and listen to see what we were doing, and on this particular occasion, amongst the others, there was John Gibson and Michael Bakewell [both producers] amongst this group of people I had all standing around the microphone all going "tsts tst tssttttst tsts" with their lips and this was the rain, of course.[46]

Briscoe ran the sound through a filter to remove the bass frequencies, and played back the treble-heavy sound into the studio live at the production. The result sounded more like light tapping on a drumhead, with very little reverberation, each iteration specifically distinct but somehow slightly distorted.

Again, I think Chion's terms are useful for describing exactly why these sounds are such "nightmare realizations." Although we as listeners can recognize the source of the sound (e.g., "rain," "bicycle," "train," "people"), these elements don't sound the way they are meant to sound. They have been rendered virtual *acousmêtre* by the nature of the change they have undergone. And it is precisely the mystery of the cause of the change that results in our tension, our feeling of bewilderment. In terms of the necessary combination of synthesis and synchronization, the sounds lack the proper synthesis to achieve synchresis; they don't contain the expected elements of the anticipated sounds. Instead we are offered a replacement, an alternate that doesn't exist in any real world. The world is possibly the world inside Rooney's head, the sound effects perhaps an example of "internal sound" (e.g., diegetic sound that corresponds to the physical and/or mental interior of a character).[47] This new version of a familiar sound exists only to upset the listener's expectations, resulting in the questioning of all aspects of the narrative. The inclusion of virtual acousmatic sound here, which previously we have discussed only with respect to science fiction, is a strong foreshadowing of most early radiophonic productions' use of electronic and tape sounds—that is, not, as one might expect, for science fiction, but rather for those projects that are trying to achieve a detached, dreamlike, alienated, mysterious feel. McWhinnie realized why radio was the perfect medium for exploring these particular aspects of human psychology when he wrote, "For the world of visual detail which the listener creates is a world of limitless dimension; the images may be vivid, but they have no specific proportions; they exist in a world which is largely dream.... It is a bridge between poetry or music and reality."[48] And again, we find that radio encourages these feelings, and these effects tend toward the ineffably "musical." Already such primitive effects were being described in terms of music, as the reviews for the production show.

Reviews were almost unanimously positive for this first production; in scope and impact most critics compared the work to Douglas Cleverdon's original January 1954 production of Dylan Thomas's *Under Milk Wood*. The effects were almost always singled out as being of particular interest and, again, as having greatly added to the production. The *Manchester Guardian* noted that "McWhinnie's production had many brilliantly judged sound effects, some of them quite new even to one who has been hearing radio dramas for many years, and all of them removed in a slight degree, from ordinary 'illustration' to a more remote plane."[49] Philip Hope Wallace, writing for *Time and Tide*, called the play "a miraculous web of sound effects.... Like a dull bad dream recounted to you by some forcible bore in a Dublin pub, [it] had a tiresome way of penetrating one's aural imagination all next day. This was a feather in the cap of sound radio drama."[50] For the *Observer* Paul Ferris noted that it "used sound effects in a most painstaking and brilliant fashion.... What made Donald McWhinnie's production especially praiseworthy was his parallel use of effects: semi-realistic, always perfectly clear but not quite normal.... It all sounds a bit arty, but the effect was completely uncontrived."[51] Finally, Harold Hobson's review in the *Times* noted the similarity in tone to the works of other authors, like Adamov and Ionesco, and observed again the musical quality of the language and effects: "Beckett... aspires... to the condition of music. He makes no precise statements. [His plays] are not exercises in thought, and have a closer resemblance to Mozart than to Ibsen."[52] It is clear that this play hit a chord with audiences eager to explore the darker and more bizarre areas of the human psyche, who weren't put off by the use of electronic sounds and tape treatment as a way of manifesting that worldview. This reaction bears comparison with the opposite way such sounds were largely received by the British intellectual community when used in a purely musical setting.

The Disagreeable Oyster

With the overwhelmingly positive response to *All That Fall*, radiophonic productions received a push. Giles Cooper's next script after *Mathry Beacon*, *The Disagreeable Oyster*, completed on August 25, 1956, was originally intended for the Home Service, but its plot seemed too fantastic, too convoluted, and too divorced from reality for Home—and this difficulty in placement was the reason it ended up sitting on the shelf for several months before it was broadcast. The plot concerns a man who spends a surreal weekend away from his wife, caught between two versions of himself (Bundy and Bundy Minor). The two sides of his personality debate and battle over what should be proper behavior. While, on the one hand, he feels expected to pursue the opposite sex, get drunk in the pub, and generally run wild, the other side, the voice of his conscience, continually reminds him—in increasingly absurd situations—of his domestic obligations: his wife, his job. Every attempt he makes to enjoy the supposed "liberatory" aspects of being ostensibly single for the weekend is thwarted by his inexperience and timidity.

Technology, so prevalent as a ubiquitous specter in *Mathry Beacon*, again takes center stage as a lobotomizing influence on Bundy and his alter ego. Bundy begins the play surrounded by comforting symbols of technology, industry, and efficiency: At his work, all views from the window are blocked except for an air shaft and a mercantile bank. His boss, the aptly named Mr. Gunn, lords over his employees at Craddock's Calculators Ltd. During the course of the play Bundy is sent as technical repairman of the VVX machine to CCW works in "the North." His internal voice betrays an internal paranoia: "I haven't slept away from home for 22 years but I couldn't tell him that." And again, while on the train, he betrays his insecurities about being away from the safety of his home by noting, "They can't fool me because all the houses look like mine, oh no, these are northerly suburbs, Eskimo land."[53]

Once in "the North" he is confronted by a sonically distorted soundworld, where sound is manipulated to refashion his environment into a threatening, "feminized" place. The idea that the technological sound can represent the exotic and feminine has been discussed in the context of space-age "exotic" records contemporaneous with this play by Timothy Taylor in his book *Strange Sounds*.[54] In these records, with titles like *Music for Heavenly Bodies* and *Music from the Moon*, women are represented as belonging to the ideological complex "space/unknown/technology," with the theremin or other electronic sounds evoking the idea of the exotic or unusual against a backdrop of masculine rationality. The association of women with this complex is apparent in cover art: in one memorable example three scantily clad female "aliens" with antennae flirt with two men in spacesuits, and the liner notes declare that "heavenly bodies, whether it be the type that whirl about us in space, or those that have the glitter of Monroe, Mansfield or Bardot, have always had a magnetic attraction for man."[55] Here the exotic is erotic, and women are reduced to an unknown but desirable phenomenon. This differs from the exotic *dangerous* women of Cooper's play, but the same signifiers apply.

In *The Disagreeable Oyster*, one of our hero's first encounters after he arrives in the north is with a feminine man named Peregrin who instantly demands to be his friend. Peregrin tells him, "Do you know there isn't a poetry reading circle for thirty three miles in any direction, nor an art-gallery, nor a string-quartet, nor even an Expresso [sic] bar. We're a desert, Mervyn, and I'm a camel." Bundy runs away from this threat of homosexuality with his footsteps sped up à la *The Goon Show*. He goes through a series of progressively more and more harrowing demasculinizing events, with more and more treated sounds piled on, until he is literally stripped naked and left in the street by a crowd of shrieking women, voices sped up and distorted. Distancing this Orphean horror from the silliness of *The Goon Show*, sound designer Desmond Briscoe insists, "We used them [altered voices] because they seemed appropriate, certainly not because the Goons had used them."[56]

The unconventional nature of the play sparked an internal debate over its suitability almost from the day it was submitted, especially concerning its appropriateness for the Third Programme. In her report on the play, Assistant Script Editor Drama (Sound) Mollie Greenhalgh wrote that the play "is going to be connoisseur's meat; the average listener will hate it."[57]

By September 19, nearly a month after it was completed and submitted for broadcast, it was decided that the production would probably be on the Third Programme, but this plan hit another snag when the script was rejected by the Third as too lowbrow. Cooper himself acknowledged the ambiguity of the piece in a letter to Barbara Bray, commissioning editor for Drama Department: "I don't know that one really ought to call it a play. It's more like a piece of music."[58] This aspect was noted and latched onto by Bray, who wrote to Cooper on December 19, 1956, wondering whether you are at all interested in the sort of technique that the French have been using for some time? We have here an album of RTF recordings which involve *musique concrète* and allied effects, which I and many others found very exciting, and indeed inspiring. I wonder whether you could come in one day and listen to them, and go away inspired and do likewise?[59]

Bray agreed with Cooper's assessment of the work, that it was more music than play, or at least a unique combination of the two, the relationship of which was similar to that of sound and music in *musique concrète*. Due to the experimental nature of the play, its producer, McWhinnie, hoped that some of the production costs could be met by the BBC's small Experimental Fund. In his capacity both as producer and as assistant head of drama, McWhinnie wrote to the controller of sound entertainment, Michael Standing, asking if this money could be made available for the production, noting, "It would be a great pity if such an amusing and enterprising attempt at radio writing could not be given a chance to prove itself in performance."[60] Val Gielgud voiced his agreement with McWhinnie, adding at the bottom of the memo, "I hope you may feel inclined and able to agree to this." Standing's main objection to providing the funds seems to have been the lack of support from either Home or Third, but shortly after the approval of the Third's director on December 14, the money (£320) was offered to the production.

Rehearsals and recording for McWhinnie's production of *The Disagreeable Oyster* occurred in the Piccadilly Two studios, the same as those used for *All That Fall*, for the same reason: it was easier to import prerecorded sound effects into the studio because of the attached control room. Cooper had followed Bray's advice and wholeheartedly embraced the use of concrete effects in his play. In many ways, the possibilities these techniques opened up matched Cooper's peculiar perspective to a T, or, in the words of drama historian Frances Gray, "The technical demands he made reflected his special vision of a reality that shifts and changes, yet is never divorced from an everyday *Gestalt*."[61]

In the production script, the effects were written in, both typed and handwritten, next to the dialogue, such as "Alice: (*Distort*) Did you remember to get a wrapped loaf?" annotated with the handwritten note "Speeded." The incorporation of recently successful techniques as an essential part of the scriptwriting led to a production that continued the move toward works that used electronic effects in a more integrated fashion. There were very few reviews of the program, but what little was said was generally positive. The anonymous reviewer in the *Radio Times* observed that "sound effects and production of a type more readily associated with *The Goon Show* than with drama productions are among the vital ingredients of Giles Cooper's play, *The Disagreeable Oyster*."[62]

Opium

Douglas Cleverdon's first real collaboration with André Almuro (as opposed to the opera *Nadja Etoilée*, which was a direct rebroadcast of its French original) was *Opium: An Essay in Musique Concrète*, recorded on February 20, 1957, and broadcast first on the Third Programme on March 18. It also used as its raw material an original RTF production by Almuro, but this one significantly reworked by Cleverdon. To do this, they worked closely together to combine the precomposed *musique concrète* with electronic treatment of the voices. The thirty-minute feature was based on Jean Cocteau's journal, which poetically describes the effects of opium, and, as Cleverdon stated, the feature "can fairly be called an essay in experimental radio, utilizing the techniques of modern broadcasting to weld together the sound patterns, both musical and nonmusical, which have come to be known as *musique concrète*, and to evoke the mood of Cocteau's brilliant writing."[63] In reality, Cleverdon's contribution was to help create the vocal effects and processing, rather than contribute in a significant way to the concrete elements. The program was not well received by the press, who had not yet experienced treated voices outside of radio comedy, and to whom such processes still had the ring of *The Goon Show*. One can infer from the tone of the reviewer for the *Sunday Times* that, at least for this critic, the idea of *musique concrète* acting as a symbolic representation of a mental state (in this case, under the influence of opium) was a suspect proposition. After comparing the voice treatments to *The Goon Show*, he notes: "Hums, whines, buzzes and psalmody ensued—and if all this was meant to suggest the effects of opium I would say to anyone thinking of trying a pipe 'Don't touch it, Jack, you're better without it.'"[64]

Perhaps the audience needed a bit more guidance, or at least some kind of explanation as to what they were about to hear. It was probably a mistake to broadcast *Opium* without any kind of preface, or explanatory material to help audiences along. These sounds and treatments were still so new, so unusual, that even for an audience of Third Programme listeners, the natural inclination seemed to be to hear them as humorous.

Private Dreams and Public Nightmares

The unsympathetic reception a work like *Opium* received parallels the initial problem McWhinnie faced in finding a place for *The Disagreeable Oyster*: there was as yet no distinct "genre" in which to place a work that was, in Cooper's words, "more music than play." McWhinnie elaborated on this new hybrid genre—one that combined traditional dramatic dialogue with manufactured, specially created sound effects—in his next production. For the first time the "tenets" of this new genre were defined and outlined before the broadcast so that audiences would be aware of what they were listening to ahead of time. This program, *Private Dreams and Public Nightmares*, broadcast October 7, 1957, was subtitled "A Radiophonic Poem" and began with a five-minute introduction by McWhinnie. He described both how the sonic effects were achieved and what the aesthetic effect was meant to be. In this introduction he had to convey both the complexity of the process and the primacy of the effect:

> This program is an experiment, an exploration. It has been put together with enormous enthusiasm with equipment designed for other purposes. It's not a masterpiece, not even a minor one, and it's not a stunt. We think it is worth broadcasting as a perfectly serious first attempt to find out whether we can convey a new kind of emotional and intellectual experience by means of what we call radiophonic effects.[65]

As a way of establishing the legitimacy of the new art, he reinforced the popular association between tape music and high technology (and thus with the supernatural or magic) by defining it as "a science of making sound patterns" capable of creating "a vast and subtle symphony from the sound of a pin dropping. . . . A sort of modern magic."

One vital point McWhinnie made was that radiophonics weren't a new thing, that people on the continent had been doing it for years and that the British had held aloof, in his opinion, "partly from distrust: 'is it simply a new toy,' and partly from complacency, ignorance too. We are saying at last we think there's something in it." Anticipating complaints from the musically conservative public that this really wasn't music at all, he disavowed its comparison to music by noting that the BBC has chosen the term "radiophonic" over the more controversial *musique concrète* and that the work they are to hear is a completely new genre, the radiophonic poem, "quite distinct from the poem on page or the poem read aloud, a poetic experience that only exists in terms of a sound complex." Noting radiophony's suitability for radio drama, indeed drama of all media, he hoped that these techniques, with their ability to create unheard-of sounds, could be free of irrelevant associations, "with an emotional life of their own."

The potentially difficult combination of text and effects required a special kind of script, one that took into account the sounds laid on them, avoiding the impression that the sounds were added to the text as an afterthought. McWhinnie made the strong point that the script, written by Frederick Bradnum, "was specifically designed to exploit some of these new sounds, and completely dependent on them for full effect." Like *Opium*, a great deal of the program's success depended on the electronic treatment of voices, a process McWhinnie defended as providing emotional effects mechanically that would be impossible for an actor to create alone. He acknowledged that some of the effects had been used already for comedy (as in *The Goon Show*) or in science fiction but argued that their potential for use in a broader range of dramatic works had yet to be explored. "It's much more difficult to manage tenderness, lyrical beauty, sweetness and light. Perhaps because of the inhuman element in the actual process of manufacture."

One can sense a certain defensive tone in both his radio introduction and the blurb he wrote for the *Radio Times*. He knew that his Third Programme audience had already in large part passed sentence on both electronic music and *musique concrète* and that the piece would be disliked intensely by most of his radio listeners, and he did his best to deflect criticism away from the techniques used, practically begging his audience to listen with patience and to accept the preliminary stage of their training and abilities: "You may detest this program, but I hope you won't dismiss it. Certainly nothing like it has come out of your loudspeaker before.... much work has still to be done before we can handle them [radiophonic effects] with style and confidence.... Clearly the new techniques must be used with discretion."[66] At one moment he even sides with his adversaries, acknowledging, "One thought does occur from time to time, not entirely frivolously, 'would it not be more illuminating to play the whole thing backwards'?"

The poem concerns the helplessness and fear experienced during a nightmare. Three voices represent different sides of the subconscious. The first voice, a female one, acts as a drone in conjunction with repetitious sound effects, representing the state of consciousness: at rest, agitated, and so on. The second voice, a male, serves as the antagonistic expression of unconscious fears and pain, most often represented at a louder volume, with harsher equalization. It continually chides the third voice, also male, who represents the conscious protagonist. The physical script depicts this integral combination of voices and sounds with the dialogue on one side, and the proposed effects on the other. Bradnum explained his approach to writing a radiophonic script in terms of certain kinds of opera libretti, particularly Wagner's: "It must have shape, and an idea, which is worked out and brought to a conclusion. It must impose strong visual images upon the mind, and these should in turn suggest sound patterns.... [Then] word and effect, can create a world of different dimensions from that created by any other art form."[67]

McWhinnie reproduced some of this script in his book *The Art of Radio*, and it offers an indication of the abstract conception of the sounds intended. This script indicates only the sound that should accompany the text; it says nothing about the specific treatment of the individual voices, or more precise indications as to how the effects are to be created. I assume that in a performance script, as in the case of *Opium*, the voice treatments would be written next to the appropriate lines of dialogue. The layout of the opening in the printed script suggests this:

Basic Effects	Dialogue
A contrapuntal rhythm	1st Voice: Round and round
	Like a wind from the
	Ground
	Deep and deep
	A world turns in sleep.
A comet-like shriek.	2nd Voice: I fall through nothing,
Acoustic change.	vast, empty spaces.
Pulsating beat.	Darkness and the
Descending scale.	Pulse of my life
	Bound,
	Intertwined with the
	Pulse of the dark
	world.
A developed sound like a cry.	Still falling, falling,
	But slower now...[68]

The actual realization of the effects was a much looser affair than the script indicates. For example, when the second voice enters, the "comet-like shriek" is the only effect utilized until "Still falling, falling," at which point rather than a "cry," a rhythm, a sped-up version of the opening idea, enters, grinding against the pattern of the voice. This rhythm (which sounds like a slowed-down spring "doooiiinggg" looped in a repeating pattern with added echo) gradually slows down to the next line of text, "But slower now, like music the way down, slow defying gravity. Almost to a stop. Almost." It's obvious that the effects written in the script were used by the production team as a guide rather than as a literal roadmap. Much of the realization was obviously determined by what they were able to achieve technically, given their limited resources in the studios at Piccadilly Two. Joining Desmond Briscoe was a studio manager from the Music Department, Daphne Oram, as well as engineer Norman Bain.

Oram had joined the BBC in 1943 as a sound engineer. Her job consisted of balancing levels for recordings and creating simple sound effects, but she had always harbored an interest in electronic music. By her own account, she would experiment at night after everyone had left the BBC, moving tape recorders together to try the techniques she had heard Continental composers use, replacing them before the staff returned the next day.[69] Oram was instrumental in preparing a document in 1956 for Brian George, head of Central Programme Operations, outlining the potential and history of electronic music and *musique concrète*, as an attempt to pave the way to establishing a studio within the BBC.

The formidable combination of Briscoe's sound effects background and Oram's musical training and experimental curiosity gave the final program a polish never before seen in a radiophonic production in England. The vocal treatments, primarily exaggerated filtering, contribute hugely to the overall effect. In addition, most of the standard *musique concrète* techniques were used: sped-up tape, backward sounds, echo effects, largely percussive tape loops. One of the most effective moments is the extended conclusion. McWhinnie had noted in his introduction the difficulty in producing sounds that were warm and beautiful, and it was one of his goals for this production to attempt sounds that weren't just nightmarish but also represented a kind of peace or joy. The moment closest to this feeling occurs at the very end, where the dreamer is finally comforted by the realization that he himself has generated and embodied all his own worst fears (music example 1.2).🔊

VOICE 3:   My fear! It was you who first made me fear, you who screamed
           that corruption when I recurled. You who placarded the head-
           lined world into my suspended cocoon of peace. You!
VOICE 2:   I? Look into my face and tell. What face do you see?
VOICE 3:   I see myself. The image is no longer divided. Like a mirror, I
           am you and you are me. In sleep our shadows cling like those
           of lovers. As lovers we can shut out the world. Not think upon
           tomorrow. Nor think upon our ruthless awakening.

The solution the production team arrived at for this concluding epiphany was to return to a sound much nearer traditional tonal music than the abstract percussive sounds used throughout the rest of the poem. What results is a drone based on the interval of a major third between D-flat ♮ and F in a pattern that undulates gently. It provides a comfortable but indefinable warmth, a shell of sound that surrounds the listener with its stability and solidity after the barrage of cacophonous sounds heard earlier. The production team had hit upon something fundamental that would have a profound impact on the way tape music would be used to best effect at the Radiophonic Workshop. One of the things tape manipulation was uniquely good at producing was this kind of low-frequency static texture, an effect that was impossible for traditional instruments to re-create and that excelled at evoking a kind of trancelike state, a scene of absolute stasis, of potentially infinite duration, with a mechanical rhythmic drive that remains frozen in one spot.

This wasn't the most memorable facet of the production to most contemporary listeners, however. It was the jarring and disturbing effect of much of the rest of the program that had the most profound impact on them. An Audience Research Department report for this production survives at the BBC, and it provides a fascinating look at how a group of ninety-seven listeners from all quarters of the Third Programme audience reacted right after hearing it.[70] The audience was asked to grade the program and provide written comments under this grade. The grade distribution was as follows: A+ 14 percent, A 20 percent, B 28 percent, C 21 percent, and C− (the lowest grade possible) 17 percent, leading to an appreciation index of 56. Not terrible, but when compared to other programs listed in the report of the same kind, only the initial broadcast of Schaeffer's *Symphonie pour un Homme Seul*—the British public's first exposure to *musique concrète*—scored lower.

The anonymous author of the report said there seemed to be a general approval that the experiment had been made but there was a wide range of opinion about the merit of this particular experiment. Most of the audience agreed that the text was a failure and "was considered weak and feeble by a sizable group." A bank official noted, "The words that were spoken were not poetic and they prevented undivided attention being given to the strange sounds: they were an intrusion and an obstacle." If the text was almost uniformly dismissed, the effects elicited a more divided response. On the one hand, a minority condemned it entirely as "loathsome," "lunatic ravings," and "cacophony," while a larger group enjoyed the performance; however, there was felt to be a lack of unity between the sounds and the voices, one of McWhinnie's greatest fears. One listener wrote, "Which came first? I sometimes thought that words were simply fitted to the sounds, although the reverse process would seem better," while another thought "there was too much talk and the 'music' was relegated too much to the background as 'effects.' I am dying to listen to a program of nothing but edited sound track, or concrete music."

On the other hand, there was a great deal of enthusiasm for the broadcast. The majority of listeners did like it, at least some aspects of it, and wished for more programs of the same kind. One listener called it "a challenging and fascinating experiment" making "a terrific impact." Another student said that "the whole work was excellently conceived and extremely powerful." As usual, the cases against this sort of program were made much more forcefully than those in favor. It is also important to notice that the audience for the broadcast was a phenomenally small 0.2 percent of the total listening public in the United Kingdom.

The mainstream press guarded its praise. Like many in the Audience Report, the reviewer for the *Times* thought the text itself was not worthy of such treatment, and spent most of its extended review slamming this aspect of the production. It is perhaps a sign of the musical establishment's slow warming to the sounds of *musique concrète* that the reviewer could write, "In England we have heard many objections to *musique concrète*, but few of the actual sounds that have provoked so much gleeful disapproval....Last night on the Third Programme, Mr. Frederick Bradnum's 'radiophonic poem'...demonstrated its power to support, indeed transfigure, the most commonplace writing."[71]

The generally more positive critical reception the work received by the press seems to be a change from the glowing but guarded reviews of *All That Fall* or the scathing reviews of *Opium*. Although radiophonics were still novel enough to startle and upset some listeners, they had, on careful listening, come to be regarded as an effective storytelling device, as valid as traditional music, and in the case of *Private Dreams and Public Nightmares*, moving beyond music to tell a more effective story than words alone had the power to do.

Despite the seemingly uphill battle each radiophonic production fought, the production team behind John Gibson's *A Winter Journey* tackled a new problem: the application of radiophonics to a dramatic production not specifically written for the purpose. For this program, the team behind *Private Dreams and Public Nightmares* returned to see whether it was possible to create a radiophonic poem out of a preexisting text. It seems, judging from reviews, that they weren't entirely successful (the recorded program no longer exists), yet it is difficult to tell whether it was the sounds themselves that offended or the imposition of the sounds on the dialogue.

A Winter Journey was the final "experimental" production made before the formal establishment of the Radiophonic Workshop in 1958. In this chapter, I have shown a gradual growth of confidence in the use of radiophonic techniques, from initial tentative steps into a remarkable level of experimentalism given the limited equipment and conditions under which the production teams worked. In the next chapter, I will discuss the behind-the-scenes events that were gradually building up momentum while these public broadcasts were taking place. There was a serious effort under way to provide a location, equipment, and staff for the development of radiophonic sound, and as the writers, producers, technicians, engineers, and musicians became more confident in their abilities, the necessity for a place where they could strike out on their own and create an art form with fewer ties to *musique concrète* became more pressing. But things weren't made easy for them in certain corners of the BBC. Every good story needs a villain, and here the Music Department fills the role admirably. They were decidedly against having any electronic studio associated with the BBC, for both practical and philosophical reasons, and were determined to thwart its creation using their considerable influence.

2

Ideological Struggles and
Pragmatic Realities

The story behind the creation of the Radiophonic Workshop reveals a complex history of compromises and collaboration faced by no other electronic music studio in the twentieth century. Out of the internal philosophical battles, economic frustrations, political dramas, and concessions, however, developed a musical style unique in several respects, one dependent to an unusually high degree on the studio equipment's idiosyncrasies and on the space in which its composers worked. A study of radiophonic music must deal with these issues, which are often ignored in other areas of research. With a more distinct impression of the space and equipment from which this music originated, an understanding of the *hows* and *wheres*, we can achieve a deeper understanding of the *whys* behind radiophonic music.

On April 13, 1956, at an Entertainment Divisional Meeting, the BBC's head of central program operations, Brian George, proposed setting up a small laboratory in order to experiment with electronic sound effects in radio productions. Shortly before the broadcast of *All That Fall*, in November 1956 he commissioned a report from Alec Nesbitt, an engineer who followed developments in electronic music, on the subject of *musique concrète* and *elektronische Musik*; in assembling the report Nesbitt received help from producers Donald McWhinnie and Douglas Cleverdon, T. H. Eckersley (assistant head of central program operations, Recording), and composers Daphne Oram (a studio manager [SM]) and André Almuro. In this five-page document they traced the history of the genres, described the existing facilities in France, Germany, the United States, and the rest of Europe, and discussed ways of establishing a similar studio at the BBC. In it they stressed the value such a studio would offer to dramatic productions, and noted that the unique application of electronic sounds to drama increased the potential for truly new ideas:

Cologne and Paris have developed this medium primarily as an art form, but in this country there is a demand by Features Department for the use of Musique Concrete [sic]....Undoubtedly, Radiophonic Music is in a primitive and elementary form and it therefore seems prudent to commence our work from the first principles, and in doing so it is probable that we will develop a facet of the technique that has been overlooked by the workers on the Continent.[1]

They argued that in addition to studio equipment, the new department would need four employees, never referred to as "musicians": an engineer capable of creating and repairing machines, and three "tape editors and devisors of special effects." They suggest that SMs could do the editing and effects, a position slightly higher than an engineer in the BBC hierarchy and one that valued creativity and originality. After examining the document, George assembled a group of producers, SMs, and other bureaucratic officials from various departments to form the Electrophonic Effects Committee (EEC), which convened for the first time on December 14, 1956.[2] At this meeting, they debated again what kind of facilities and staffing were needed for the proposed unit, who would direct it, and what its administrative structure would be. Donald McWhinnie had recently traveled to Paris to meet personally the composers behind *musique concrète*, in preparation for his work on *All That Fall*, and on behalf of this committee McWhinnie submitted a report to George wherein he noted the necessity of

obtaining facilities for private experiment and for making recordings which may never be broadcast. Clearly the exact requirements would have to be worked out in detail with a technical expert and in consultation with the *Club d'Essai*: I should say that the basic essentials would be a room containing two or three tape reproduction machines, turntables for slow speed of 78s, a tape-recorder, facilities for echo, filters, etc., and a small studio with two or three microphone points, an old piano, various percussion instruments and space for two or three actors.[3]

Since the committee found the extemporaneous qualities of sound effects especially important, they noted that "perhaps it might be stressed that the ability to improvise will be a quality preeminently to be looked for both on the technical and production sides of the team."[4] They also questioned in this initial meeting whether they wanted to "loan" SMs and engineers to the new department or create permanent appointments, tentatively settling on the former. (Later documents indicate that the committee believed musicians/engineers would be able to deal with electronic sound effects only for a limited amount of time before succumbing to mental instability!)[5] In this description of the potential duties of staff in the studio, there is a remarkable similarity to the fears first voiced about the staff of the BBC's earlier Research Division in the 1920s and 1930s: "Whilst a free hand must be given to those working in the section, it will be necessary to exercise a strict, but understanding control over their work. Self-discipline is most important as their work will be erratic and will not follow a normal shift pattern."[6]

Cleverdon and Searle's production of *Night Thoughts*, from December of the previous year, was said to have been "restricted owing to the limitation both in the numbers and the performance of our existing tape machines," and the document concludes by suggesting that "once basic techniques are mastered, discussions should commence with Features and Drama Departments," then offering a tentative shopping list for the basic equipment necessary for setting up a studio. Basing their list on Continental models, they included as many pieces of equipment as possible, knowing they wouldn't get everything they asked for. George followed up this optimistic list by noting that "you perhaps set your sights a little bit too high in terms of staff and technical facilities, bearing in mind the present financial stringency."[7] Up to this point, all of the members of the EEC were representatives from sound broadcasting. On March 6, 1957, they agreed to ask a representative from television, Leonard Salter, to join them.[8] They also decided to change the name of the subject under discussion from "Electrophonic" to "Radiophonic," because the former term was currently used in brain research. They agreed on the change and subsequently changed their name to the Radiophonic Effects Committee (REC).

At the same time these decisions were made, in his enthusiasm to teach others within the BBC about the potential of electronic and tape effects and music, producer Douglas Cleverdon organized a monthly listening group for the playback of electronic music, starting February 19, 1957. He devoted the first evening to *Nadja Etoilée* by French *musique concrète* composer André Almuro.[9] Another typical evening's playlist consisted of Jim Fassett's *Symphony of the Birds*, Karlheinz Stockhausen's *Study II*, Herbert Eimert's *Etudes Übertongemische*, Luciano Berio's *Mutazioni*, and Bruno Maderna's *Notturno*. That night's listening concluded with *Ruisselle*, an hour-long radiophonic poem with words by Roger Pillaudin and music by Maurice Jarre. Cleverdon sent out invitations a week before the event, announcing it as a playback of "experimental recordings in the fields of electronic music, musique concrète, and other forms which may generally be described as radiophonic music."[10] Cleverdon was on the lookout for composers, technicians, poets, or SMs who might be interested in the techniques and equipment available to them at that time.

Location

One of the biggest obstacles facing the REC in setting up an electronic studio was the lack of a viable site. They sought a location that would provide "adequate daylight, large rooms, little interference with other people, peaceful surroundings, and... not too easily accessible to keep away people not connected with the work."[11] The need for several soundproof rooms, free from interference and noise, with close access to echo rooms and existing studios, made the search more difficult than it might otherwise have been. They considered Nightingale Square, a huge Victorian-Gothic nineteenth-century building in Clapham that had been a convent for elderly Belgian nuns before being taken over by the BBC Engineering Department.[12] (It had the advantage of being close to electrical equipment and facilities.) The most desirable site, though, and the original thought of the committee, was the Maida Vale studios, where the majority of the BBC's music was recorded in five large studios. The BBC had used the huge art nouveau Maida Vale complex, built in 1909, since the 1930s, when they had it converted from a large sunken roller skating rink, the Maida Vale Roller Skating Palace and Club, into a multipurpose studio complex for use by the BBC Symphony Orchestra, chamber music groups, and dance bands. Since then, it had housed all of the BBC's major music recording studios. Although it offered the perfect location, there was initially no available space in that facility. Four months after the REC began making inquiries, however, a small collection of rooms was offered to the fledgling studio, situated in the old balcony of the sunken rink.[13] The Engineering Department cleared two rooms to house the new Radiophonic Workshop: the first, Room 13/14 (created by knocking down a center dividing wall to create a large working space), and the small adjoining studio, Room 15.

My purpose in dwelling on the materiality of this space is to create a dramatic sense of the conditions of production at the Workshop. It is easy enough to describe the details of the original rooms; what I hope to do instead is to describe how these details combined to create the specific environment needed for the creation of the radiophonic sounds under discussion. I want to emphasize that I am not concentrating on material specifics to prove a "perfect conjunction" of elements, or a "unique combination" of people and equipment banding together to create works of universal genius. Although it is certainly true that these works can be judged by some set of standards as either good or bad, successful or unsuccessful, that is not my primary goal. Rather, by simply showing the hidden details of production in their original context, I will demonstrate the idiosyncratic nature of these works' creation.

Today Room 13/14 betrays nothing of its radiophonic past; the equipment has long since been evacuated and the space converted into office cubicles. But as the winter of 1958 turned into spring and the Workshop's opening approached, the REC and the Engineering Department began filling this newly created space with electronics. The room was about twenty-five feet long and fifteen feet wide, with two frosted windows on the south side, and doors leading into the main hallway directly opposite on the north. The ceiling was low, with a thick supporting beam running its length and concrete arches extending from it on both the east and west ends of the room, making for an irregular work space. Short carpeting covered the floors, and a series of soft lights illuminated the space. The lack of ventilation in the room was immediately a cause for concern. It could become very stuffy, because the source of outside air was often blocked to eliminate sound from the busy Delaware Road outside. Located right next to this room (usually just called Room 13) was Room 15, which was not so much a room as a utility space. Because of its small size and its lack of outside windows, it was most frequently used to record sounds in isolation for later treatment. Engineer Dick Mills told me once that if more than one person used the room at the same time, "we almost had to take turns to go outside and breathe!"

Having solved the question of location, the committee turned its attention to matters of equipment and staffing. Although Nesbitt, in his initial report, had offered suggestions as to which recorders, filters, and other equipment the fledgling studio would require, and although he had given his opinion on the best method of staffing such an organization, the REC could not go ahead with his plans, as the next section will demonstrate.

Opposition from the Music Department

The Workshop's supporters and opponents were clearly divided. Predictably, the strongest criticisms of the Workshop came from the Music Department, particularly from Light Music. The Music Department had resisted supporting electronic and concrete music since it had first been developed, leaving the Drama Department to pursue its own course. The antagonism between departments had developed as a result of the BBC's difficult mandate to cater to large audiences while at the same time "educating" the public in the repertoire of classical music. By the late 1950s this had produced a persistent middle-of-the-road approach to broadcasting. Predictably, certain staff members quickly dismissed avant-garde trends or experiments offhand as of too limited a utility.

By this time, those in power at the Music Department must have known of British composers' growing desire to experiment like their American and Continental colleagues with the developing medium of electronic music. After the success of Beckett's *All That Fall*, they must have also felt within the BBC the growing impulse to create a separate, internal department for the creation of electronic sound effects for drama and, most threatening to them, music. One can detect the Music Department's careful drawing of the boundaries of *musique concrète* in the minutes of the first meeting of the REC on March 6, 1957, during which the second item under discussion was the terrain of each department. The committee agreed that the sounds under consideration should fall into two categories:

A. Those produced on instruments played by musicians which may include electronic devices, but the music of which can be expressed in existing forms of musical notation.

B. Sounds, produced by technical methods, embracing the techniques already developed in other countries, e.g. electronic music derived from oscillators and for which the composer cannot use existing forms of musical notation, and music concrete based on natural sounds.[14]

It can be easy to miss the significance of this seemingly arbitrary distinction, between "notatable" and "nonnotatable" music, but they were trying to find in electronic music features of the "traditional" music with which they were more familiar. When it came to dividing the work to be done between the various Drama and Music Departments, discussions became more politicized. They agreed that the Music Division would be responsible for "all music effects under 'A,'" while the "Entertainment Division" (the Drama and Feature Departments) would "be responsible for sounds in 'B.'" This implied that if a sound could be notated, it would belong to the Music Department. In other words, it was then, in fact, "music." And naturally, the opposite was also true: if the sounds were not notatable, they did not constitute music. This easy way for the Music Department to create boundaries for electronic music (and especially *musique concrète*, which was of particular interest to British composers) only temporarily satisfied young composers who wanted a chance to experiment with new equipment outside the confines of dramatic productions.

Faced with what they must have seen as an inevitability, the committee decided to defuse the burgeoning movement for a full-fledged electronic music studio with a plan of their own. For the idea to work, however, the Music Department had to satisfy the Drama Department's needs, as well as those of eager composers and advocates of electronic music, without sacrificing their ideals of maintaining the musical high ground. They attempted to do this by purchasing a unique new instrument that created electronic sounds but kept the comforting form of an organ. The head of Light Music Programmes (Sound), Frank Wade, along with F. W. Alexander (both committee members), requested the purchase of this new musical instrument, which could create music electronically and yet was more suited to the tastes of less marginal audiences. They received permission to order the construction of a special "Colour Tone Instrument" or "Multi-colour Tone Organ" from the firm Musical Research Ltd. (a division of the Miller Organ Co.) at a cost of £3,000. In a letter to the accounting office dated February 11, 1957, Wade wrote that in Europe, and to a lesser extent in America, "where musico-electronics remain under control of scientists and have no really practical musical application, we are convinced that we should concentrate on being the first country to combine electronics with live instruments in the production of real music."[15] One of the supposed benefits of the instrument was that it had a keyboard just like an ordinary organ, with a single manual, and could function as an organ, conforming to "established musical patterns."[16] Wade hoped that the instrument would help existing musical ensembles to save money and that the novelty of its electronic sounds would increase the number of BBC listeners.

The Miller Multi-colour Tone Organ could also produce "electronically generated 'effects' sounds useful in plays, features, etc." and thus was considered a perfect concession to the Drama Department.[17] This multipurpose instrument could be used to "experiment with electronic sound as a musical language and to expand the colour tone box into a musical instrument in its own right," so it seemed to make the Workshop redundant.[18] The Music Department recognized the use of electronic sounds in their Drama productions as legitimate; this was not the problem. It was more threatened by the potential use of electronic sounds to create undesirable *music*, because such music threatened to undermine the careful cultural work they had undertaken.[19]

With the purchase of this instrument, the question of electronic music seemed, to the representatives of the Music Department, to be answered. They could see no reason to continue participating in a discussion geared toward creating an electronic studio; they did their best to fight the promotion of music they felt jeopardized the moral musical culture of Britain. However, the purchase of this instrument as a supposed solution to the electronic music problem did not diminish composers' and producers' desire to see the BBC create studios like the ones existing in Europe and America.

An amazing collection of memos and letters survives in the BBC's archives showing just how divided the Drama and Music Departments were over this issue. One particular event fanned the embers of controversy that had been on the point of igniting for some time, bringing the most conservative members of the Music Department in contact with the most radical proponents of electronic music for the first time, with Drama representatives seemingly caught in the middle. On February 12, 1957, four members of the BBC's upper staff met with representatives of the Society for the Promotion of New Music (SPNM). The BBC contingent was composed of Bernard Keefe and Frank Wade (representing the Music Department), Douglas Cleverdon (Drama), and M. R. G. Garrard (the "number two" of Studio Operations, responsible for the staffing of the Workshop). After the meeting, both Keefe and Cleverdon reported to their bosses. Cleverdon, who had lunched with the chairman of the society on the day before, had nothing but enthusiasm for the organization and was eager to accommodate the needs of its composers. He saw collaboration between the SPNM and the BBC as leading to useful cooperation, taking for granted the need to pursue in-house electronic music production. Cleverdon reiterated his plan to conduct monthly playback sessions of experimental music (the first of which, Almuro's *Nadja Etoilée*, was scheduled for a week after the meeting). He saw these sessions as a means of exposing young talent to the new techniques of electronic and tape music "with occasional demonstrations of new BBC gear as it becomes available. This would help us to get to know young composers with the necessary enthusiasm and elementary technical knowledge, who might in due course undertake experimental work for us."[20]

Note that Cleverdon had no qualms about calling the creators of electronic work "composers." The ideological baggage surrounding the traditional notion of the composer was not nearly as important to Cleverdon, detached as he was from the intricacies of musicians' union politics, individual musical biases, and institutional prejudices that had grown up around experimental music within the Music Department.[21]

Keefe and Wade's response was not nearly as optimistic. Wade added a handwritten addition to the bottom of Cleverdon's memo confirming that the Music Department wanted to be allowed to pursue electronic music in its own way. At the same time, Wade indicated that he respected Cleverdon's position: "It seems desirable in view of the many lines of approach to electrophonic effects of which the above is only one example that as soon as possible a further meeting of the committee might be called ... to assure coordination." His insistence that the sounds under discussion be labeled "electrophonic effects," rather than music, and his subtle attempt to make sure "his people" were included in the discussions betray a fear that the "lunatic fringe" would take over the more musical commissions.[22] Keefe expressed this fear more explicitly in his letter to the controller of the Music Department, R. J. F. Howgill, and his more musically conservative assistant, Maurice Johnstone. From his discussion with the SPNM, Keefe was able to establish two positions. First, he expressed his and Wade's belief that electronic sound should be "limited at present to the technical facilities necessary for compositions of electronic music and *musique concrète* used in conjunction with features and drama productions." This way, there could be no misunderstanding of the boundaries between proper "music" and this new subversive form. Second, Keefe resented the composers, two of whom he felt were urging the BBC to "spend every penny it could lay its hand on to build an electronic studio to outdistance those at Cologne and Milan.... My personal impression is that one or two of the composers were anxious to have a toy to play with, not that this was the only instrument by which they could realize their imaginative dreams."[23] Keefe did not object primarily to the idea that composers would take advantage of the BBC's generosity. Rather, he dismissed these composers for turning against the ideals of British music. These traitors, in his eyes, were merely small symbols of what he saw as a larger threat to the newly established "British musical tradition." He articulated his beliefs further in the memo, which bears reprinting in full, for it represents a perspective and philosophy widespread among musical conservatives in the Music Department at the time:

A comparison between the situations in Germany and England was continually emphasized [in the meeting], suggesting that the BBC was hopelessly conservative. I think the comparison was false: in Germany composers had experimented in atonal and dodecaphonic music to a degree beyond which the human element was inadequate in performance, and electronic devices offered the only means of realizing the mathematical complexities their music seemed to need. Webern himself said that he could go no further with traditional means. Such a situation has not arisen in this country. Twelve tone composition has been used by very few, and without any marked success. At this stage I think the BBC should beware of providing what will be little more than an opportunity to escape from a stylistic impasse.... The situation, I think, is comparable to that of a few years ago when every composer thought he should write another "Ring," and demanded eight horns, Wagner tubas, four harps, etc.[24]

Keefe articulated a narrow position, ignoring British twelve-tone advocates Elisabeth Lutyens and Humphrey Searle, to say nothing of younger up-and-coming composers. He argued that although electronic sound was rapidly evolving into a necessary element in drama and features, it should be restricted to these areas. He urged the administration to prevent any further encroachment of electronics into the sonic world of the BBC. Drama and Features had to remain firmly separated from Music; this was essential to their position. Musical conservatives like Keefe saw electronic music as just the serialist composer's latest attempt to gain a foothold in Britain. Electronic music was thus irredeemably associated with the ideological battles being waged throughout the Continent, which Britain had managed to avoid, largely due to the exclusionary policies of the BBC.[25] Keefe's and others' anxiety over musical technique coincided with a uniform belief that the composers of this music were largely charlatans who sought a style that could disguise their lack of ability. Keefe presented the case cryptically, and in a diplomatic fashion. But there was nothing cryptic about the memo Wade sent a day later to Howgill, in which he rearticulated this position unmistakably:

> In Europe, in my opinion, it is already *vieux jeu* to make electronic noise for its own sake. There was of course, heavy pressure from the more extravagantly minded (and less erudite) composers for the BBC to provide them with an expensive toy. But Mr. Keefe and I endorse each other in the view that the [BBC] should continue its two-pronged policy:
>   A. To provide an electronic instrument that can be combined musically.
>   B. To supply Drama and Feature's legitimate requirements of background and effects.
>   Our inability to supply the Society for the Promotion of New Music, etc. with the £150,000 toy they demanded does not seem terribly important to me. *Guardianship of rational development of musical aesthetics in this country does, however, seem to be of paramount importance* [emphasis mine].[26]

Finally, the gloves had come off. Nothing less than the musical integrity of the nation was at stake. As protectors of the country's music, leaders of the BBC's Music Department took their responsibilities very seriously; that is where their Multi-colour Tone Organ came in. It allowed electronics to be used in a way that "[could] be combined musically." Wade sarcastically dismissed composers' desire to take advantage of the musical tools of their Continental colleagues with a barely concealed contempt for their perceived inarticulateness.

On March 19, Wade outlined the Music Department's position in a letter to the controller of Entertainment (Drama and Features). This letter included a "Statement of Purpose," which Wade forwarded to all of the important figures in sound broadcasting at the BBC. Acknowledging both the inevitability of establishing a Radiophonic Effects Unit and the desire of "musical" composers to utilize the equipment housed there, he then revealed that Music Department heads had recently decided they needed to exert control regarding electronic music: "A watch will be kept to safeguard the rational development of musical aesthetics in this country, and at the end of the year selected composers only will be given the opportunity to experiment."[27] He cited Frank Howes's summary of electronic music in the *Times*, which had said that "the scientists and trautonists are therefore not yet dealing with music, which is an art, but only with its raw material."[28] Using Howes's remarks as a tacit endorsement of his ideas, Wade went on to claim that the primary and "legitimate" concern of the Music Department was to protect how "art" and "raw material" were combined. He proposed the electronic Multi-colour Tone Organ as the solution to this problem.[29] With it, "appropriate results" could be injected into the art form. Although Wade acknowledged the legitimacy of electronic sound effects and said that laboratory work might be required for such projects, he added:

> We are also very concerned that the sterility, which has resulted in
> Europe from expensive laboratories being at the disposal of secondary
> musical composers who have produced little beyond freakishness, should
> be avoided here. In due course we shall doubtless emerge at a point
> where the results of the sound effect operation can have some bearing
> on the future of the music art form. But that point will be some time
> ahead.[30]

The decision to house the Radiophonic Workshop at Maida Vale was a coup for those who believed in electronic music as music, and it had political implications outside the realm of electronic sound production. With its close proximity to traditional musicians in the orchestral studios, the Workshop inevitably became associated more with music making. Such geographical proximity enabled the kind of back-and-forth communication between the Workshop's composers and engineers and those associated with more traditional music. One can only imagine how the Workshop's output would have differed if it had ultimately found a home at the Engineering building at Nightingale Square. At the time of Wade's memo (March 19, 1957), the decision on where the Radiophonic Workshop would be housed was still three months away and could thus still be influenced by the Music Department (although, ultimately, practical considerations outweighed any philosophical ones). Music's goal was to maintain two distinct strains of development for electronic sound, as Wade made clear in the conclusion to his memo: "May we ask that it be ensured that the two parallel lines of development be pursued and that there be no undue haste to exploit sound effects, under a pseudo-musical label, for their novelty, freak or feature value."[31]

It was up to forces outside the sphere of the Music Department to advocate in favor of electronics. Two weeks later, in a spirit of reconciliation, the head of Features, Lawrence Gilliam, wrote a carefully worded response to Wade's letter, directed to all recipients of that Statement of Purpose.[32] Gilliam, a longtime supporter of experimental techniques, "strongly support[ed] [Wade's] view that the radiophonic equipment should not be used by secondary composers who (have failed perhaps to establish themselves in more traditional forms) wish to cash in on this new technique." But he gingerly admonished Wade for assuming that just because experiments on the Continent had ended in "sterility," British composers would naturally end up with the same results. "The younger generation of composers is interested in these possibilities; and inasmuch as the BBC is the only organization in Britain with the necessary equipment, there is a certain obligation on the Corporation to let them see what they can achieve." With a bit of rhetorical sleight-of-hand, Gilliam then described the situation of three respected "art music" composers—Peter Racine Fricker, Humphrey Searle, and Michael Tippett—who had all expressed an interest in composing electronic music for Features but were severely limited by the lack of available equipment. The pig-headedness of the Music Department was now affecting the output of Features, Gilliam seemed to be saying. No one could deny that Tippett was a respectable composer. Gilliam knew that the BBC Music Department's shortsightedness had been in some way responsible for the bad reputation of English music in Europe. Only by encouraging the more experimental paths of those other studios could England hope to compete. Comparing the Music Department's members to an earlier generation of art critics, Gilliam noted that "the early cubists were often accused of 'sterility and freakishness,' but no informed person would now dare to deny their formative effect on such modern masters as Braque and Picasso." As if to prove the Music Department's reactionary position invalid, Gilliam reminded of the BBC's poor showing in recent Continental music competitions by reminding them that "we cannot blink the fact that, in the view of the Italia Prize juries, the BBC music entries [meaning the entries from Music Department] so far have all failed to exploit the potentialities of the radio medium." Hoping to bind the sound broadcasting world together, Gilliam finally reminded them of the elephant in the room, television, whose growing market share threatened to eliminate radio altogether if it did not begin to explore new, more dynamic techniques: "In the present situation of Sound broadcasting, it is surely self evident that we must pursue with energy, determination and ingenuity a new technique that belongs to the realm of imaginative creation in the Sound sphere."[33]

Gilliam's note calmed the Music Department, or at least made them reconsider their public opposition. In private correspondence, their antagonism toward the Workshop continued unabated. Over a year after the Workshop opened in April 1958, Wade wrote an angry memo to Pip Porter, who was responsible for scheduling commissions for the Workshop's services, after receiving a cost estimate for the Workshop's services that had apparently been sent around to all production departments as a way of recruiting business. In it he reiterated:

> It should be quite clear that this department would never use the Radiophonic Workshop and is, in fact, offering much more economic facilities through the Colourtone Instrument now installed in Maida Vale 3.... I shall be more than interested to know how the overall cost of the Radiophonic Workshop to the Corporation could be reduced by proper consideration of the facilities now available in MV3 via the Colourtone Instrument.[34]

Porter responded immediately to Wade's letter by agreeing that it would be nice if the Workshop staff could use the "Colourtone Instrument" but that no one knew how to use it![35] However, Wade, responsible for the Light Programme, perceived only part of the threat of the Workshop. What he and others in the Music Department did not realize was that radiophonics was ultimately to abandon whatever tenuous claims could be made for it as part of the "contemporary music" scene and tread directly into the territory of Light Music. Gilliam's claim that electronic sound "belonged" to sound broadcasting also held true for only a short time; within a few weeks of the Workshop's opening, television began exploring "special sound" with equal enthusiasm as radio.

In the last two years of the decade, however, there was a slight but noticeable shift in attitude toward electronic music in the music culture of the BBC, at least in terms of acknowledging its importance on the Continent. Cleverdon commented in a meeting of the Third Programme board that "although Music Department seemed to be willing to put on recordings of electronic compositions from the continent, they did not seem to be so anxious to encourage British composers in this field." He then wondered "whether electronic composition in fact really came more within the scope of Features Department."[36] His concession that his department might be responsible for support of the fledgling art form indicates his resignation to Music Department's continual opposition to the creation of new electronic music within the BBC. But his acknowledgment of this music's value was an important step for the department, anticipating an important philosophical shift brought about there by a new leader. In winter 1959, William Glock was appointed controller of Music. With this change in management came a huge change in programming direction. In contrast to his predecessors, Glock was famous throughout Britain for his advocacy of contemporary music, and particularly for his enthusiasm for young avant-garde composers. He had created *Score*, Britain's first journal devoted to the study of contemporary music, in 1949. To further the promotion of new music, he had also established in Dartington at the beginning of the 1950s, with the help of other leading composers, a summer school on the model of Darmstadt. This school emphasized the study of both contemporary and early music. In this new climate, those in Light Music (and the more conservative individuals within the larger Music Division, such as Howgill's second-in-command, Maurice Johnstone) were forced to rethink their aggressive tactics.[37]

Staff and Equipment: Stocking Rooms 13/14 and 15

It is not easy to inventory the equipment that ultimately ended up in the Radiophonic Workshop's initial studio in April 1958. Since no records survive detailing the specific machinery in their entirety, this sort of precise list is impossible to assemble. Nevertheless, by using records, photographs, and the memories of those involved, I have attempted to reconstruct as closely as possible the limited inventory of the Workshop at the time of its creation. Again, such detail is necessary, as it was those specific pieces of equipment that were to determine the nature and sound of the Workshop's output. One thing is certain; the task is made much more difficult by the haphazard methods by which the Workshop gathered equipment. From the moment the REC secured a home for the Workshop, the committee began asking around in other departments for obsolete or redundant and used equipment. After receiving the overly optimistic equipment list suggested in the initial proposal, the committee was faced with the realization that they would receive only £1,900 for "minimum purchase of essential equipment not obtainable from redundant plant."[38] This meant that although they would be receiving *some* money—"start-up" money, as it were—most of their equipment needs would have to be met by soliciting other departments or by requesting through the Equipment Department a search of the redundant plant, a storage facility for over-stocked items or equipment too obsolete or old-fashioned to be wanted by anyone else.[39] These items still had to be paid for, but could be purchased at a reduced price. They managed to scrape together some pretty exotic things, in particular some equipment from the recently upgraded Royal Albert Hall, including an enormous ornate wood-carved mixing desk. The Equipment Department sent them a list of available items: a shabby collection of secondhand, unwanted gear including microphones, amplifiers, jackfields, filters, and other assorted studio essentials, but very few large items.[40] Once they had established what kind of material they would obtain from other departments, the REC was able to begin shopping for new equipment, which they purchased from their £1,900 budget. George summarized the final approved budget to McWhinnie on February 25, 1958, and included a chart of the essential equipment to be ordered (table 2.1).[41]

Table 2.1. Initial Radiophonic Workshop Purchases

Item	Manufacturer	Type No.	Approx. Cost
Two Reflectograph Industrial Model Recorders (variable speed)	Rudman Darlington (Electronics) Ltd.	RR 102	£241
One Reflectograph Twin Channel Data Recorder	Rudman Darlington (Electronics) Ltd.	RR 102	£250
One Decade Oscillator	Muirhead	D-650-B	£313
One Square-wave Shaper	Muirhead	D-783	£70
One Variable voice frequency filter with amplifier	Albiswerk Zurich S.A.	502/50	£480
Two Lenco four-speed Transcription Units complete with pick up and band location service	Goldring Manufacturing Co. (Gr. Britain) Ltd.	GL56	£46
Minor equipment which cannot be specified in detail at this stage			£500 Total: £1,900

R.V.A. George to Donald McWhinnie, memo, February 25, 1958, WAC R97/9/1.

George was overly optimistic about the opening day for the Workshop, yet the contents of his list were purchased without delay. The equipment listed above, together with the redundant equipment "adopted" by the Workshop from other departments, constituted an effective bare-bones basic studio, even though the equipment was almost entirely secondhand and ill-functioning. These obsolete and antique items constantly needed repair and/or adaptation to fulfill the demands of the composers. This was another reason that, when issues of staffing arose, it was necessary to have a highly skilled engineer who worked full-time keeping the equipment in working order.

Tape Recorders

In the classic tape studio, tape recorders are the single most important pieces of equipment. The Workshop ended up with a unique combination of such machines. The most interesting and eccentric pieces were the two German-made Motosacoche tape recorders (figure 2.1). To enable dubbing back and forth, these huge machines, about four and a half feet tall and three feet square, were linked by a central controlling unit, making for three huge boxes. They were the first non-steel tape recorders bought by the BBC and took fifteen seconds to gear up to the correct speed.[42] They were very reliable machines, however, and could run all day without problems. The Motosacoche company was

Figure 2.1. The two German-made Motosacoche tape recorders, with central controlling unit. Copyright © BBC.

known for their motorcycles, and an interesting feature of these recorders was that their "hoods" could be raised by electric motors and steel ribbons to above head height for repair and motor replacement!

The BBC had also modified the original machines in order to modernize them. They had replaced the original open-platter format from which the magnetic tape spooled with less precarious closed-tape reels, and adapted them in the interest of tape economy to run at 15 inches per second (ips) rather than their original Continental standard speed of 30 ips.[43]

The EMI BTR/2 tape recorder was only slightly less bulky than the Motosacoche but required no separate controlling unit. This British machine had been the professional standard recorder at the BBC since 1953 owing to its versatility, ease of operation, and durability.[44] Extremely reliable, the BTR/2 was about four feet tall and provided an exceptional frequency range (50 to 15,000 cycles per second). It had adjustable speeds that could play at either 15 ips or 7.5 ips.[45] The main drawback was their prohibitively expensive cost: new machines were selling for £850. By 1958, these machines had largely been replaced by the cheaper EMI TR90, which were half the cost, making the BTR/2 an uneconomical choice. I can only assume the Workshop was able to get one of the BTR/2 machines after it had been replaced with the cheaper TR90 in another department.

The Reflectograph 500 was a new model of semiprofessional mono tape recorder that recorded at a slower speed than the Motosacoches but had the advantage of variable speed, adjustable anywhere between 3.75 and 7.5 ips. This meant that recording pitch could be raised or lowered in interesting ways. At about three feet square by one foot deep, with detachable lids, they were also fairly portable. One of the Reflectographs acquired by the Workshop was a special model that could record two separate tracks onto the same piece of tape. While it was different from a stereo recorder, since it couldn't record both channels of sound at once, it was still the first "multitrack" recorder the Workshop possessed.

At the bottom of the quality scale were the Ferrograph recorders. These portable workhorses were used in the Workshop for recording sounds in isolation or on location. They were common throughout the BBC and had been used before the Workshop opened in the studios in Piccadilly, and particularly at Piccadilly Two, where *All That Fall* had been recorded.

Turntables

In the late 1950s, tape was still a very new medium. The vast majority of recording at the BBC, including all programs recorded for rebroadcast, was still done on disc. Most stations around the globe still required disc copies of BBC programs; these were provided by the BBC transcription service, which recorded them onto special larger discs that required special turntables. The Workshop acquired a set of internally built machines known as the TD/7 Transcription Disc players, which were the standard machines used to play back these discs. The Workshop required these turntables not only for playback but also to rerecord tape recordings onto disc for playback on TD/7 machines. In order to play back standard records, the Workshop acquired a set of turntables by Lenco, a company that specialized in high-quality turntables for broadcasting.

Sound Generators and Miscellaneous Equipment

Following methods developed in earlier productions, most of the actual sound creation in the Workshop in the early years was done by manipulating existing sounds in the manner of *musique concrète* rather than by producing it electronically through oscillators. The north wall of the Workshop, in between the two doors, was devoted to three large rack-mounted units holding miscellaneous pieces of equipment for sound manipulation, mostly signal amplifiers and filters. Attached to the racks on the right was a small workstation where portable components (filters, oscillators, tape recorders) could be combined to create new sounds.

Before any sound could be recorded, its signal had to be amplified. The Workshop owned two kinds of amplifiers: line and trap-valve. The line amplifier is a basic amplifier that simply boosts a weak signal. The slightly more complex trap-valve amplifier isolates a signal. Each individual signal was fed into the trap-valve amplifier in order to separate it from the other sounds. At this point its level was adjusted independently of other sonic components.

Various filters were acquired to alter the quality of sound signals. Usually filters are used either to amplify or attenuate specific aspects of a signal. Amplifying the low frequencies, for example, makes the sound much richer. Attenuating the middle frequencies, on the other hand, hollows out the original sound, making it appear disconnected and ethereal (like the sounds created for *Private Dreams and Public Nightmares*).

The most useful filter was also the most basic. Known as a Portable Effects Unit (PEU), it was initially used within the BBC to remove irritating low-frequency noise heard frequently during phone calls. It could filter out low- or high-frequency sound, but could also function well in drama as a filter for making a regular studio microphone sound like a voice heard over a telephone. It was also surprisingly useful for creating the kinds of alterations in voices effectively demonstrated in *Private Dreams and Public Nightmares*. It is a perfect example of a piece of technology being used in a way never intended by its creators. It was passive, which means it didn't contain an amplifier and had no external power source; it was simply plugged into the microphone and adjusted before the signal reached the mixer. Since it was also so portable, no permanent place was given to it on the equipment racks; it floated around the studio, usually resting on the mixer or on top of larger machines.

Another filter, slightly more high-tech than the PEU, was the Variable Correction Unit. Again, it was not originally created for the artistic manipulation of a signal but, rather, was designed to reduce disc hum in turntables and to act as a primitive noise-reducer on high-noise disc recordings. This filter's controls enabled users to add or remove the high or low frequencies of a sound. By means of a central switch, users could instantly add or remove the filter's effects.

The Workshop initially acquired two high-quality oscillators. Generating their own sound electronically, most oscillators of the 1950s (before the advent of the voltage-controlled synthesizer) could produce only a sine wave, consisting of only a single tone, with no overtones to muddy the sound. A sine wave would then often be treated to complicate the sound. The Muirhead Decade oscillator could create an audible sine wave on adjustable frequencies and was so named because it had preset controls that produced frequencies set in units of tens or multiples thereof. Along with this was the Muirhead Square Wave Shaper, a smaller box that converted the sine-wave signal from the oscillator to a square wave. The Workshop also bought a beat-frequency oscillator known in-house as the "Wobbulator," which was originally designed for engineering acoustic tests but was also quite useful as a source of raw material. It created a sweeping tone whose pitch was continuously varied by a second internal oscillator, creating moving patterns of electronic sound. The range of the sweep was controlled by a large central knob. One could also add to the moving sound a set amount of pitch "wobble."

The Workshop created reverberation in two ways. The first, and most basic, was by using a small echo room in the basement of Maida Vale, the technology and idea for which had been around since the beginning of radio. The room had a loudspeaker at one end and a pickup microphone on the other, and its smooth, bare walls created natural reverberation. The echo thus created was "authentic," although of rather short duration. To create a more exaggerated echo, a new machine created within the BBC was used. This Artificial Reverberation Unit utilized a rotating drum with tape oxide on its outer rim. Multiple playback heads (as used in tape recorders) read the signal from the drum, and each was controlled individually. The playback quality was less than ideal, and for the Workshop composers, the machine worked best when the rotating motor was switched off during recording to achieve even longer durations of echo.

Mixing Desk

The Workshop composers and engineers controlled sound sources' inputs from a massive oak mixing desk obtained from the refurbished Albert Hall. This unit dated from before the Second World War and contained the obsolete modular components of the outside broadcast amplifier known as the OBA/8. The OBA/8 had been designed in 1938 and comprised three components. The smallest box was a simple power supply amplifier (known as an MU/3A), providing power to the rest of the unit. The larger box was the OBA/8 itself, a component for combining various sound signals. The longer box, known as MX/18, was a four-channel mixer. It allowed the user to adjust the volume of up to four separate signals at once before it entered the OBA/8 and from there into whatever recording media was used. The Workshop's mixing desk contained three separate MX/18s enabling the mixing of up to twelve signals at once. Figure 2.2 shows Daphne Oram with the old Albert Hall OBA/8 unit. Note the

Figure 2.2. Daphne Oram, Desmond Briscoe, Richard "Dickie" Bird, and Donald McWhinnie in Room 13/14. Copyright © BBC.

PEU units on top of the mixer. The photographer was in the claustrophobic tiny studio attached next door.

Staffing

The question of how to staff the Workshop troubled the REC from the very beginning. The initial document proposing the studio in November 1956 suggested "three tape editors and devisors of special effects" and one "recording Engineer...experienced in construction of apparatus."[46] This was followed up on March 6, 1957, with the suggestion of combining staff from the production and engineering departments, but not exceeding three or four people. But a month later, Garrard reported to the committee that in the few radiophonic productions that had been created up to that point, staff had complained about how fatiguing it was to devise radiophonic sounds. He also acknowledged that the time-intensive process of creating sounds was a necessary part of the learning process and should not be hurried. He thought "it would be necessary to use larger numbers of people and change them frequently. The recent experiments in 'Radiophonic Effects' had aroused widespread interest throughout all units... and it was proposed to let as many interested people as possible try their hand at the work."[47]

In an attempt to find those staff members most adept at radiophonics, Garrard organized and designed a two-day course to teach potential senior SMs and selected members of their staff in the techniques of electronic music. The first day was spent demonstrating recordings of Continental and U.S. studios and describing their apparatus. During the afternoon, the class assembled their own effects "involving the primitive methods at our disposal."[48] This project was then completed on the second day. Garrard hoped that the course could be conducted on a regular basis. Whether or not the course was ultimately successful is unknown, since no records survive, but one can assume it was the prototype for later, more hands-on courses taught to prospective composers; records do survive for these later courses.

When the wiring of the studio began on December 30, 1957, its staffing still had not been decided. At this point it was planned that the staff would consist of two SMs and two engineers (one senior and one junior). The engineering staff organized the installation of the equipment; the new SMs were not present until the installation was complete.[49] Ultimately, the solution to the problem of fatigue was solved by the decision to introduce two SMs along with one engineer, with a third SM arriving six months later as a replacement for one of the managers, and continuing in rotation, every six months, "for rest and refresher," and to maintain "continuity of work and thought."[50] According to future Workshop director Desmond Briscoe, the reason employees were constantly juggled around was more than a little political: the powers that be hoped that this shifting would prevent the musical "lunatic fringe" from gaining a foothold within the Workshop.[51]

Engineering work was not considered as "fatiguing" as the supposedly more creative work done by the SMs. They were not to be shifted as often; in fact, no provision was made for the moving around of engineers. In a demonstration of the BBC's notorious scaled hierarchical job system, the engineers were thought to have a less stressful job, "merely" realizing the more mentally draining artistic vision of the SMs.

Daphne Oram was the committee's first choice as one of the studio's SMs. She had by far the most experience with radiophonic production and had expressed an interest in the field long before the establishment of the REC. Oram, a skilled musician, had been employed initially as a BBC "music balancer" during the war. Oram also trained as an engineer and by the early 1950s had been promoted to Music SM. In this capacity, she campaigned for electronic music facilities and was one of the contributors to Brian George's initial

proposal to the EEC in 1956. On January 26, 1958, a radio adaptation of Shaw's
Heartbreak House featured radiophonic effects by Oram. This was preceded by a
discussion of *concrète* effects on the program *Monitor* immediately before, so a
great deal of publicity had been given to the production. In March of that year,
Oram composed music and effects (constructed with sine-wave oscillators, a
single tape recorder, and homemade filters) for *Amphitryon 38*, the first television program to use radiophonic effects.[52] In the months leading up to the
opening of the Workshop, Oram added radiophonic elements to several other
plays, including *Prometheus Unbound*. She was clearly electronic music's most
experienced and enthusiastic advocate among the Music Department's SMs.
Her musical training and experience also gave the fledgling Workshop a much-
needed dash of musical credibility. Oram's great hope was that the Workshop
would use the success of its productions for the Drama Department to encourage
the creation of more straightforward musical works and that it would eventually become a center for electronic music creation rivaling that of Paris, Cologne,
Milan, or Columbia-Princeton. That she was the first person considered for the
job is clear from a letter from staffing executive Pip Porter, who specified that
if she was around, she could "impart the know-how so far gained" to the other
"suitable types."[53]

The choice for the other SM was equally easy. It made sense to employ
someone from the Drama Department, since so many of the commissions would
come from there. The manager with the greatest experience, Desmond Briscoe,
had worked on Beckett's recent success, *All That Fall*. Since Beckett's play, Briscoe
had worked on Giles Cooper's *The Disagreeable Oyster*, as well as *Private Dreams
and Public Nightmares* and *A Winter Journey*. In essence, he had participated in all
of the major dramatic productions featuring radiophonic sound up to that point.
Although he wasn't trained as a classical musician in the same way as Oram, his
practical experience in electronic sound effect production made him the logical
choice. His bureaucratic deftness and showman-like personality were also highly
valued in the politically sensitive world of the BBC.

The senior engineer assigned to the Workshop was Richard "Dickie" Bird, an
elderly man with over thirty years of experience at the BBC. Bird had begun his
engineering career maintaining slot machines in pubs and cafes. Although he
maintained equipment with an astonishing degree of dedication, he also had
continued a successful career moonlighting as a sound recordist for feature films.
His technical expertise and love of machinery made him the ideal choice as the
Workshop's permanent engineer. The shoddy and precarious condition of most
of the equipment meant that Bird would be required to take apart, repair, and
reassemble almost anything at a moment's notice. He was also required to fulfill
the artistic needs of the sometimes technically vague SMs. It was his duty to help

Figure 2.3. Daphne Oram, surrounded by the first generation of Workshop equipment. Copyright © BBC.

them realize their creative visions in a practical way and to let them know whether an idea was in fact possible.[54]

A friend of Oram's, Jeannie MacDowell, was employed as a junior engineer and assistant to Bird. She was from the Control Room, but also had experience working in electronic sounds due to her relationship with Oram.

In the beginning, the SMs and the engineers fulfilled two completely separate roles. This had as much to do with political and class hierarchies within the BBC as with the actual work undertaken. Despite the changes occurring in British culture in the late 1950s (as more women entered the workplace, and class distinctions began to blur), the BBC attempted to maintain as rigid a class structure within its walls as was legally possible.[55] Operating on a graded scale, BBC jobs were categorized according to their relative difficulty, that is, whether it was skilled or unskilled work, creative, technical, or clerical. Such distinctions intentionally or unintentionally maintained the larger class divisions of society at large. Dick Mills, who joined the Radiophonic Workshop in 1959 as an engineer, only half facetiously observed the distinctions between the "first class" of employees—the SMs, producers, and so on—and the "second class," the engineering staff. He noted that "the first group consisted of 'arty' folk who knew about the loftier aims in life, which knife and fork to use at 'dinner,' could probably recite Shakespeare, play the piano and took the *Daily Telegraph* or *The Times*. (Calling each other 'Luvvy' came later!)" The engineers, by contrast, worked mostly in the Control Room, which was like a telephone exchange center, receiving the signals from the various studios and outside broadcast units and recording them. The Engineering Department had to maintain all of the equipment and understand the machines' workings inside and out. Their services were then invaluable to the more "artistic" staffers, whose knowledge of technical matters could be less than adequate. In an atmosphere that was, in Mills's words, "typical of the British class system, each department was looked down on (or up to) by the others. Studio Managers obviously thought Control Room staff couldn't hold a tune, whilst recording staff felt that Studio Managers couldn't wield a razor blade for fear of hurting themselves!" Because of this fear, it was decided that each new project at the Workshop would be realized using one SM and one engineer working together.

Despite all the careful planning, it was impossible to tell what the actual job descriptions would be for the initial staff. Pragmatic decisions made fairly early on reflected more accurately the necessities of production. This included having visiting SMs in the first year—like Norman Bain, who returned in a more official capacity in 1960 and whose experience in engineering made him a useful colleague for the Workshop's initiates, and engineer Ken Squires, the resident engineer at Maida Vale. He was essential in getting all the new equipment powered and operational in an unpredictable fifty-year-old building. In general, after the opening day, a more flexible attitude toward Workshop appointments was adopted by BBC staffers. This of course makes it much more difficult to tell who did what: many creative minds were able to work on the various projects always in continuous circulation through the studio. This feeling of communal work was encouraged by Oram and Briscoe. Nearly all Workshop projects are credited in broadcast credits to the "Radiophonic Workshop" rather than to an individual composer or engineer who actually worked on it.

Table 2.2 summarizes those major works produced and broadcast between November 1956 and April 1958, when the Workshop officially opened its doors. Each of these works contributed something to the ongoing development of electronic sound in radio and with *Amphitryon 38*, the first use in television. As each project attempted more and more ambitious sound and musical effects, there began to evolve an aesthetic unique to the BBC, one that involved a distinctive combination of words and sound.[56]

As the Workshop took over these productions, the variety of the commissions demanded versatile staffing. The log book from the first six months of the Workshop's opening, shown in table 2.3, shows both the balance of labor and the various roles each staff member played. Daphne Oram operated as a full-time composer, while Desmond Briscoe combined composition with public relations. Dickie Bird served as their engineer, with Norman Bain assisting. This list also shows the sheer variety of projects undertaken and the speed with which they were completed.

In addition to an overt spirit of cooperative composition, what stands out in this calendar is not only the sheer volume of composition, but also its variety and innovation. Note that less than a week after the equipment had been installed, Workshop staff were already hard at work on the first official productions, *The Heritage* and *The Ocean*.

Table 2.2. Key Pre-Workshop Radiophonic Projects

Date	Title of Work	Producer	Sound Designer/ Composer/Engineer
1/11/57	*All That Fall*	Donald McWhinnie	Desmond Briscoe, Norman Bain
3/18/57	*Opium*	Douglas Cleverdon	André Almuro
8/15/57	*The Disagreeable Oyster*	Donald McWhinnie	Desmond Briscoe, Norman Bain
10/7/57	*Private Dreams and Public Nightmares*	Donald McWhinnie	Desmond Briscoe, Norman Bain, Daphne Oram
10/27/57	*Metamorphosis*	Michael Bakewell	Franz Reizenstein, Desmond Briscoe, Norman Bain, Daphne Oram
2/24/58	*A Winter Journey*	John Gibson	Desmond Briscoe, Norman Bain, Daphne Oram
3/2/58	*Amphitryon 38*	Harold Clayton	Daphne Oram, Norman Bain

Table 2.3. 1958 Logbook Activity

Date	Project or Task Performed	Radiophonic Employee
4/8	Equipment installation	
4/9	Equipment installation	
4/10	Equipment installation	
	Effects for *Antarctic Wind*	Daphne Oram, Richard Bird
4/11	Equipment installation	
4/14	Equipment installation	
4/15	Equipment installation	
	Recorded basic oscillator notes	Oram
4/16	Equipment installation	
	Recorded basic oscillator notes	Oram
4/17	Equipment installation	
	Recorded basic oscillator notes	Oram
	Effects for *The Heritage*	Oram
4/18	Collecting materials, tapes, etc., from various places, taking to Maida Vale	
4/21	Effects for *The Ocean*	Oram, Desmond Briscoe, Bird
4/22	Effects for *The Ocean*	Oram, Briscoe, Bird
4/23	First demo for Radiophonic committee	Oram, Briscoe, Bird
	Playback of *The Ocean* for Donald McWhinnie, producer	
4/24	*The Heritage*	Oram
	The Ocean	Oram, Briscoe, Bird
4/25	*The Ocean* for McWhinnie	
	Meeting with producer to discuss *Arabian Nights*	Oram
4/28	Visit by publicity officers	Oram, Briscoe, Bird, Norman Bain
4/29	Demonstration for BBC controllers	Oram, Briscoe, Bird
	The Ocean	Oram, Briscoe, Bird, Bain
	Playback of *The Heritage* for Gibson, producer	Oram
4/30	*The Ocean* recording in Studio 3 Maida Vale with cast	Oram, Briscoe, Bird, Bain, Nesta Cathn
5/5	Effects for *I Talk to Myself*	Oram, Bird, Denis Lewell, A. Henderson
5/7	Effects for *I Talk to Myself*	Oram, Bird, Denis Lewell, A. Henderson
5/8	Effects for *I Talk to Myself*	Oram, Bird, Denis Lewell, A. Henderson
5/9	Effects for *I Talk to Myself*	Oram, Bird, Denis Lewell, A. Henderson
5/12	Effects for *I Talk to Myself*	Oram, Bird, Denis Lewell, A. Henderson
5/13	*Private Dreams and Public Nightmares*, playback and copying	Oram, Bird, using Motosacoche
5/14	*Mr. Goodjohn and Mr. Badjack*, discussion with producer	Oram
5/15	*Mr. Goodjohn and Mr. Badjack*, creating and recording effects	Oram
5/19	Press photographers visit	Garrard, McWhinnie, Oram, Bird, Briscoe

5/27	Planning and prep for *The Talking Bird*	Oram, Bird
	Visit by member of *Hebrew Section*, demonstrations for *Hebrew Section*	Oram, Bird
5/29	Oram goes to Broadcasting House to pick up Pakistani and New Zealand visitors, gives demonstration of equipment	Oram
5/30	Effects for *Talking of Films*	Bird
6/3	Effects for *Studio E* (television program title)	Oram, Bird, director Len Chase
6/11	Work on Howard Blair television program	Oram, Ken Squires (Maida Vale in-house engineer)
	Work on *Children's Hour*	Oram, Squires
	Effects for *The Jack in the Box*	Oram, Squires
6/16	*Radio Show* (TRW#1012)	Oram, Bird, producer M. Garrard
6/30	Ken Squires gives demonstration to Mr. Crawford (superintendent engineer, Sound Broadcasting)	Squires
7/1	Preparation for *Under the Loofah Tree*	Briscoe
7/2	Discussion with producer for *Under the Loofah Tree*	Oram, Briscoe, McWhinnie
7/4	Effects for *Under the Loofah Tree*	Oram, Briscoe, Squires
	Effects for *Towie Castle* "two inserts radiophonically treated and replaced on original tape"	Oram, Briscoe, Squires
7/5	Incidental Music for Edinburgh Festival [8 short pieces for Adamov's *Invasion* for Oxford Arena Theatre]	Oram
7/7	Incidental Music for Edinburgh Festival	Oram
	Effects for *Ballad of Mari Lwyd*	Oram
7/12	Edinburgh Festival with producer, Bryan Izzard	Oram, Izzard
7/14	Bird "treating television news with PEU...to try and increase body of chimes. Original tape quality poor with distortion and tape flutter."	Bird
7/17	Trial effects for *The Language of the Sea*	Bird, producers Thomson, A. Henderson, H. Catlin, J. Johnson
7/22	Recording *Under the Loofah Tree*	Briscoe, Bird
7/23	Recording *Under the Loofah Tree*, with time in Echo Room	Briscoe, Bird
7/24	Recording *Under the Loofah Tree*, with time in Echo Room	Briscoe, Bird
7/25	Recording *Under the Loofah Tree*, with time in Echo Room	Briscoe, Bird
8/5	Completes music for Edinburgh Festival	Oram
	Clearing up after recording *Under the Loofah Tree*	Bird
8/6	Music for *The Creation of the Animals*	Briscoe, Oram, Bird, producer Douglas Cleverdon, composer André Almuro
8/13	Music for *The Creation of the Animals*	Briscoe, Oram, Bird, Cleverdon, Almuro

Opening Day

The Radiophonic Workshop officially opened on April 1, 1958, although, as the chart shows, it had begun tentative projects several days earlier and was not completely operational until April 14.[57] In fact, after the main equipment had been set up, it had to be calibrated and master tapes of various electronic sounds prepared. This happened in the first three weeks of April. On April 15, 16, and 17, for example, Daphne Oram recorded basic oscillator notes for future use, making a stock of individual pitches that could be reused, to save her the task of setting up an oscillator each time a specific note was required.

The REC met for the first time *in situ* on April 23 to discuss the first few weeks of the Workshop's operation and to sort out remaining problems. The Workshop opened with £500 in the bank, but staffing remained a problem. Although Oram, Briscoe, Bird, and MacDowell were all to stay for the present, only Oram's position could be guaranteed; staff shortages signaled that the other three could potentially be sent elsewhere if needed. Oram, as unofficial "head," was to remain "for some time to preserve continuity."[58] Perhaps because of this it seems that the majority of the earliest projects in the Workshop were realized by Oram rather than Briscoe, who mostly acted as a liaison to the outside. In addition to creating the basic oscillator tapes, Oram also realized most of the effects for the first production to come out of the newly christened Workshop, *The Heritage*. These effects must have been minimal, because the next production, an adaptation of James Hanley's novel *The Ocean*, occupied most of the rest of April and was a group effort.

The BBC called a press conference on May 22 to announce the Workshop's opening. It released a four-page description of the new service with the heading "BBC Opens Britain's First Radiophonic Workshop." The publicity material goes to great pains to distinguish between what the Workshop was doing and *musique concrète* or electronic music: "Although some of the techniques are similar, radiophonic sound is not an art in itself—it is used to provide an additional 'dimension' for radio and television productions."[59] They still acknowledge the dual function of the effects, however, by noting that they "provide an aid to productions which neither music nor conventional sound effects can give."[60] In light of the battles between the Drama and Music Departments, this distinction was particularly important. By calling the Workshop's output neither literally music nor sound effects, but acknowledging its capacity to be both, the BBC effectively hedged its bets. In the daily newspapers, the arbitrary distinction between "music" and "sound effects" again caused some confusion. Some, like the *Times*, merely reproduced the BBC's description of the Workshop's output as "providing an imaginative background to drama productions which cannot be obtained from ordinary music or from the stock-in-trade of sound effects."[61] Other papers, however, weren't nearly as certain of this distinction. Several prominent papers, after considering the output of European electronic music studios, hoped that the composers of "radiophonics" in Britain, "a team of enthusiasts, led by musician and technician Daphne Oram," would "yet dazzle their continental counterparts by their independent discoveries and ambitions."[62]

As the team settled into their jobs, they grew more confident, and the composers' and engineers' ability to create the abstract worlds promised by the Workshop's publicity soon became apparent. As discussed in the next chapter, productions like Giles Cooper's *Under the Loofah Tree* and an adaptation of Jean Cocteau's film *Orpheus* demonstrate the fluency and indeed mastery over *concrète*-style abstract effects that the BBC's press announcement had emphasized. It was the next generation of works for television and radio, however, that would direct the emphasis away from abstraction and into a more "musical" world, albeit one far from the ivory tower of the contemporary classical centers.

3

The Golden Age of Special Sound

First Projects

What philosophy, if any, guided the use of radiophonics during the first years of the Workshop? Searching for a generic semiotic "meaning" for radiophonic sound during its early years can be a project fraught with difficulty, since its use varies so strongly from commission to commission. But standing back and observing the studio's output from the distance of time, we can see certain general trends emerge. For example, over a fifteen-year period, from the late 1950s to the mid-1970s, there was a broad shift in how projects used radiophonic sound: radiophonics moved away from representing disturbed or altered states of consciousness, alien threats, and future dystopias and toward signifying an optimistic future filled with technological promise. Yet if we think of this trend as simply representing a cultural zeitgeist, we overlook the gradual nature of this shift and in turn diminish the roles of the various individuals, producers, composers, and engineers who, working on discrete commissions each with specific demands, contributed to the overall teleology of the Workshop's sound.

The early obsession with frightening, disturbing, and alienating sound can be traced partially to the techniques available to the first group of composers at the Workshop. It was, as producer Donald McWhinnie had noted in his introduction to *Private Dreams and Public Nightmares*, frankly easier to make sounds that came across as horrific than to make sounds that were warm, inviting, soothing. Yet it was also true that the popular conception of the relationship between the arts and sciences was largely an antagonistic one. C. P. Snow's 1959 Rede lecture, "The Two Cultures," had hit a chord with the public and seemed to articulate to the British press and its readers a real disconnect between the optimism of scientists and the ambivalence of the contemporary arts toward them. Productions from the BBC, such as the *Quatermass* and *Andromeda* series, reflect this disconnect in their portrayals of a cold scientific elite, while at the same time in their soundtracks, particularly in the final *Quatermass* installment of the 1950s, they problematize a simple understanding of this division with a "scientific"-sounding electronic music that seems to attempt to unite the worlds of the arts and science, or at least to create a "scientific art form."

It is these larger philosophical and cultural questions that haunt and shape the changing form and function of electronic music during the first years of the Workshop's existence. The evolution of the sound produced at the studio demonstrates a threefold shift from more abstract, *musique concrète*–based pieces to works that are driven primarily by tape-loop-created rhythmic patterns and finally to a combination of these rhythmic structures and tonally based composition.[1] This move is gradual but persistent, and the works I examine are both chronologically typical and exemplary demonstrations of those changes. Thus, a primary task of this chapter is to discuss and analyze in detail individual works using transcriptions, film and sound theory, aesthetic theory, and, when useful, basic harmonic analysis in an effort to explore radiophonic sound's unique power for blurring the distinctions between diegetic and nondiegetic noise, and using the nonrepresentational *acousmêtre* in more complex ways than is possible in traditional music and sound effects.

Yet it is also possible to draw broader conclusions about the nature of British modernism in the period under discussion as it is manifested in the pieces produced by the Radiophonic Workshop. One approach, perhaps the standard one, is to see the works through the lens of the traditional narrative of contemporary postwar music, in which they are perceived essentially as watered-down examples of Continental modernism, with its notions of the supremacy of musical autonomy, dissonance, and "difficulty." Another approach is to reconcile the various conflicting elements in the Workshop's output. After all, its primary function was to provide television and radio productions with sound and music, a function that Continental art-music composers viewed as an unacceptable concession to antimodernist aesthetics. Yet the Workshop's output resists these approaches. Its style combined rhythmic regularity, tonal progressions, recognizable structural forms, and familiar, albeit treated, sounds with the modernity of contemporary recording methods, electronic sound production, and truly challenging timbres, a "difficulty" which, in spite of bouncing melodies, left its audiences with an experience of the modern. Apprehending the Workshop's extraordinary achievements in this way enables us to form a new understanding of the works as modern and challenging *within the context of their creation*, and their potential value as effective, moving, complex works of art within a uniquely British populist modernism should be judged on these new sets of criteria. This modernism is content to reference qualities of Continental postwar musical modernism and sample them freely—a little dissonance here, a little electronic sound production there—without committing itself to the musical, cultural, and political implications of high modernism.

Almost immediately after its establishment in April 1958, the staff of the Workshop began asking for more money for equipment. In particular, they wanted funds to set up a separate studio for the production of electronic sounds. For the first year or so of the Workshop's operation, there were only limited possibilities for producing electronic sound: for example, through the Muirhead oscillators. As a result of the paucity of equipment, the kinds of pieces composers tended to create in the beginning were less tonally precise. They were more abstract and atmospheric—the kinds of works made possible by slowing down and speeding up existing sounds. Such sounds worked well as backgrounds for programs, but limited the potential creativity of the Workshop's composers, who were anxious to explore the kinds of techniques they had heard in works emerging from other studios around the world.

Three kinds of compositions were required of the Workshop. First, following the mandate of their founding, they continued to contribute to Drama Department productions with radiophonic sound effects, or "special sound," as it was frequently credited, although it soon became clear that the boundary between special sound and incidental music was tenuous at best. Second, they needed to provide "interval music," to be played either during the beginning or end of the broadcast day or between programs. If on television, the interval music was accompanied by a moving clock. Finally, and perhaps most problematically for the nature of their equipment, they needed to compose signature tunes for the opening and closing credits of radio and television productions.

The Ocean and Under the Loofah Tree

The Ocean exemplifies perfectly the kind of early commission that blurred the distinction between "music" and "effects." After producer Donald McWhinnie explained what the production required, Desmond Briscoe, Daphne Oram, and engineer Norman Bain worked together for seven full days creating the sound effects and atmospheres. James Hanley's drama concerned the crew of a World War II ship adrift in a lifeboat, with radiophonic sound evoking the ubiquitous sea. Two notes from an E♭ clarinet, a G♯ and F♯, served as the source for the majority of the effects. The producers combined and then treated these sounds, sliding the pitches downward between the G♯ to the F♯, then reducing that pitch to half-speed to sound the lower octave, producing a three-note sequence. While the noise obviously sounds treated, it is also harmonically functional, demonstrating a movement from the second scale degree to the tonic, G#–F#, and a final reinforcement of that tonic with its lower octave. These three notes are looped in a slow repetitive pattern that is at once harmonically soothing and uncanny. This sensation is reinforced in turn by the heavy filtering of the narrator's voice, which, as in *Private Dreams and Public Nightmares*, attenuates all the lower and middle frequencies to give a thin, reedy quality to the disembodied storyteller. In an article published in the *Radio Times* McWhinnie described how difficult it was to translate for radio a novel set entirely at sea: "Clearly, conventional methods would not do—one must evolve a radio style which would blend poetry and realism, drama and reflection."[2] Remembering the attitude of the press after *Public Dreams and Private Nightmares*, he again apologized in advance for the program's possible lack of success: "The wonderfully creative team of technicians have spent hours in blending realistic and radiophonic effects. Don't shoot me either; just switch off."[3] The reviewer for the *Listener* received the production warmly, singling out the radiophonic sounds as its strongest element: "This . . . made surrealist sounds serve the script. The three-note phrase [was] something like the slow swell of the sea but also like a groaning dirge from some inhuman voice . . . and as effective as an audible equivalent to nightmare."[4] An unnamed critic even went so far as to note that "few who heard it will forget the haunting theme which so aptly conveyed this impression."[5] See music example 3.1. ☙

The Ocean was an important testing ground for the facilities of the Workshop in its opening days. A greater challenge for Oram, Briscoe, and Bain was to come with Giles Cooper's follow-up to *The Disagreeable Oyster* (discussed in chapter 1). Inspired by the success of that play, Cooper wrote *Under the Loofah Tree*, capitalizing on those elements of his earlier comedy that had made use of tape manipulation and other relatively rudimentary techniques. Whereas his earlier productions had been assembled using whatever equipment happened to be available, he now had access to a unit dedicated to the creation of radiophonic sound, and as a result, Cooper let his imagination run riot, working closely with the production team to unify the sounds and words organically.

Perhaps it was good that the first major production undertaken in the new Workshop dealt with a subject familiar from earlier projects, namely a cloudy, surreal world, introduced through a Theatre of the Absurd–like narrative, describing life in a distorted postwar Britain. In *Under the Loofah Tree*, Cooper invented a hero who was terrified of the world outside the four walls of his bath. As he had in *The Disagreeable Oyster*, he used his protagonist's paranoia to explore issues of domesticity and the outside world, and larger issues of masculine and feminine spaces, although in *Loofah*, the reclamation of the hero's domestic space is the central theme.

A popular theme in modernist discourse, the postwar battle over domestic space deserves a bit of explanation. Throughout the 1950s, the definition of a location as masculine or feminine became more and more culturally significant, due in part to shifting workplace models and modernist aesthetics that reinvented the floor plan of the home. Throughout the twentieth century, as men sought entertainment outside the house through the development and proliferation of masculine spaces, including clubs, mass sporting arenas, and pubs, they gradually lost their hold over domestic space. In his essay on the postwar hi-fi sound system, Keir Keightley quotes housing historian Margaret Marsh, who observed that suburban homes "came to represent togetherness by reducing the number of rooms and opening up floorplans....the important new idea about domestic space was that the house should express togetherness and family activities, not provide special spaces for individual activities....However, husbands were heard to say that togetherness made them feel trapped."[6]

Anxieties about the loss of private space, both at home and in the larger world, led men to try to recover some of their lost turf. Enter the bachelor pad. Keightley describes how a male culture developed that deliberately and specifically masculine space, which also came to include backyard tool sheds, garage workshops, and, in Britain, the allotment. Artificial *sonic* spaces of privacy (and, by extension, masculinity) were created by the newly developed hi-fi sound systems. Although the actual hi-fi equipment was compact, it allowed men, using already masculinized "exposed wire" technology, to reclaim the feminized living areas of the home through sheer amplitude. A key point of Keightley's assessment is that men were using technology as a means of "realizing [their] repressed, true self, of momentarily abandoning the sham, pretense and rationality of a compromised age in favor of authentic emotions and unbridled experience."[7] Ironically, technology in some ways conveyed a more authentic experience than the one men experienced in their lived suburban existences. More than this, though, men were able to redefine their material arenas, recapturing their territory simply through technologically mediated sound. And what could represent this newly reclaimed masculinity better than *mechanized* sound? Sounds treated electronically are inherently infused and imbued with traces of technology. They cry out, "I once was boring, natural; now I am treated, better, scientifically enhanced, made manly." The new electronic sound had masculinity literally hardwired into it. Similarly, Cooper's plays rely on technological "innovation" to critique the masculinist worldviews his characters embodied and perceived as threatened. Technology didn't necessarily empower his characters, but in his productions it was vital to the redefinition of their physical or mental space.

In *Under the Loofah Tree*, the negotiation of sonic spaces is of primary importance. Locked in the bathroom for the duration of the play, Edward Thwaite paints different scenarios and locations in his imagination, à la Walter Mitty, including a great military victory on the Loofah fields. All the while he is constantly interrupted in his sanctum by a rotating cast of characters, including his wife, a traveling salesman, a bill collector, tax men, and more. His imagined sonic experiences are contained within the material space of this small room, signaled to the listener as hallucinatory "vision." Cooper thus uses radiophonic sound to both expand and constrain Thwaite, as we see in the final montage (music example 3.2). 🔊

EDWARD: But how? (*An intensely menacing rumble begins in the distance. It comes closer and closer until it fills the air with its heavy throb*) ...
(*Fade in a tape recording so speeded up as to be merely a series of squeaks. It slows down to a growl*)

CHORUS: Thwaite, Thwaite, Edward Thwaite, Mr. Edward Thwaite, our Ted.
(*It is now so slow as to be unintelligible*)

EDWARD: What are they saying about me?
(*Cross fade from this tape to the sound of the sea*)
What are the wild waves saying behind my back?
(*All the following voices are away from Edward, talking to someone else, unaware of his presence*)

WOMAN: It's a boy. Seven and a half pounds.
(*Fade in trams clashing and clanking over points and grinding uphill*)

MOTHER: He can talk but he won't.
(*Someone whistles "Bye Bye Blackbird"*)

FATHER: There's no sense taking him. He'll only be a nuisance.
(*Fade in "The Music Goes Round and Around"*)

GIRL: He's just like all the others. Only wants one thing and that he won't get—not with all those spots.
(*The throb of his heart continues*)

MAN: Oh no, we don't want *him*. Surely there's someone else.
(*Fade in a chorus of "Roll Out the Barrel" intoned with an air of tuneless gloom*)

SERGEANT: They're coming on quite well, sir, most of them. There's *one* not up to standard, only *one*.
(*Fade in "All Clear" siren*)

MAN: He says he was with us before the war, but I don't remember him.
(*Fade in "Here Comes the Bride"*)

WOMAN: She's never marrying him. Whatever for?
... (*The heart-throbs are going very fast now and behind them is a high single note, increasing in volume until it is unbearable at which point there is a mighty splash*)[8]

As the excerpt opens, Edward Thwaite is taunted by the dead soldiers with whom he served during the war. They accuse him of cowardice but assure him he will get his chance to die soon. "But how?" Thwaite asks. At this point a low, indefinable tone plays in the background, much as the Deflector had in Cooper's earlier, pre-radiophonic play, *Mathry Beacon* (1956). It fills the space, removing the ambient bathroom noise that had sheltered and reassured him throughout the rest of the play. Voices, treated with tape echo and processed through a PEU filter to remove key frequencies, taunt him to drown himself, their technologically augmented nature highlighted by their abrupt cutoff as Thwaite's voice reenters. As he plunges under the water, with a sound far more expansive than realistic, the low tone is replaced by a more insistent pulsing, ostensibly a heartbeat, but just as likely the sound of machinery. "My whole life passed before me in a flash," he says. His life is depicted as a document preserved on magnetic tape, as the whirr of tape spins round and round, eventually slowing. All of the people who then talk are individually defined, before their voices appear, by a sonic marker of the space they inhabit. Some are more material than others (realized by varying degrees of frequency filtration). For example, the sounds of a nightclub presage a girl who once rejected Edward's advances. A miserable chorus of singing soldiers introduces Thwaite's sergeant, whereas a wedding march plays before a woman expresses her disappointment over Thwaite's inadequacy. As in *The Disagreeable Oyster*, technologically altered sounds, sounds rendered into virtual *acousmêtre*, can just as easily signify an internal paranoia. But in this case, the sounds seem external to the protagonist, representing "hypermasculinity" as an unattainable goal, the inescapable pressure of an unrealizable normality.

As the underwater sequence comes to a climax, each voice is treated differently, reflecting different aspects of Thwaite's insecurity and different threats to his masculine autonomy. As if to emphasize the supremely alienating effect this has on him, a high-pitched electronic hum enters the texture, gradually gaining in intensity. This is the first immediately identifiably electronic sound heard, until Thwaite bursts back into the highly reverberant safe space of his bathroom with a desperate emphatic assertion of himself: "There's always me!" This electronic element, the high-pitched hum, functions with particular effect because it is the first time that the technological world has made its bare self audible, that the technology has peeked out from behind the curtain to make its presence known even as the play grapples with relationships between modernity and alienation, between human agency and a society based on industrial capitalism. Cooper's plays not only explore new technologies in their writing and their production, but also examine the ways in which technologies affect and change peoples and cultures.

Change and Signature Tunes

Yet for all of the innovation and possibility the Workshop expressed in the production of *Under the Loofah Tree*, the mandate of the Workshop, combined with its limited technology, led to some personnel shifts. Daphne Oram, frustrated at not being allowed to work on more strictly musical projects, left six months after the studio's inception to set up her own electronic music laboratory in an old round oast house, "Tower Folly," in early 1959. When she left, she took engineer Jeannie MacDowell with her. Rather than replace Oram outright, the Radiophonic Effects Committee (REC) thought it would be better to follow the original idea of bringing in a rotating field of studio managers (SMs) and engineers to work for a brief time. In the first five years of the Workshop, these included Maddalena Fagandini, Dick Mills, Jimmy Burnett, Phil Young, Dennis Morgan, John Harrison, John Baker, and Delia Derbyshire. Due to the overwhelming success of the new Workshop, however, the BBC decided to increase the regular staff to ensure the timely completion of the ever-growing number of commissions.

On leaving the Workshop, Oram developed her theories of what she called "Oramics," a method of creating music through oscillators connected to photoelectric cells. In some ways operating similarly to a process created by Percy Grainger for his Free Music Machines of the 1940s and 1950s, and by the Soviet composer Yevgeny Alexandrovitch Sholpo in the 1920s and 1930s, Oram's self-manufactured instruments consisted of cells that read an image drawn with black ink onto plastic sheets, converting the image into sound. Eventually Oram applied this technology to personal computers, developing software to exploit the possibilities of Oramics. One can read about Oram's position on the process of composition, and her ideas about music more generally, in her fascinating and eccentric book *An Individual Note*, written in the early 1970s as she worked through the implications of her Oramics system.[9]

Given her importance and influence as the primary musician responsible for the establishment of the Workshop, and as the first woman in the world either to open an electronic music studio or to construct electronic instruments, I am disappointed and frustrated that Oram occupies such a small place in my discussion of the Radiophonic Workshop. This is due to several factors. The first, and most practical, lies in the plain fact that very little of her music from her time at the Workshop survives in the BBC's archives, and what does survive remains inaccessible because of the fragile nature of the material.[10] (Magnetic tape, once touted as "indestructible," tends to have a remarkably short life span.) One project in particular, the visual portion of her adaptation of *Amphitryon 38*, the first to substantially use radiophonic sound in television and the first given a special "Radiophonic" credit in the *Radio Times*, no longer exists, like so much of the BBC's output from the earliest years up to the late 1960s. Given Oram's status as the sole "trained" classical musician among the early Workshop crew, and the only SM from the Music Department—certainly the person with the best knowledge of Continental techniques—a fuller knowledge of her approach would enrich any study of the history of electronic music.

I would love to know how Oram approached scoring for television; certainly the electronic film scores she composed after leaving the Workshop, such as her uncredited collaboration with Georges Auric on 1961's *The Innocents*, betray a subtle understanding of the ability of manipulated sound to frighten and to generate an atmosphere of unease. The acquisition of Oram's archives by Goldsmith's College hopefully heralds an exciting future for the study of this key figure in the overwhelmingly male-dominated world of electronic music, as they contain not only documents related to Oramics, but also other inventions, such as plans from 1957 for an early multitrack tape recorder.[11] By her own account, she had experimented with electronic music already by 1949, on a thirty-five-minute composition for two orchestras, five microphones, and manipulated recordings, and met with BBC officials as early as 1952 to discuss the establishment of an electronic studio.[12]

Histories of the Workshop tend to downplay Oram's role in its success. One reason for this was a rather strange feud between her and Desmond Briscoe that arose during the writing of his account of the Workshop's first twenty-five years. When he sent her his original draft of his manuscript covering her time at the studio, she wrote back calling it "a shabby account, giving little credit to those who worked hard to bring the fruition the electronic dreams of the 50s."[13] Specifically, in her complaint to Briscoe, where she objects to his omitting most of her contributions, she makes some claims not necessarily backed up by other records, including that in 1957 she personally "was now called the Radiophonic Unit, and given the share of an office, Room B6, 5 Portland Place (part of Staff Training recommendation)." She goes on to state, "I had 'secretarial' assistance during the day from a junior SM, Alec Nesbitt," the same man charged with writing Brian George's original report on electronic music.[14] Most bizarrely, she claims that Briscoe "was not fully involved in Radiophonics until 1962" and was deliberately not giving her editorial control over the writing of the section concerning her, giving her only twenty-four hours to make corrections, and no chance to correct later versions; "such treatment ensures that Mr. Briscoe has his way. I sense in this a degree of insult."[15] Briscoe claimed that the editorial cuts he made to lessen her presence in the book were the result of a decision to focus on the history of the Workshop after its opening, but regardless of the reason, her presence in the book is compromised by this acrimonious exchange, and reading it one senses the carefulness with which she is mentioned. After her scathing letter, legal advisers are mentioned more than once by various BBC bureaucrats, and there is a real feeling that they felt it was better to omit her than to risk her misinterpreting what *was* there.[16]

It is a shame that her role was downplayed in the only published history of the studio until now, since her position as the first woman electronic composer is vitally important. Unlike many other divisions within the BBC at the time, the Workshop employed an almost equal number of women and men, and this should be acknowledged as one of its many great successes.[17] But there can be no doubt that in the 1950s, women in so-called "men's jobs" at the BBC faced a great deal of condescension if not outright prejudice from many of the more old-fashioned male staff. Delia Derbyshire, for example, when she was resident at the Workshop, is reported to have worked only after the "suits" had gone home to avoid having to deal with the wonder they faced at the prospect of an "attractive" woman doing a job traditionally identified as masculine. Although, as Maddalena Fagandini acknowledges, there had been a tradition in the BBC of hiring women as engineers and technical people in radio, these same women faced "quite a cutback after the war when the surviving gentlemen came back and wanted their jobs."[18] Certainly these prejudices were still very much in place in the mid-1960s, while Delia Derbyshire was at the Workshop. The following newspaper account of her "remarkable" presence in the Workshop is typical of attitudes toward women in technical and intellectual jobs: "Here in this almost wholly male scientific preserve works 27-year-old Delia.'... I went up to Girton College, Cambridge, to read maths. At least that's how it started out. ...It was the old story of it being too much like hard work. Anyway, maths isn't very useful to a woman,' she ended with a spurt of feminine logic."[19]

The institutional sexism would lessen throughout the years at the Workshop but would never entirely disappear. I've been told in interviews with both male and female composers how female employees were told in no uncertain terms, by varying levels of administration, that they were hired only because they were a woman, or that their gender made them unsuitable for certain aspects of their technical work. Despite this continuing pressure, or perhaps because of it, the presence of so many women, as well as a significant proportion of out, gay composers, must have played some part in controlling the atmosphere at the studio.

Quatermass and the Pit (TV, 1958–1959): Briscoe, Mills

It might seem that different interpretive methods are required in order to write about music for television as opposed to radio. But as I suggested in chapter 1, the two mediums operate in a very similar manner, semiotically using audio in much the same way. Indeed, it is difficult to think of any aspect of film or television music that doesn't have an equivalent in radio drama, regardless of film music scholarship's central position in this discussion.[20] On the surface it might seem as if the visual nature of film and television offers a unique opportunity for music to comment on the silent action of the moving image (and as our experience of moviegoing and television watching reveals, this is an opportunity film composers often take advantage of). We perceive the primary function of film and television music to be to emulate an experiential phenomenon, relating and reflecting the essence of that experience in aural terms. But is there a substantial difference between the musical evocation of a visible emotion (as in a film) and one implied by radio's dialogue or an actor's reading? Determining the relationship of music to text is, of course, one of the oldest problems in music history, traceable back to the first musical settings of text. One inevitably links the nature of the melody to the words, and the two interact in what Claudia Gorbman, speaking about the interaction of film visuals and film music, called "mutual implication."[21] Whether or not the music comments on the text, or vice versa, it is clear they are irretrievably intertwined—and this is true for music for radio drama as well.

If one of the basic functions of so-called "media music" is to represent the internal thoughts and feelings of the characters and their struggles in the onscreen drama, then another function must certainly be its utility in symbolic representation, that is, music operating not to directly express emotion, but rather to signal something more abstract, like the film's genre.[22] Unlike musical shorthand that expresses "real" emotion in music through its apparent simulation, musical shorthand in this case is employed to convey genre conventions instantly. For example, audiences respond to tremolo strings with a feeling of suspense because audiences have learned to expect that such an effect *signals* suspense. Film music holds, by its manipulation of generic signs, the ability to generate the emotion itself, evincing from its listeners the feelings required to place the film, radio play, or television show into whatever category it wishes to be placed. The signs, as complex as they are, present film music scholars with a problem, as film music scholar Caryl Flinn notes, wondering "how to talk concretely and specifically about the effects generated by a signifying system that is so abstract."[23]

This kind of detachment includes by extrapolation any musical representation of genre, mood, or tone, as a stereotype, such as "sentimental" (strings), "heroic" (diatonic brass), and, of course, "frightening" (dissonance or electronics). The establishment of these characteristics' symbolic meanings often dates far back into musical history, predating film. But some of these meanings date only to the creation of the sound-producing machines themselves, and in the case of electronic music, this is a quite recent date. Creating commentary through symbolic sound bites is one of film music's most powerful tricks. Such commentary can be equally effective without visual components, for once a convention is established, an audience no longer even needs to *see* what it is reacting to: the music does all the work.

The case of electronic music/special sound is of particular interest here. If always-diegetic electronic sound effects are symbolic representations of how something imaginary is supposed to sound (paradoxically both futuristic and "the unknown," acousmatic or synchretic acousmatic),[24] then we might conclude that electronic music that is nondiegetic can be a symbolic internalization and aural expression of both emotion and the "mood of the film." The question then, in the context of this study, becomes whether or not an electronic noise can pass from sound effect to nondiegetic music. In other words, can a sound act as a sound effect and at the same time act as music, in much the same way source music contributes to "mood," diegetic or not? By using the term "special sound" to describe the unique material produced at the Radiophonic Workshop, the BBC already acknowledged this potential confusion, and no program demonstrated this better than the hugely popular *Quatermass and the Pit*.

Quatermass and the Pit premiered on BBC Television on December 22, 1958, at 8 p.m., slightly later than the early slot to which science fiction was traditionally relegated. Writer Nigel Kneale had a reputation as a political writer, because of his 1954 adaptation of George Orwell's *1984* and his prior two Quatermass adventures, with their decidedly "Green" perspectives. As such, he was considered an author of "serious" science fiction. The third science fiction serial involving the popular Professor Quatermass of the Rocket Research Group, *Quatermass and the Pit*, told in six thirty-minute episodes the story of Quatermass's thwarting of an attempted invasion of Earth by the psychic force of a group of ancient Martians.

For the serial, Desmond Briscoe devised several radiophonic cues that could be used as music or sound effects, in combination with a traditional orchestral score composed by Trevor Duncan. Throughout the first episode, Duncan's traditional brass-heavy "suspense" music accented the growing tension between the military establishment and the "rational" scientists. The military leap to easy conclusions about the bizarre phenomena experienced when a large mysterious container is discovered buried in Central London. The scientists, however, wish to study the object more before offering an explanation of its origin. Duncan's music is a mixture of brief stings punctuating startling revelations and quiet, dissonant music reserved for mysterious moments. Only four cues by Duncan are used in the series, and each of them is repeated many times, conveying different feelings or emotions. The general, nonmelodic nature of the longest "atmospheric" cue lends itself to this kind of reuse. Yet rather than seeming merely repetitious, these cues convey the overall suspenseful nature of the program as a whole. A fanfare-like theme opens and closes each episode, as well as dramatizing the climatic moments in the story. Typical of the kind of music written for television at the time, each of these cues was flexible in meaning and use, as well as duration. For example, a cue used most often as a sting, while fading slightly after the initial burst, can continue for an additional twenty seconds if required, providing additional suspense.

Not until halfway through the third episode does the first radiophonic cue enter, and when it does, it takes the listener—and characters—by surprise. Two soldiers, standing around chatting, are in charge of starting the generator that powers a large drill used to bore into the mysterious buried ship. Suddenly, quietly, an upward-moving sine tone, modulated with vibrato, rises into the sound texture. The soldiers look around—they obviously hear the sound—and wonder where it is coming from. It seems to emerge from nowhere, neither from the ship they are guarding nor from any specific location. They look around, they look upward, and as quickly as it arrived, the sound is gone. "Did you hear that?" one of the soldiers asks the other. Before he has time to answer, another soldier yells at them to switch on the generator. Against a backdrop of mechanical drilling, a whole complex of radiophonic sounds emerge, again from no fixed location and representing no specific kind of sound other than purely "alien."

The *acousmêtre* asserts itself not only through sheer volume (it is deafening) but through the very timbre of the competing sounds. Beginning as before with an upward-rising sine tone, it continues rising further and further until it is taken over by a bass rumbling, processed through tape feedback. This particular kind of feedback sounds like a kind of distorted echo and, while heard here for the first time in television, had become a staple of radiophonic radio broadcasts. It involved playing a recorded sound back onto itself, and repeating the process again and again, manipulating the sound by altering it until it no longer sounded like its original source. In this process, a sound (fed from an oscillator) is recorded and played on one machine, then played on a second machine, then fed back through the original recorder, adding that replayed sound to the original tape, the entire process repeated potentially endlessly.

In *Quatermass*, the original sound has also been slowed down, creating a churning, chugging sound. This chugging, and combinations of chuggings from other recorded tape feedback loops oscillating at different rates, increases in amplitude (Briscoe and crew achieved this by hand-spinning the tapes to achieve an uneven rate of pitch rise) until the characters cry out in pain. On top of this, extremely high-pitched electronic screams, like the cries of hyenas, yelp out of the texture. In a perfect example of an *acousmêtre*, the radiophonics capture the situation's ambiguity. There is no discernible reason for the sound; it emerges from nowhere and seems to represent no material object or technology. Yet there is a material analogue to the sound in the physical presence of the buried ship, and it is the attempt to understand its elemental structure that causes the sounds to emerge in the first place. The soldiers' frustrated efforts to penetrate the shell of the ship exemplify the inability to understand it. The ship can't even be described to any satisfaction; the soldiers alternatively refer to it as "greasy," "plastic," "metallic," "like diamond," and "crystalline," and their descriptions mirror the incomprehensible radiophonic noises that repel them and are similarly beyond their understanding.

Yet this sound effect as cue also performs a double function, however, acting as music has traditionally functioned in drama, when we encounter the alien "consciousness" for the first time. Although they are always diegetic, the effect of hearing these sounds corresponds to the effect of hearing a piece of contemporary music for the first time: the sounds are purely "sound," without associative quality, and the listener struggles for comprehension, lost in a sea of unfamiliar sonic signs, listening for melodies, rhythms, anything that helps impose a formal design. The disorienting sensation, mirroring the character's disorientation on the screen, offers both a suspense similar to and a timbre foreign to Duncan's more traditional score, absent in this section.

When Duncan's music appears with Briscoe's radiophonic score later in the production, the effect is impressive. The end of episode 4 features another psychic attack on a worker near the buried ship. The scene takes place late at night; a lone mechanic is busy setting up machinery for the next day's work at the site inside the ship when a wrench beside him starts moving by itself, accompanied by a quick pulse of a sine wave. It is unclear whether or not the sound attached to the wrench is heard by the worker. More likely the sound serves two functions. On the one hand, it acts as a kind of radiophonic Mickey Mousing, a "technological" (read: alien) explanation for the sudden movement. On the other hand, and perhaps more important, it also serves to remind the audience what genre they are watching; electronic sounds encourage a "science fiction" reading of the phenomenon, fulfilling and rewarding the viewer's expectation and generic knowledge. The worker's face screams terror, accompanied by a dramatic sting of Duncan's brass music. The worker's reaction is a response to the physical phenomenon, seemingly unaware of the sounds that surround him. He runs out of the ship and tries to escape the increasing chaos of his surroundings; tools, boards, equipment all fly through the air, and radiophonic and brass music combine cacophonously through it all. Rapidly moving flute lines connect crunchy dissonant brass chords, and underneath this both rumbling tape feedback loops and bent sine wave attacks follow the worker as he tries to outrun the phenomenon, as seen in video example 3.1.⊙ Here it is impossible to separate the diegetic and nondiegetic, the acousmatic from the atmospheric: even if the radiophonic noises are meant to be heard as sound effects, their commingling with the brass and flute make such a unified "music" that the result sounds like a traditional evocation of both "suspense" and "science fiction."

This triumph of early television science fiction succeeds in large part because of the radiophonic element, forging a firm connection between the mysterious, the alien, and the electronic that would continue for decades at the Radiophonic Workshop. Later projects would expand on the conflict inherent in the ambiguity between sound effect and music, but here at the beginning of science fiction television in Britain, we see the dilemma emerge fully formed.

Outside (TV, 1959): Briscoe, Fagandini, Mills

The first television documentary to commission the Workshop was a thirty-minute program called *Outside*, first broadcast on February 19, 1959. It followed a discharged prisoner, John Morris, for six months after his release, depicting the realities of life outside the prison walls. For the program, Briscoe and newcomer Maddalena Fagandini offered director David E. Rose a sound sculpture that combined fixed pitches with abstract noise. From the thirty-nine-second clip included on the twenty-first anniversary album of the Workshop and reissued on the BBC Radiophonic Workshop Retrospective CD, it is clear that the music represents on some level the experience of facing an unfamiliar world. Unfortunately, the program itself no longer exists, making a discussion of the interaction between the sound and the drama impossible.

The clip divides into three main segments: the first, approximately eight seconds long, includes the unpitched and untreated sound of keys and a mumble of voices (see example 3.1). Suddenly, all sound drops out, and the clattering of locks transitions into the second section. Here pitched, gonglike banging in an irregular meter and emphasized by percussive tapping in the background alternates up and down, never resolving. The feeling of tottering instability is reinforced by the fading in of a piano playing a quickly moving ostinato on notes dissonant to the alternating B–A♯ of the gongs, and the A, B♭, D♭, E♭. The piano builds in intensity, six notes of the scale all clashing against each other. Finally, all these sounds are interrupted by a loud gonglike sound (like, and yet vaguely unlike, as if the gong were being heard underwater) firmly on B. With its sheer solidity and loud echo, this is the resolution to the conflict of the central section.

3.1. *Outside*—(TV, 1959)—Briscoe, Fagandini, Mills

The Workshop team clearly opted to try to evoke the prisoner's sonic experience, offering a symbolic interpretation of his world, in much the same way that Desmond Briscoe had in Beckett's *All That Fall*. There, you will recall, Briscoe constructed sounds that conveyed the distorted worldview of the protagonist, Maddy; sounds appeared as distorted, altered versions of themselves. What the listener heard was a reflection of that sound passed through the mind of the protagonist. In *Outside*, the relatively untreated sound of the opening eight seconds depict the sounds of prison life, which are familiar to this man. The sounds emerge from his mind relatively unchanged and unfiltered, as an unremarkable example of the sounds he hears everyday.

These sounds drop out, however, with the turning of the key, and the shifting of the locks, when they are replaced by the indefinable pulse, throb, and hum of specific pitches. Suddenly, all the known world, the world of direct sonic realization, evoking Ludwig Koch's BBC "Sound Portraits" of the 1940s and 1950s, disappears at the precise moment of the prisoner's release. The level of unfamiliarity is so great that the recognizable sounds that had surrounded him (and, by proximity, the listener) vanish, replaced by completely alien sounds. But these are not quite *just* sounds, either. What we hear is in fact pitched music, as if that which had been sound (sound effect) had been mentally rendered into the more abstract form of music, in order to convey the sheer level of confusion in the mind of our protagonist. With every frame of reference gone, his mind resorts to that most abstract, least representational art, music, to explain his experience, with only the shadow of his actual sonic diegesis remaining in the persistent, abstract clicking. Each click, *almost* pitched, is accompanied by an artificially generated echo rhythmically establishing both its place in the real world and its distortion at the hands of the world "outside." Finally, the concluding gong again is unrecognizable as a real sound in the world, but is at least not complicated by other sounds. It exists in isolation, and as such is indefinable as either/neither music *or* sound effect. This can be interpreted, if the sound reads as music, as supremely alienating, a conclusively distancing finale to our released prisoner's experience, an inescapable hopelessness. Having found nothing in the outside world to relate to, he is reduced at last to one unknowable chime. If, however, the sound reads as sound effect, it is a victory, an emergence from the fog of alienation as represented by music into a world of potentially identifiable sounds again. If the gong isn't quite familiar, it is still recognizably a gong, and that must be regarded as something. This multiplicity is unique in this period of radiophonics, and while we'd like to have the completed piece—drama and music— to interpret, the piece indicates that if by this stage radiophonics had not entirely codified this dual modality of sound effect/music, it had at least become aware of the representational power and possibilities of the multiplicity available in this form of representation.

Science and Industry (Radio, 1959): Young, Fagandini

Phil Young and Maddalena Fagandini were two of the most promising new SMs brought in to work at the Workshop after Daphne Oram left. Young's work, both in composing signature tunes and incidental music for television and radio, is among the best of the early Workshop compositions. He was expert at adapting the techniques already in practice and expanding on them, especially in the use of more tonally precise music (which uses actual pitched notes instead of abstract sounds).

Fagandini, one of the Workshop's most prolific and creative early composers, began her career at the BBC as a typist before getting a job on the "technical" side of production, working on general programs (news, talks, disc shows). After a few years, she was transferred to the Drama Department with a view to an eventual attachment to the Workshop. She had had musical training as a child, and after the war briefly studied composition using Hindemith's textbooks. Her bosses realized that with her combination of technical skill and musical training, she was perfect for radiophonics. One of the first assignments for Young and Fagandini together was the signature tune for a BBC World Service program, *Science and Industry*. The result is credited as being the first completely electronic signature tune in radio, although it uses both electronic and *concrète* sounds.

The piece is in four brief sections and opens with the sound of a tinny hammer against a bass throbbing in counterpoint. In a tritone (A–D$\sharp$) interval separated by several octaves, the two parts alternate a rhythmic pattern, emphasizing a strong beat on every pulse by filling in at the eighth-note level each space in the texture. This alternation has the effect of quickly establishing a rhythmic beat. The bass quietly drops out after about four seconds, and the second section begins with its replacement by the high-pitched sound of a sine wave on a single pitch (nearly a quarter tone higher than the A that had been in the bass, and only a fourth below the hammered pitch). This sine tone shifts up to an F$\sharp$ after about eight seconds. A descending minor triad (B–G–E) in a mid-frequency range is introduced, articulating a rhythm unrelated to the initial pattern against the continuing regular tapping of the treble hammer. This descending triad, produced by the square wave oscillator (buzzier, less soft than the sine wave), increases in amplitude, as does the persistent sine wave, periodically punctuated by brief, apparently random high-pitched electronic swoops of sound, almost like birdcalls.

The square wave pattern fades out, overlapping the beginning of the third section at around seventeen seconds. The treble hammering also fades, and in its place another collection of sine tones on a rich F♯-major chord gently chimes twice. Another sine tone provides a delicate dissonance, introducing an upward-moving swoop from C♯ to E that repeats slowly against the sustained F♯ chord. The random electronic noises continue in the background texture. Finally, all these sounds drop out with a concluding bass throbbing in a new rhythmic pattern—one that repeats the motive of the first (shorter notes as pickups to strong downbeats), only this time in a duple rather than triple meter.

In the signature tune, the composers have only a few seconds to convey their intentions. They depend on the listener's recognition of key conventional signifiers, since without the help of visuals, in a radio signature tune the music contains all the information the listener receives. In *Science and Industry*, Young and

3.2. *Science and Industry*—(Radio, 1959)—Young, Fagandini

Fagandini expertly deploy these signifiers, delivering a clear message as to the content of the program. Despite the constant activity, the spaciousness and austerity of the texture is always apparent both through the continuous use of echo effects and the harmonic distance between notes and through drastic differences in dynamic levels between foreground texture and background. The resulting combination of simplicity and rhythmic regularity in lieu of textural filigree and ornament embodies the spirit of the modern age. It is a functional demonstration of "science and industry," the field it attempts to reproduce.

To this end, each of the sounds, either electronic or *concrète*, contributes somehow to the evocation of science or industry. The initial "hammering" sounds, which originate in the sound of a piano processed through filters to remove all bass frequencies, as well as the accompanying bass (throbbing in the rhythm of an assembly line), and finally the electronic sounds, including both the "tuning" frequencies of the random slides and the single sine tones as signifiers of technology, were all chosen for their quick associative qualities. Here again we have the alternation of function between sound effect (hammers, bass throbbing, random electronic sounds, as if a functional element of some advanced piece of equipment) and tonally based music. The rapidly descending minor triad after the introduction of the "sounds of industry" is a musical evocation of physical movement, of technology racing along, while the introduction of the sine tone and random electronic "tweaks" emphasize the importance of technology in this process—in the best tradition of film music. The fact that the triad itself is electronic only highlights the "progress" message of the theme: nothing so romantic as a melodic theme is needed; the streamlined workings of the modern factory contain the maximum effect with the least romance. The eventual success of the combination of science and industry is ultimately demonstrated by the electronic consonance of the static F♯-major triad against the still "hard at work" electronic whirrings of the upward-moving third quietly behind it.

Rhythm and Music: The Interval Signal

The interval signal genre was music of an indeterminate length to be broadcast on either radio or television between the scheduled programs, or when there was an unscheduled break in broadcasting. It could not be too adventurous or abstract, since it had to both mark the passage of time and maintain the attention of an audience tempted to switch channels. As a result, these pieces were often rhythmically interesting, and the genre enabled Workshop composers to experiment and to develop their abilities to construct complex rhythmic patterns out of tiny pieces of magnetic tape. In turn, these individual patterns could be combined with other rhythmic constructions in complex polyrhythmic tape loops of varying length. The person most adept at these early process pieces was Maddalena Fagandini, whose interval signals rivaled in popularity anything produced in more conventional genres. Given the function of these works, Fagandini described their necessary final sound as "less abstract than other work because they are for the general listener or viewer rather than a modern drama audience."

The straightforward quality demanded by the interval signal resulted in an ironically complicated history for one of her first examples of the genre. Originally commissioned by the Television Department and composed by Fagandini in October 1960 to introduce the political speakers at a series of televised debates, this tune, given the descriptive title "Music for Party Political Conferences," found its way back onto television as an interval signal for the rest of the year. There it was heard by future Beatles producer George Martin at EMI, who arranged through Robbins Music to compose an orchestral accompaniment to the radiophonic track, now renamed optimistically by the BBC as "BBC Television Theme No. 1."[25] Robbins bought the rights to the tune in April 1961 and subsequently renamed it "Tune in Time," later revised to "Tunin' Time."[26] In the buildup to its release later that month, Parlophone Records unleashed a barrage of publicity about the single derived from this tune, capitalizing on the "futuristic" nature of the tune's production. "Electronic music—that slightly disturbing sound of our times which is produced amid a complex of tape recorders and electric wiring—is about to attack the hit parades," noted one newspaper.[27] Never once in the coverage, however, do the reporters refer to the Workshop's output as music, or the employees as composers. Rather, Martin strategically marketed his latest novelty by appealing to the public's curiosity about this mysterious new phenomenon, offhandedly suggesting possible sequels, in order to highlight the "engineers'" and "laboratory staff's" supposed scientific detachment from popular culture. He noted, "We've sent the radiophonics people some records by The Shadows so that they can pick up the sort of thing we want."[28] By the time of the single's release, Martin had perfected his angle, renaming the record one final time to "Time Beat," and listing the performer as "Ray Cathode." The songwriting credit went to "BBC Radiophonics." Since credit for radiophonic compositions almost always reverted to the Workshop rather than the individual who composed them, Martin could not only ignore Fagandini's contribution and authorship, but also in her place credit a fictional (male) science fiction composer: "The artist on this record is virtually an electronic brain guided by human hands."[29] The coverage of this single shines a spotlight on the pervasive image electronic music held in the public imagination. In February, in preparation for the story, the *Daily Mirror* had sent a photographer and the writer of their record column to look around the Workshop, but "did not take any pictures, nor did they show any particular enthusiasm for the Workshop as such."[30] When the article eventually ran, the Workshop's existence was disguised behind a description of "Ray Cathode": "He is a collection of electronic sounds. To meet, he is a mass of valves, dials and wires. To hear, he is a delight, producing a mechanical rhythm as faultless as any human."[31]

For another of her interval signals, Fagandini took the sounds of a clock as her guide, to mirror the image usually displayed during their broadcast. (See example 3.3.) Within a four-bar framework, she constructed six different rhythmic loops. For this exercise in loop combinations, the tone color remained limited to one kind of sound: a wood block. Although the tape manipulation produced intervals, the intervals served only to articulate an abstract change of pitch (up or down) rather than a more specific interval relation. All but the first loop are on the same "chord" (composed of intervals outlining a C#-major triad), which makes the

[Pattern Combinations]

3.3. *Interval Signal*—(TV, 1960)—Fagandini

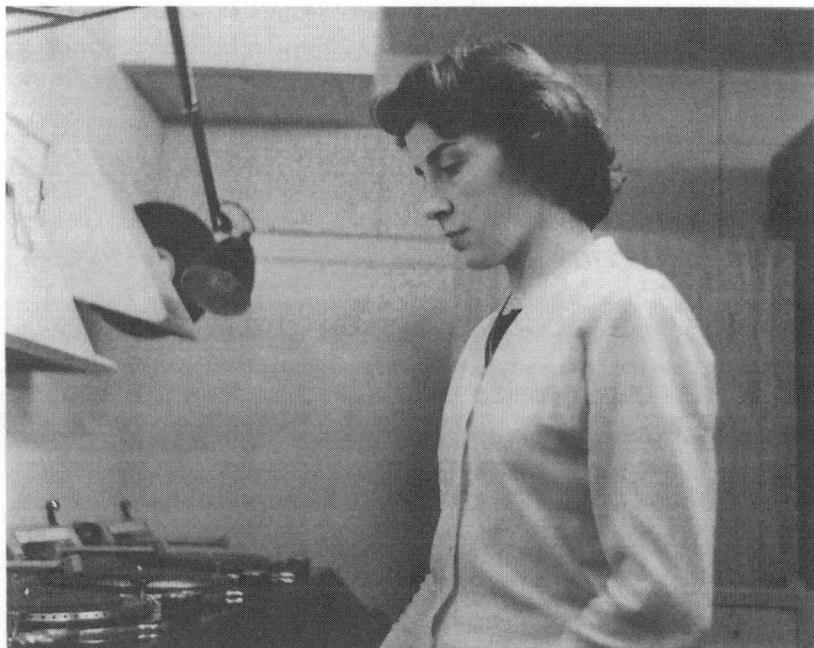

Figure 3.1. Maddalena Fagandini operating a bank of grams. Photographer unknown.

shifting between the first loop and the others another area of "change." More important, each bar is geared toward generating tension in its first half and resolution in its second. Five of the loops have a strong downbeat on beat 3, while the single loop without a strong beat on 3 uses syncopation to surround it.

Because the piece has no tonal direction, and because it essentially "cadences" halfway through each measure, the interval signal works in much the same way as many minimalist works of the 1960s (although it predates the earliest of La Monte Young's similar pieces). That is, without a teleological imperative, the interval signal works by accruing and discarding disposable modular elements in a process procedure. The texture is the work. If the ticking of a clock was the initial inspiration, this interval signal elaborates on that imagery, imagining an eternal clock of infinite variety, but with each loop working toward the same goal, each "tick" (beat 1) leading inexorably toward the concluding "tock" (beat 3).

Although the piece could conceivably continue forever, Fagandini constructed the interval signal around a larger repeated loop of six four-bar groupings. Within this larger grouping there are internal repetitions of loop combinations, showing a reflexive relationship. Fagandini eliminates the possibility of any larger sense of teleology (by "terracing" levels, for example) by making the four-bar groupings relate to each other in a simple mirror relationship.Yet this method of construction organizationally demands closure of a certain kind: if it were to conclude without its final iteration of a single pattern, the piece would remain structurally unsound.

Orpheus (Radio, 1961): Fagandini

In 1961, Fagandini provided music and radiophonic sound effects for Douglas Cleverdon's radio adaptation of Jean Cocteau's film Orphée.This production provides an excellent example of the period in the Workshop's history when composers combined complex rhythmic and concrète methods with the beginnings of tonally based melody. Although the scale of the work (almost ninety minutes) precludes any serious in-depth analysis here, I would like to draw attention to several of its most impressive moments. Sadly, the production was not released commercially and has not received repeat broadcasts in recent history. Its excellence, however, urges me to discuss it and my argument and evidence draws on the readily available film on which the program is based and transcripts of major music cues I provide in the music examples, as well as brief excerpts at this book's Web site.

Cocteau's Orphée script is a contemporary telling of the legend: Orpheus lives as a poet, misunderstood by both the public and his wife, Eurydice. Death, personified as "the Princess," enters into the world and falls in love with him. Her assistant, Heurtebise, both pities and loves the neglected Eurydice. As he sees his popularity fading, Orpheus starts obsessing over cryptic messages broadcast on his car's radio, ignoring his wife's pleas to disregard them. The messages are, in fact, from the Princess, who attempts to draw his attention away from his dying wife (dying, one assumes, from neglect). After Eurydice's death, and against the wishes of the Princess, Heurtebise helps Orpheus rescue her by descending into the Underworld. Overcome with guilt about abandoning his wife, and despite his growing feelings for the Princess, Orpheus eventually recovers Eurydice, but on the condition that he never look at her again. This proves impossible as Orpheus succumbs again to the ambiguous messages on the car radio, finally glancing at Eurydice while scolding her through the car's rearview mirror. As a result of their interference, both the Princess and Heurtebise are put in front of a mysterious tribunal and are forced to restore both Orpheus and Eurydice to life.

More than rethinking Cocteau's film in an electronic music idiom, Cleverdon and Fagandini abandoned Georges Auric's original score, choosing instead to incorporate portions of Gluck's opera *Orfeo et Euridice* (1762), Wagner, and French jazz as well as original music cues. Taking advantage of the Workshop's knack for appropriating the meanings of aural signs, the radio play deploys these musical elements as if they were signs of the things themselves, cultural ubiquities that need no further explanation: if Gluck's *Orfeo et Euridice* once depicted Orpheus's descent into the Underworld, then now all that is needed are a few chords from the recorded opera to effectively symbolize the same. So well-known is Gluck's opera that it can exist both in the world of the score, nondiegetically, and as source music, diegetically. This diegetic use occurs often; whenever a character turns on a radio, this is what is playing. It is music that is understood to be known to all—a "classic" that exists in some respects as aural wallpaper, and in another as a very real signifier of certain experiences: lost love, longing, romance.

One of Fagandini's primary challenges involved Orpheus's descent to the Underworld, and to evoke it, she excerpted Gluck's music from three key places in the opera. First, the fanfare opening of act 2: with a quickly rearticulated unison on E♭, it evokes nothing but itself as "Gluck's opera." In the opera, Orpheus has at this point arrived in the Underworld and has yet to experience anything. Poker-faced, the music betrays none of its eventual torments and, as such, is the perfect excerptable moment—uniquely recognizable for the memorability of its unison and yet lacking conventional emotive significance. Fagandini uses only a few seconds of this music—just the first four bars, for key moments, and like a fanfare.

The second and third excerpts both occur just moments later in the opera, but in tone they evoke a very different mood. Two sections featuring harp arpeggios—the first immediately after the opening full orchestral phrase, and the second after the Dance of the Furies—are looped to remove the voices and provide an endless progression. Again, the music is used as a quick reference to remind listeners they are in the Underworld or, even more generally, in the world of "Orpheus the myth," using Gluck as signifier.

These references are the most obvious, being direct, unaltered samples of actual recorded music. Another reference hides deep in the texture of Fagandini's originally composed score. She wrote two musical themes for the Princess, realizing, in her words, that the Princess's effect on Orpheus "required a musical quality (as opposed to an 'effect')." She was looking for an unfamiliar sound, though, and so explored several Greek enharmonic scales, finally settling on one consisting of three intervals: a third and two semitones (originally quarter tones). She recalls: "They were all a bit too recognizable for me [the Greek scales], except one which is very short, only four notes and three intervals... which of course you can split apart by an octave or two. I confined myself to just those four basic notes."[32] After composing several variations using the four-note scale, she plucked out the intervals on the nine-foot concert grand piano in Studio One Concert Hall in Maida Vale, holding the pedal down "to get maximum harmonic richness and reverberation." This was to be the raw material for the majority of the themes, although when she got back to the Workshop, she realized how much more interesting the sounds were when played in reverse, when the initial attack faded out. In addition, she used sample tones from the Muirhead oscillator and performed another set of variations on marimba.

The play opens with a trilogy of musical evocations: first an excerpt from Gluck, one of the quiet harp moments, followed by three brief sine-wave melodies (see music example 3.4).🔊

The opening concludes with a segue into the action: a quiet guitar blends into the final seconds of the sine-wave melody, and eventually a voice joins the guitar, singing a ballad in French. The next music cue for the first time initiates movement reminiscent of what will be the First Theme, but never explicitly outlines it. The marimba is used here, playing formless patterns, wandering around a limited thirteen-note range (see music example 3.5).🔊

The first theme proper (music example 3.6), heard almost seventeen minutes into the play, unfolds in two parts and an introduction. After a brief opening section utilizing a backward-treated build from a pianissimo E to a sforzando A, the final two elements are constructed in an antecedent-consequent phrase—the first

3.4. *Orpheus* 1—(Radio, 1961)—Fagandini. Three sine melodies

3.5. *Orpheus* 2—(Radio, 1961)—Fagandini. Wandering proto-first theme

3.6. *Orpheus 3*—(Radio, 1961)—Fagandini. First theme

half of the melodic theme, A–F–E–D♯, is followed by its answer, B–G–F–F♯. These patterns both consist of the original Greek-inspired intervals, but have been manipulated to occupy various octave placements. The two motives are similar in their tonal abrasiveness, mostly on account of their chromaticism. First heard as the Princess declares her love for Orpheus, the positioning of the intervals instantly evokes the opening of *Tristan und Isolde*'s identical pitches in the cello: A–F–E–D♯. This outrageous bit of "sampling" again relies on the audience's familiarity with the opera, on the one hand a perfect example of Third Programme highbrow ideals, and on the other, an excellent shorthand for the forbidden nature of the Princess's love for her mortal subject.

The second theme occurs just over ten minutes after the first (see example 3.7)🎵 and again comprises an antecedent-consequent phrase, four notes each, with a drone underneath. The antecedent is a diatonic four-note motive that is answered with a motive reminiscent of the first theme, only a half step higher. The entire phrase sounds less abrasive than the first theme, largely because of the drone below it. This drone increases in volume until just before the end of the first section, dying off before rearticulating itself at the end of the whole phrase. Its dissonant C♯ against the rest of the phrase (which starts as a tritone) resolves into a major third by the end.

The rest of the play uses cues based around these two basic themes, often with minor melodic variation, or slight tape treatment, speeding the music up or slowing it down. Occasionally, as in *Orpheus* Transcription Five

3.7. *Orpheus 4*—(Radio, 1961)—Fagandini. Second theme

3.8. *Orpheus 5*—(Radio, 1961)—Fagandini. First and second themes combined

(see example 3.8)🎵, Fagandini combines the two themes, playing them at the same time, altering the first theme with the variable-speed tape recorder so it sounds an octave lower.

Even the basic *musique concrète* sound effects evolved out of careful planning, with the emphasis on internal cohesion rather than eventual perceptibility. When Orpheus is torn apart, the screams of the Furies, treated with reverb and rearticulated echo and filtered to remove bass frequencies, serve as backdrop to the altered cries of Orpheus. His almost-inarticulate shouts were achieved, Fagandini remembers, "by recording separately each syllable of the author's name, "JE . . . A N . . . COC . . . TEAU." The pitch was altered, and tape feedback and echo were applied to give each syllable an unnatural quality, extending it and deepening it. She recalls: "Back in the Workshop, I simply chased after the infinite possibilities the material offered—until, that is, the producer said that whatever I'd prepared was it because he was doing the final recording and editing for transmission. There's nothing like a transmission deadline to concentrate the mind!"

Orpheus was received with greater acclaim than any recent Radiophonic production, with an extended review in the *Musical Times* written by skeptic Reginald Smith Brindle (author of the earlier *Musical Times* article "The Lunatic Fringe," which had been critical of the possibilities of electronic music). In this review, Brindle lauded the BBC for attempting something beyond the mere "sound effect," noting that the program "reveals a definite move towards true radiophonic music-drama. It would seem that the BBC facilities are still rather primitive, inferior to pre-1952 Germany and Italy. . . . However, *Orpheus* indicates that someone is trying hard under difficulties, and rather than discourage him, I wish him more power to his elbow."[33]

The reviewer recognized the shift from less-integrated sound effects to a complete collaboration between sound and story, with sound incorporating both effects and all the emotional range music can offer. The passing of the blame for the production's few shortcomings to the BBC rather than the (presumed male) composer indicates a real sympathy for the plight of the Workshop: understaffed, overworked, and with outdated equipment, the studio was ill-prepared to move in a more musical direction, but, ready or not, that was exactly where they were headed.

Music!

In 1963 the Workshop celebrated its fifth operational year, and by this time it had acquired additional rooms and equipment. Getting the large Room 12 (next door to the existing studio) in 1961 had allowed for the opening of a second studio, making it possible to work on more commissions at the same time, and four additional rooms acquired at the same time housed a basic tape library and offered administrative and maintenance space. In 1962, six more rooms were acquired for editing, storage, and repair space, and, for the first time, a locker and break room for the Workshop staff.[34] This meant that by 1963, the Radiophonic Workshop occupied an entire wing of the Maida Vale studios: Rooms 7 through 16, plus Rooms 29 and 30. Throughout this period, there seems to have been a relatively constant push to get more equipment and more space, and, largely because of the unit's success and the relentless PR work of Desmond Briscoe, it generally got what it asked for.

With its workload continuously increasing, the Workshop's staff increased as well. Briscoe, whose position title was now senior studio manager, assigned individual projects to staff, or producers requested specific staff to work on their productions. The team was usually a combination of SM and engineer, although the engineering staff was often pulled in many different directions, largely as a result of their ambiguous position within the Workshop. It was clear that SMs were meant to be the "creative" ones, writing music, shaping sound; what was less clear was how many facets of this process were dependent on the talent and creativity of engineers. Engineers were primarily responsible for maintaining the aging (often antique) equipment in the Workshop, but they also invented several innovative pieces of equipment themselves. It should come as no surprise that the Workshop's engineers were required to build a lot of their own equipment; it was simply impossible to purchase equipment that fulfilled the requirements of most radiophonic productions. The keying units, discussed in more detail in chapter 4, are one example. Another example of technology developed specifically for the Workshop were the special optical faders installed in a mixing desk, renamed the "Glowpot Desk" invented by lead engineer Dave Young. These kinds of innovations didn't just add new options for composers at the Workshop. They were in many ways what made it possible for the limited staff to accept the continually growing volume of commissions coming in from radio and especially television. Desmond Briscoe reported, at a meeting of engineers, "a steady increase in the demand for Radiophonic Sound[,] noting that 150 commitments had been completed in 1963 and that 18 commitments had been worked on the first month of 1964." He continued optimistically, "This output could be maintained and possibly increased with the existing staffing and equipment situation, provided that the rate of technical development can be continued."[35] This optimism on Briscoe's part disguises the real frustration felt by the engineers throughout the early 1960s. In 1961, chief engineer "Dickie" Bird had written numerous memos complaining about the ambiguity of their position. Although he had the capable help of his two assistants, Dick Mills and John Harrison, an ailing, elderly Bird was barely floating above water. Harrison, who was not there on a permanent appointment, was constantly being called away at a moment's notice by his "parent" department, Engineering, to work on other projects. Although this situation reflected a general engineering staff shortage at the BBC, it also demonstrated the precarious position of Workshop engineers. Essentially "on loan" from their departments, they could be recalled at any time. The engineering staff situation reached a head in 1964, when there were four permanent SMs and only two engineers. Ultimately the only solution to the problem was for the SMs to learn more about engineering, and as a result, the role of the engineer was reduced in the scheme of musical production. SMs learned to do basic repairs on their own and became more familiar with the equipment and its operation. In addition, there was the shift on the part of some of the engineers, particularly Dick Mills, from engineering to composition. In part, these shifts in responsibilities had become possible due to the growing standardization of production methods in the mid-1960s, including the reuse of prerecorded sound elements for the streams of commissions that were growing more and more traditionally "musical."[36]

Giants of Steam (1963, TV): Hodgson, Mills, Grainer

The television documentary *Giants of Steam* exemplified this shift toward traditionally "musical" composition. Broadcast in April 1963, this program detailing the history of the steam train in Britain featured a collaboration between composer Ron Grainer, the "Master of the Signature Tune," and the Workshop.[37] Assigned the task of working with Grainer were Brian Hodgson and Workshop veteran Dick Mills.

Hodgson joined the BBC as an SM, mostly in the Drama Department, where he worked on numerous plays, including *Orpheus*. After two years in Drama, he was inspired by a visit to the Workshop and requested a three-month attachment; he ended up staying nearly twenty-five years, not counting a brief time away, and eventually became head of the studio. Hodgson was not trained as a musician, but

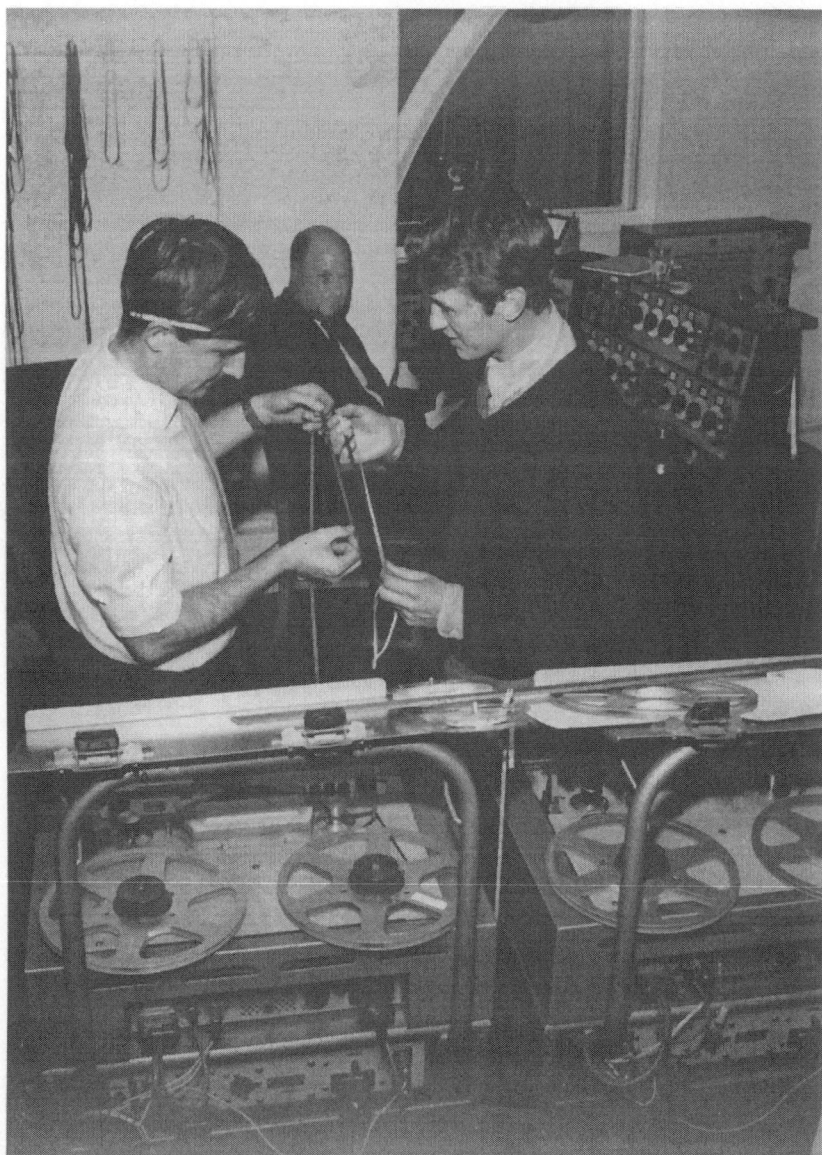

Figure 3.2. Dick Mills (left) and Brian Hodgson (right) compare tape edits. Desmond Briscoe (center) looks on. Note the loose tape loops on the wall behind them. Copyright © BBC.

had an extensive practical knowledge of electronic music and electronic sound creation and had experience working in the theater with composers like Marc Wilkinson. Rather than creating extended musical works based in tonality, Hodgson's forte was finding and assembling the right noises—the right component sonic elements that combined create unique timbral collections for a work—and as such he was the perfect person to work on *Giants of Steam*.

Hodgson and Mills assembled their musical tracks to approximate and symbolize the regularity of a steam train's sound. This worked partially to eliminate a potential problem, as Hodgson remembers: "[Director] John Read...wanted to use a lot of silent archive film and this country is full of railway geeks who would shriek and volubly protest if they heard the wrong sound with a picture of a railway engine so it was decided that all the sounds of engines would be stylized." To do this, they combined tiny pulses of white noise from Room 13's white noise generator and sounds taken by pounding on an old oil drum, constructing an elaborate multitrack tapestry of polyrhythm.[38]

Once the Workshop was commissioned to provide these sound effects, Briscoe suggested to Grainer that perhaps the rhythms could be incorporated into the music, reflecting a more "musical" interpretation of the loops. Grainer liked the idea and chose about a dozen of the rhythm loops and composed around them. He wrote several cues—a combination of brass fanfares, pastoral harmonica folklike tunes, and elegiac melodies for sections about the "end of the steam age"—and conducted his band against a backdrop of the Workshop's rhythmic creations.

While the reviewer in the *Listener* compared Grainer's music unfavorably with Honegger's *Pacific 231*,[39] the *Radio Times* described it as Grainer's "most ambitious work yet for television, and a brilliant interpretation of the railway saga," and within the BBC the results were thought of highly.[40] The success of the score resulted in the rerecording of the main theme for Decca Records with the aim of an eventual release as a pop single, along the lines of "Time Beat."

This second attempt at commercial success represents the desire by some at the Workshop, particularly Briscoe, to shift the public perception of the studio from that of an abstract, Third Programme avant-garde sound house to a more mainstream, more musical recording studio. Modernist concert music had, around this time, begun to start sharing electronic music's stage with more popular forms. Electronic music's novelty had been discovered by rock and roll, which, since the lessening of R&B as a primary source of inspiration for some branches of popular music, had looked to the novelty of unique sound sources, one of which, obviously, was electronic music. The idiosyncratic sounds emerging from the Workshop had perhaps begun to sound less unique to audiences now, its familiarity brought about both by the saturation of BBC productions with these sounds and by the popularity of those same weird noises in other forms of music, so much so that a reviewer in the *Observer* quipped that the Radiophonic Workshop "have surely become enough of a routine to make their self-conscious title expendable."[41]

While the release of a single based on Grainer's *Giants of Steam* signature tune never happened, the success of this collaboration inspired Grainer and the Workshop to work together again less than six months later on a project that would give the Radiophonic Workshop a higher profile than anything else in its nearly thirty-year history and prove to be its biggest success—the signature tune to the science fiction program *Doctor Who*.

Doctor Who (TV, 1963–1989, 1996, 2005–): Derbyshire, Mills, Grainer

Although certainly the most famous tune to emerge from the Workshop, and arguably the most famous British signature tune ever written, the *Doctor Who* theme in most ways was assembled using the same techniques as earlier Workshop projects. We are fortunate that due to the popularity of the theme, dozens of discussions exist about it and its composition.[42] For that reason, my examination will primarily place it in the larger oeuvre of the Workshop and in the long trajectory of works that move gradually toward more rhythmic complexity and, above all, more tonally melodic language.

The two composers most responsible for completing the shift to tonality are Delia Derbyshire and John Baker. Their music for the Workshop frequently employs harmonic progressions consistent with traditional tonality. However, although many works could now be said to work within a tonal framework, this never altered the Workshop's emphasis on unique sound. In other words, even though signature tunes were now *tunes*, the sounds forming the tunes were uniquely constructed *musique concrète* creations, and the works' power and effectiveness usually lies in these individual sounds.

The biggest difference between the collaboration on *Giants of Steam* and *Doctor Who* lies in the production of the music itself. For *Giants of Steam* Grainer both wrote the music and performed it, leaving the radiophonic element for the underlying rhythmic ground. In *Doctor Who*, Grainer is said to have "scribbled a melody and bass line on a piece of paper," leaving it to the Workshop staff to "realize" his score completely using electronic sound.[43]

The unique character of the program itself led to the initial decisions about the signature tune. The original cast comprised four main characters—two humans and two aliens. The aliens, who by all outside appearance look perfectly human, were "the Doctor," a mysterious figure about whom little was known, and his granddaughter, Susan. They travel through time and space in a ship known as the Tardis, which, in theory, should be able to disguise its appearance and blend in with the surroundings. The ship is broken, however, and is stuck in the shape of a blue police telephone box (a familiar sight on the streets of England in the 1960s, although there are few in operation today). The ship also has the unique quality of being larger on the inside than the outside. The two human characters are two of Susan's schoolteachers who stumble upon the Tardis and begin traveling with them through time and space. According to the original series' guidelines, the weekly exploits of the travelers would find them going from the French Revolution one week to a far-off planet in the distant future the next. The key element that first-time producer Verity Lambert wanted to focus on was the axis of "familiarity/difference" that the Doctor and his granddaughter navigate. Initially the characters appeared to contemporary audiences as perfectly recognizable figures, but when the alienness of their origins was explored, they quickly came to represent both difference as well as familiarity. The ship itself, familiar in shape yet different in substance, also carries this idea.

In keeping with this train of thought, Lambert wanted the signature tune to represent this motive. "I wanted something melodic, but yet didn't sound like any conventional grouping of instruments. In other words, I didn't want anything recognizable used at all."[44] She recalls: "I had wanted to use music, whether electronic or otherwise that had a melody rather than just *musique concrète*."[45] She wanted music the audience could relate to, could hum, and yet know that it was not generated by normal means.

On July 12, 1963, Lambert asked the Music Copyright Department to contact the New York–based agent of the French avant-garde composers Jacques Lasry and Francois Baschet, with an aim to commission their group, Les Structures Sonores, to compose the signature tune.[46] Among other techniques, Structures worked with glass rods mounted in steel to produce a ghostly sound. At the end of July she was advised by the head of TV Music, Leonard Salter, to contact the Workshop before engaging the much more expensive group, but the Workshop had to prove it was as capable of tunefulness as of uncanniness. Brian Hodgson recalls, "We were all very impressed by the sounds made by Les Structures Sonores, who had appeared on the BBC TV arts program *Monitor*. But whereas they made new sounds on glass rods set in steel, we used sine and square wave generators, a white noise generator and a special beat frequency generator."[47] Ultimately, Lambert remembers talking to the head of the group, who said they were extremely busy and couldn't do it, leaving the job open for the Workshop if they wanted it.

In her first meeting with Desmond Briscoe, Lambert told him about the importance of conveying the idea of "familiar but different" in the signature tune and explained that she wanted something "radiophonic, with a strong beat."[48] She also requested that Ron Grainer be assigned to the program. It was decided that Grainer would write the tune and that it would be realized at the Workshop by an SM. Hodgson recalls:

> Desmond Briscoe was the man who set the ball rolling. Having agreed to Verity Lambert's request he contacted Ron Grainer, who composed the music, and the Workshop composer, Delia Derbyshire, took over from there to actually perform the piece. Dick Mills worked alongside Derbyshire on the signature tune, as at that time we nearly always worked in pairs.[49]

Delia Derbyshire was still fairly new to the Workshop when she was assigned *Doctor Who*, having only composed three pieces prior to the commission.[50] She studied math and music at Cambridge and, after applying to Decca Records and being told that "they didn't employ women in the recording studio," toured for a time with a stage production of *Julius Caesar*, providing offstage electronic sound effects.[51] After joining the BBC, she spent much of her time as an SM visiting the Workshop, and often asked Briscoe if she could "just sit in the back and watch."[52] Once employed there, she quickly learned to combine her love of music and mathematics to create new sounds. One of her standard methods involved analyzing complex concrete sounds using an oscilloscope, then reconstructing the sounds using banks of Jason valve oscillators.

Lambert had already commissioned the visuals for the title sequence, so Grainer was able to see what images his music would accompany. Bernard Lodge and Joe Starie, responsible for the opening titles, had used a new technique called "positive feedback" or "howlround," which is the glowing image received by a video camera when it films its own broadcast on a monitor. Starie shone the light of a penlight into the camera while at the same time generating howlround. The result captured on film was the impression of white cloudlike formations moving toward the viewer quickly in random patterns. Over this effect were displayed the program's titles.

Derbyshire remembers her first encounter with Grainer: "The title sequence was done first, so Ron had a chance to see it before he created his score. He watched the opening graphics and did all of the timing with a stopwatch. It was when Verity [Lambert] and Waris [Hussein, the first episode's director] brought in the title graphics to show us that I met Ron for the first time."[53] Grainer had told the team that he wanted the music to sound "like the visuals," which he described as "wind bubbles and clouds." Mills recalls: "All we got from Ron Grainer was one sheet of paper. He did the tune with a theme right the way through it and the bass line. We just filled in the gaps."[54] Hodgson also has memories of Grainer's contribution: "He scribbled a few bars on a piece of manuscript paper he'd torn off from something else he was working on, leaning against this filing cabinet.... About a month or so later, Delia had finished it, and Ron came and listened to it and said, 'Gosh, did I really write that?'"[55] Derbyshire, with Mills, took Grainer's melody and slowly pieced together the tune. Mills remembers, "We created the sounds with an electronic sound generator [Jason oscillators], recorded a section and then cut it together onto one of the three tape machines that we were using."[56] In an interview, Derbyshire detailed her procedure in a typically precise manner: "It was a matter of translating notes on the page into cycles per second. Then translating the duration of notes into inches of tape at fifteen IPS.... We used some old valve oscillators to generate the initial sound. It was very hit and miss, in fact it was a nightmare."[57]

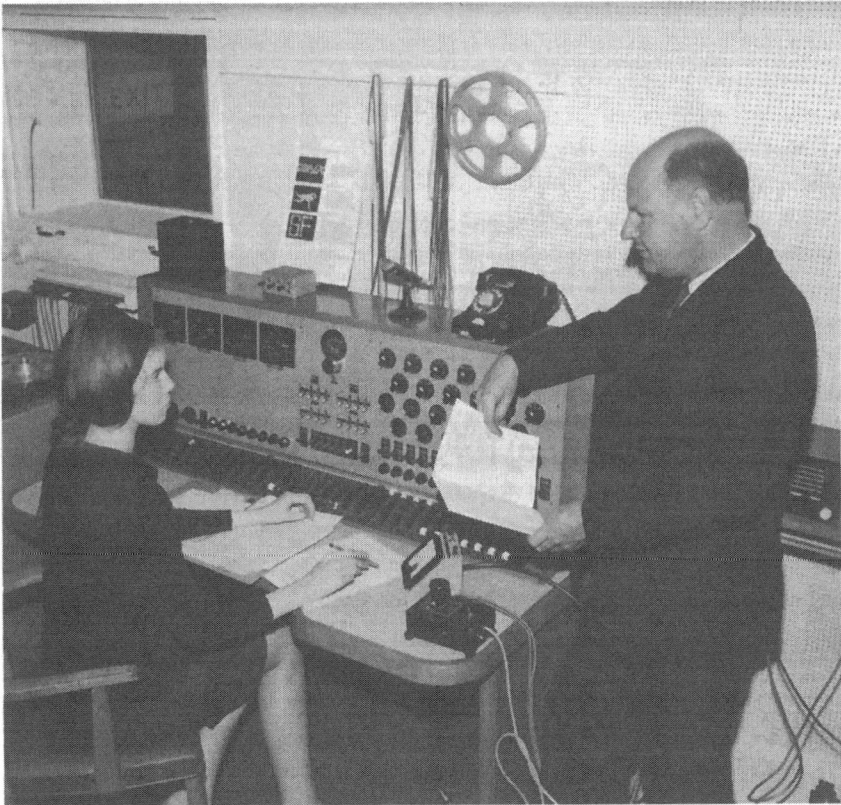

Figure 3.3. Delia Derbyshire making notes for the (ultimately unused) signature tune for *Out of the Unknown*. Desmond Briscoe is to her right. Copyright © BBC.

One of the composers' concerns was that it would sound too inhuman, which was something they didn't want. Although the signature tune was supposed to sound "different" (i.e., alien), it was also to have a touch of fallibility. To achieve this, they added tiny imperfections to the realization. According to Mills,

> There was a certain robotic quality, a sterile quality, which, if you like, could only be found in outer space where there's no atmosphere, and no coloration.... It's very easy to listen to musicians—they bring a piece of music to life by putting their own performance onto it. And although they are in rhythm 99% of the time, it is the little 1% that makes it a human being playing it and not a machine.... So when we did the *Doctor Who* music, we tried to creep in one or two, not wrong notes, but imperfections, like a little bit of tremolo in the tune. We may have shifted the beat slightly just to make it sound as though it was played by somebody with feeling, rather than a stitched together music job.... The *Doctor Who* tune swoops up, it doesn't go in precise notes. It sort of slides from note to note, and it does give it a bit of a spacey feel.[58]

The original signature tune is commonly heard in two versions: one for the opening credit sequence, which is around thirty seconds, and a longer closing credit sequence that contains a bridge and lasts around one minute. The tune is in E minor and in 4/4 time, beginning with an eight-bar introduction that consists of a four-bar ostinato bass pattern. Over the second repetition of the ostinato, a high-frequency electronic sweeping sound is heard, as if moving toward the listener. When the main melody enters at the end of bar 8 by means of a half-step descent, the bass jumps from V to i. The melody is of a completely different character than the bass. The bass is almost like a chugging engine, and indeed does sound like no recognizable instrument. The melody, however, is a pure sound, almost like a bowed vibraphone. Fulfilling the mandate from Lambert to create music that sounded "familiar but different," Derbyshire found her ability and interest in "re-creating" natural sounds electronically very useful indeed. The sonic effect is exactly one of vague recognition. Both the bass line and the melody are eminently hummable, yet the sounds that comprise the tune are utterly unidentifiable. My earlier distinctions between "music," "sound effects," "acousmatic," and "synchretic acousmatic" lose some of their relevance when talking about a thing it is difficult to experience as anything but music. The *Doctor Who* theme clearly *is* music. One finds oneself following the rhythmic pulsations as one does a pop tune: the melody has a regular phrase structure; the piece itself has a traditional eight-bars-with-bridge structure. But the individual radiophonic sounds contain the "alienating" elements.

The popular contemporary conception of the *Who* theme's construction fit into the same mythology as Fagandini's interval signals. It was understood as an attempt to "modernize" popular music through the magic of technology, science, and scientists. An article in the *Daily Mirror* two weeks after the premier of *Doctor Who*, for example, examined the signature tune through the eyes of its young producer, Verity Lambert. "Verity's Tune Is Way Out!" the headline blazes. After describing how Lambert walked into the Workshop "and said 'I want a new sound... way out and catchy!,'" the article continues by explaining that "Mr. Briscoe and his team looked at the notes and went to work... without using a single musician or musical instrument. They did it all with electronics.... This is the first time electronics have been used to produce a recognizable tune that's way out and catchy."[59] Casting the Workshop as a white-labcoat-wearing "think tank," modernizing popular music for the masses in a way impossible for the general public to imagine, this assessment depicts the music as mirroring the ideas of the program itself, with its enigmatic hero, a time traveler from space.

That the resulting arrangement was a success was obvious to the tune's composer. Originally, Grainer had intended to hire a backing band to play behind what Derbyshire had created, but he decided against that when he heard the final version. Derbyshire recalls her reaction when she finally heard the completed version: "In those days people were so cynical about electronic music and so *Doctor Who* was my private delight. It proved them all wrong.... [Ron Grainer] said 'I can't believe you've been able to do this! I want you to have half my royalties.' Unfortunately, that wasn't allowed."[60]

That the Workshop itself realized the special quality of this signature tune is apparent in an internal memo sent to the Radiophonic Technical Subcommittee two weeks before the first episode's broadcast. "This commitment is of special interest because apart from the special effects relative to the whole series and the special sound for the various story locations, the title music which was composed by Ron Grainer was realized in entirely electronic terms at the Workshop."[61] Alongside the Daleks, *Doctor Who*'s memorable villains introduced six weeks after the premiere of the first episode, the signature tune was the most talked-about aspect of the new program in its first year.

Although a new program could afford to be relatively experimental in its signature tune, especially since part of the function of that tune is to grab the attention of the casual viewer, the same is not necessarily true for the incidental music. The original incidental music for the early years of the program (with a few notable exceptions) tended to be scored for a small group of traditional instruments or derived from library records. One way of introducing the science fiction element into the program was through the use of the Radiophonic Workshop to create the program's electronic sound effects, which were labeled "special sound" and included such things as alien speech, spaceships' engines, and any other aurally unusual element that a specific serial might require. This tradition, using the Workshop for special sound, continued from 1963 until the show's initial cancellation in 1989, with Brian Hodgson filling the role from 1963 to 1973, and Dick Mills from 1973 to 1989. As we have seen, though, the boundary between "music" and "special sound" is fluid, and through the incorporation of the Workshop into each and every episode of *Doctor Who*, the program was able to realize a more unified electronic atmosphere than would have been possible without their help. This enabled the program to code itself as "science fiction" even when the budget didn't stretch to cover expensive visual effects. Examples that provided continuity within the long life of the series include the internal Tardis hum and the Tardis dematerialization sound, both designed by Brian Hodgson. To realize the latter, Hodgson dragged his mother's house key across the strings of the Workshop's old piano and treated the resulting sound.

After the success of the *Doctor Who* theme, and the publicity it brought about, specifically to Delia Derbyshire, more attention than ever was given to the individual composers within the Workshop. This was contrary to the prevailing notion of anonymity advocated in the beginning by Desmond Briscoe, but the new spirit of individuality was encouraged by four composers in the 1960s, Delia Derbyshire, Brian Hodgson, John Baker, and David Cain. These Workshop members were four very different types, with four widely divergent, distinctive styles, and together they worked to create a greater sense of artistic independence.

Amor Dei (Radio, 1964): Derbyshire, Bermange

While already by the mid-1960s the highbrow dramatic radio commissions responsible in large part for the Workshop's creation had started to dry up, several high-profile projects increased the Workshop's visibility. Of these probably the most important were the four *Inventions in Radio*, a collaboration between playwright Barry Bermange and Workshop composer Delia Derbyshire. "The Dreams," "Amor Dei," "The After Life," and "Evenings of Certain Lives" each used a similar collage technique to explore single themes. In the premier *Invention*, "The Dreams," like the others on different topics, Bermange interviewed a diverse group of ordinary people on their thoughts related to dreaming, recorded their comments, and edited and shaped the responses into a cohesive whole. The resulting product resembled a scripted work. Specially composed radiophonic music by Derbyshire then provided the background to these spoken-word collages, often occupying quite a substantial role in them, with purely musical interludes separating individual sections and topics and, more important, creating an artificial musical glue that held together and unified the often disparate voices. Each of the four *Inventions* followed this same procedure, with interviews on a topic edited together according to specific themes and tones, Derbyshire's music providing cohesion throughout. The end product of each is a self-contained reflection on a large issue, discussed in vernacular terms by ordinary people, musically rendered in a nontraditional way that serves to heighten the already alienating and mysterious mood created by the disembodied quality of the voices.

While it might seem that the text, or rather the shaping of text into poetry, was Bermange's primary focus, what he makes clear in contemporary interviews is his intention that these be considered first as musical inventions. Given the multiple "movements" contained in each, a more apt comparison might be with the symphony. The contribution from the Workshop, then, provided much more than just background sound over which the voices would express their sentiments. In almost the same way that the visual material and film score work together in a movie, here the words and music combine to create a mutual implication. That is, each adjusts and controls the other's meaning, or, as one critic of the *Inventions* put it, the addition of the radiophonic sound resulted in "the monster...being tamed."[62]

Although Bermange maintained director's control over the entire project, he gave Derbyshire only vague instructions and left her to create the musical portion of the program based on his generalized suggestions to her of the work's structure. Bermange, while acknowledging that he didn't actually create the music, felt that his musical input was vital: "I'm at the controls of the music, I can control the volume of the music. I can bring in the sounds I want to bring in."[63] This is contradicted by Derbyshire's notes for these works, in which she has indicated fairly precise musical timing notated from her initial meetings with Bermange. When he states that he would "ask for certain basic sounds to be produced for me and from these, as with the voices, I make a selection of the kinds of sounds I think would suit the particular movement that I'm engaged on," he denies the active role played by Derbyshire in the creation of those sounds. Further complicating attribution of authorship, of course, is that despite efforts by Workshop composers to claim their contributions as their own, Derbyshire is given no credit for her work on these productions. Instead, as was still standard practice for the Workshop in the mid-1960s, individual composers' contributions are still credited as "BBC Radiophonic Workshop" as if an abstract team of scientists were hard at work forging these sounds in a top-secret laboratory.

A closer examination of the second *Invention* can serve as a demonstration of the type of program at which the Workshop excelled in the years immediately before voltage-control synthesis changed many aspects of the studio's operation. It is at its core a work based on the manipulation of recorded sound, and as such it explores most of the options available to Workshop composers in an idiom and style unique to the BBC. It also demonstrates the fundamental differences between the output of the Radiophonic Workshop and other academic electronic music studios, in that while the techniques and concepts behind the music might be superficially related, in this work at least, the final sound of the work much more closely resembled traditional music. We are also lucky in that Derbyshire's original notes and makeup tapes survive for this composition, giving us an insight into the working process. It is a rare chance to follow a Workshop commission from initial discussion to broadcast.

In "Amor Dei" (The Love of God), Derbyshire was responsible, as she had been for "The Dreams," for constructing the radiophonic accompaniment to Bermange's collage of voices, who were this time discussing the role God plays in ordinary people's lives. Whereas the first *Invention*, although unusual in its creation, had been on a topic familiar to the Workshop, that is, the dream state, an abstracted state of consciousness, "Amor Dei" posed a much more challenging scenario. Rather than representing a dark, menacing threat, or altered mental states, Bermange was constructing a spoken collage based on a discussion of the way ordinary people related to God. This meant Derbyshire's music had to convey a sense of wonder, awe, and mystery, but also overwhelming love. In one sense, then, the choice of radiophonic sound was obvious: the abstract nature of God's love and people's belief (or disbelief) in him could be captured in an equally abstract musical way. However, these sounds had also to represent the concrete reality of God to many of the commentators. They must have a very real sense of beauty. They also must somehow portray the important element of tradition so vital to many of the commentators' views of religion in general.

Even without considering the more literally musical aspects of its radiophonic score, the overall program is structured in a way that mirrors traditional "classical music" forms: the work is built out of four overarching topics, which Bermange labeled "movements."[64] In the eight-minute first movement, Bermange assembled a speech collage of interviews taken for the most part at the Old People's Welfare Council of Hornsey conveying the interviewee's impression of the nature of God—in particular, their belief that God is always connected inseparably with the infinite. A sense of God's ineffability is generated by linking differing impressions using similar words in a disorienting way. For example, a fast-moving sequence using the word "something" offers many differing, contradictory impressions:

MAN: Something which makes flowers grow.
WOMAN: Something inside you.
WOMAN: Something that I feel.
WOMAN: Something which envelops everything.
WOMAN: Something which is completely outside of myself.
MAN: Something working through man.

Occasionally, Bermange uses the disparate voices to construct a teleological sequence, as when each speaker advances an opinion on what "God is..."

The second movement, also around nine minutes, concerns the way individuals perceive God in their lives, and the various ways he is manifested in them, starting primarily in the material world, such as "in flowers" or "a newborn baby" shifting to more abstract representations: "how everything is ordered," and "when you pray." The text is constructed along similar lines to the first movement, in that a sequence is often linked by similar initial words, such as "When I see a lovely sunny day," "When I am close to nature," or "When I am by the sea."

The third movement lasts fifteen minutes and provides a contrasting atheistic viewpoint. Opening with an extended single speech outlining a basic frustration with religion and people who put their faith in God, this movement's texture quickly fragments into short, incomplete thoughts. For these speakers, the overwhelming feeling is one of despair, shared equally by those who rely on God to make decisions in their lives and by those who cannot optimistically rely on blind faith.

Finally, the fourth movement, fourteen minutes long, begins by expressing a believer's frustration and pity at the nonbeliever's lack of faith. It then proceeds to list all those aspects of life that are thought to be better with God, shifting to a discussion of how prayer allows a close connection with him. As the speakers become more introspective, the speech seems to slow down, the words emerge more slowly, and the individuals' thoughts are allowed to be expressed in more extended passages, in segments of several sentences. The movement then concludes as the first movement did, with four brief sentences contrasting the more extended section preceding it:

WOMAN: God is in every one of us.
WOMAN: He is inside everyone for—everyone to find.
WOMAN: We all have God within us.
WOMAN: And I love him.

Bermange's initial directive to Derbyshire was to produce "the sound of a Gothic altar piece."[65] It was agreed that unlike their first collaboration, "The Dreams," "Amor Dei" would, unusually, have no electronically produced sounds at all. All radiophonic sound would be derived from the sound of the human voice. In this, Derbyshire was guided by Karlheinz Stockhausen's *Gesang der Jünglinge*, one of the foundational works of electronic music, and a work Derbyshire admired. Perhaps due to her study of mathematics at Cambridge, Derbyshire loved using complex formulas to construct elaborate structures for even the simplest of signature tunes. This may have been an attempt to push people to take her and her works more seriously. Certainly within the Workshop the Bermange commissions were considered the most "highbrow" Third Programme broadcasts to be undertaken there in quite some time. Consequently, Derbyshire must have felt the pressure to deliver the artistic goods, filling the work with as much high-modernist paraphernalia as she felt she could muster. Of course, this desire for the creation of "highbrow" art is in direct conflict with the Workshop's larger mission to create a more accessible, British form of electronic music, and she never intended to create a difficult work, only one that could resemble the difficulty of Continental music. Her art is an accessible parody of modernism, drawing on the tropes of high modernism without sacrificing the satisfaction of traditional dominant-tonic tonal relationships or dialogue-heavy narrative closure.

Once the decision had been made to use only the sound of the human voice, Derbyshire then hit upon the idea of emulating Stockhausen's famous piece further by using a boy soprano as the source material. At the top of the first page of notes for this work is outlined the Dies Irae melody, but she quickly settled on a library recording of the more expansive Advent antiphon "Rorate coeli desuper et nubes pluant justum" (Drop down dew, ye heavens, from above, and let the clouds rain on the just).[66]

In her notes for the construction of this piece, she writes on the first day: "Take 'rorate,' make detailed analysis (serial, statistic and linguistic), rebuild a fragmented variation, serially organized fragments of voice. Find best tech for cutting fragments: normal cut, switched, scanned, long cut, spaced fade up, etc. Very very fast at first in short groups, then in breathtakingly long complex dramatic sections."[67] From these basic ideas, throughout the last weeks of May 1964, she began working with the prerecorded chant, first rerecording it, isolating each individual pitch, as heard in music example 3.7.

Derbyshire never intended for her music, unlike Stockhausen's piece, to be considered an independent artwork; it exists entirely in collaboration with its *other* text, Bermange's collage. She also never intended to create harmonies that were outside traditional diatonic harmony. Consequently, she maintains the Dorian mode of the chant in the construction of her own melodies built out of the original recording, adding no chromaticism not already present in the chant. This must have had an influence on her choice of "Rorate" in the first place, since it uses every pitch of the Dorian mode, then offering an easily sampled choice of each note. Music example 3.8 shows Derbyshire's original edit.◐

Once she had isolated each pitch, she created a loop based on a reversed, filtered combination of several syllables, removing the consonants to create a smooth texture on one pitch. This looped single pitch was then used to re-create each pitch of the Dorian mode expanded to two octaves, created by matching each pitch to the Workshop's frequency counter. She divided the mode into three groups: the first group comprised the fifth E and B over two octaves; the second was a minor triad built on C♯, F♯, and A, repeated an octave higher and completed with a final high C♯; and the third was built out of the fourth D♯ and G♯, also repeated an octave higher, as heard in music example 3.9.◐

Having constructed three "tone rows," Derbyshire then divided her mode into groups of two and three pitches each, moving stepwise up diatonically two octaves beginning with the lowest pitch, C♯. She recorded each group as a tone cluster separately, working her way through all fourteen combinations up two octaves. Dynamics, while largely determined by the volume of the speaker's dialogue, were arranged according to six values, of six decibels difference between each, an influence she attributes to Stockhausen in her notes. Both the individual looped pitches and the clusters would serve as her final material for the broadcast, joining more heavily filtered and ring-modulated versions of individual pitches.

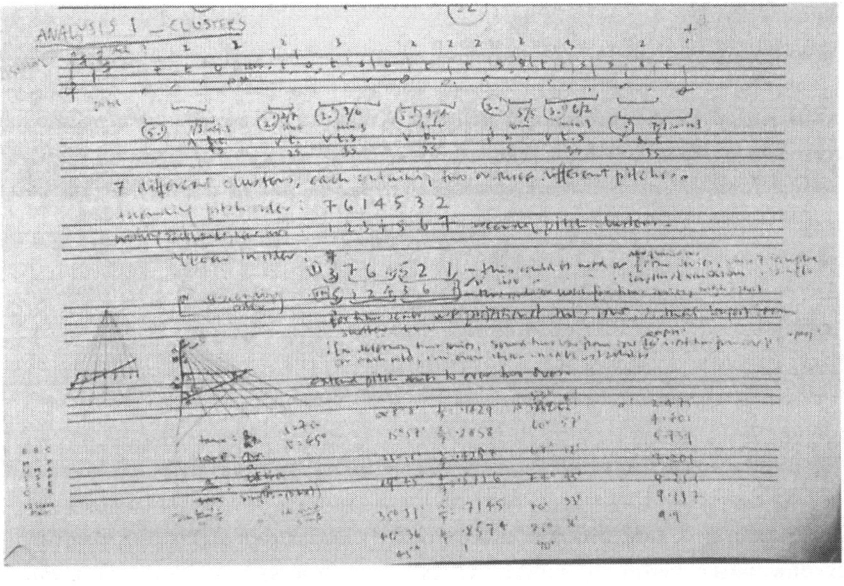

Figure 3.4. One page of Delia Derbyshire's notes for the composition of *Amor Dei*.

In the first movement in particular, Derbyshire seems keen to disguise the human origins of her music, making the vocal aspects essentially unrecognizable and forging, as in her *Doctor Who* theme, a mysterious sound impossible to identify. The movement opens with a very slow rocking between the pitches A and B, back and forth, creating a mild sort of tension until a plateau is reached on C♯ falling right before the words "God is my friend and I love him." This tune continues to rise an additional pitch to D♯ before giving way to an unpitched falling wave of sound. Derbyshire's technique here matches Bermange's textual technique, gradually accumulating tension before a comforting release through tonal resolution. In this case, extending the progression by an extra pitch and adding the long wavelike fade, the music serves as more of a comma than a period, while still offering the listener a satisfying sense of partial closure. It also marks out as special the first occurrence of the text "God is my friend," a phrase that recurs throughout the program and ultimately concludes it.

In the second movement, however, Derbyshire deliberately gives away her game by opening with the chant, clear and distinct for the first eight pitches, before layering multiple iterations of this opening melody on top of itself in a loop. The delay, or repetition of the recording, begins after the fourth pitch and is suggestive of nothing so much as a reverberant cathedral, as heard in music example 3.10.◗

After this clear and unambiguous use of the chant melody, Derbyshire isn't nearly as hesitant to use more recognizable versions of it throughout the rest of "Amor Dei." During an interlude midway through this movement, she combines the more abstract background sounds of the first movement with the clearer treatment of individual pitches she had designed earlier.

It is in the third movement that she gets the most creative with her use of the original chant. The problematic topic of atheism in a program about God inspired Derbyshire to further abstract the original chant melody: using the variable-speed tape recorder, she constructed a pattern based around falling half steps and wind. Unlike the Mixolydian sections that preceded it, the third movement is filled with uncertainty. What starts off as a stable note inevitably slides a half step down, often against the background of a similarly sliding "windy" bass texture. In addition, this is the only time the musical treatment seems to infect the speakers, with dialogue treated with echo, distancing these speakers from the earlier believers. About five minutes in, though, as believers start to talk about how empty life would be without God, the half step tends to progress further down a whole step. The texture starts to thicken out so that the windy bass begins to resemble a bass drone, while the descending pattern is established as a 3–2 progression that never quite resolves on the tonic. Eventually this is diffused and the bass fades into the background while the melody returns to its half-step motion as the nonbelievers' dialogue takes over again.

As the believers' pleas return at the end of the movement, the steady pitched bass also returns and, more spectacularly, the looped chant melody from the beginning of the second movement reappears, this time at the end of the chant phrase, offering a Dorian cadential pattern at last. Relief is short-lived, however, as the bass begins to mutate into a less stable and louder abstract, pitchless noise against the backdrop of a more and more abstract chant loop. This cacophony slowly fades, ending a movement based on instability and lack of faith on a note of profound uncertainty.

With the return of certainty in the final movement (opening as it does with the words "There *is* a God! There *must* be a God! There *is* a God!") comes the return of our four-note motive (A–B–C♯–D♯) from the first movement, beginning this time on the fourth pitch of D♯. At first it remains unclear where this D♯ is going, but with a downward leap of a major third, it begins to become clear that this movement will take full advantage of the built-in whole steps. The music operates quite differently in this more confident movement, which, rather than rocking between two pitches, rises only to a major third after building sufficient tension, and breezily moves up and down these two interlocked major third configurations, as heard in music example 3.11. ♪

After a few minutes, the sliding whole step progression from the third movement is layered on top of the four-note progression, as well as a more treble drone soaring above the lower layers. This music, played quite high in the mix, continues on like this for around ten minutes. Finally, much of this texture fades, and the looped chant melody rises out of the background, initially quite abstracted but settling into a more recognizable looped pattern. The voices of the speakers end with the final repetition of the words "And I love him," giving way to a purely musical conclusion, a radiophonic collage rather than a textual one, comprising clear but complex mixtures of different aspects of the chant. It concludes not with the end of the chant but, rather, with an extremely long fade lasting over a minute that lets the chant simply melt into the background noise.

Of course, what Derbyshire is doing throughout this piece is manipulating the standard rules of tonality. Whole steps equal tradition, goodness, stability, faith, God; half steps equal the different, rational, lack of faith, and atheism. Ultimately, what makes this an exciting example of radiophonics is the way Derbyshire was able, with a technology traditionally associated with scaring audiences, to manipulate tape to create, in her words, "the most beautiful sound I've ever heard."[68]

Although a Technical Committee memo from 1965 notes the "recent good publicity which the Workshop had received for some of the more serious aspects of its work," highbrow works like "Amor Dei" represented only a very small percentage of their output in the mid-1960s.[69] The majority of their work consisted of short contributions to programs like the Brian Rix vehicle *Dial Rix*, or school broadcasts such as Vera Grey's *Music, Movement, and Mime* series. The Workshop also wrote signature tunes for a bewildering number of programs. In fact, after the sudden success of the *Doctor Who* theme, it seemed that everyone wanted a radiophonic signature tune. But after all the ridiculous *Who* coverage, Derbyshire and Hodgson were concerned that the Workshop wasn't getting good press for their more serious projects. They invited the press to visit the Workshop on March 25, 1965, for a "day of radiophonics," using the Bermange programs as examples of their methods. The staff of the Workshop had increased yet again and by early 1965 was composed of Briscoe as senior studio manager, four SMs (John Baker, Delia Derbyshire, Brian Hodgson, and, on a short-term attachment, Keith Salmon), and three engineers (David Young, Dick Mills, and John Harrison), all present to host the special day.

That day the composers described to the press what the Workshop did by starting with the sounds they all would know, specifically its special sound for *Doctor Who's* Daleks, before moving effortlessly on to the more "high-end" spectrum of their output: "It produces anything from Dalek voices through Signature Tunes to Background Scores for such programs as 'The Dreams' 'Amor Dei' and 'The Making of the Bomb.'"[70] They also emphasized this on the day, demonstrating specific techniques used to produce the Bermange works:

> These programs have already attracted considerable interest in the artistic world: *New Comment* on Wed, 30th December 1964, included an interview with Bermange about his Inventions for radio; "Monitor" is preparing a visual background for "Amor Dei," and German version are being planned in Munich by Der Bayerische Rundfunk.... We feel that this plan can but have a beneficial effect on the "informed public image" of the Radiophonic Workshop, and indeed on that of Sound Broadcasting.[71]

The public perception that the Workshop had been gradually shifting from "sound" to "music" can be mapped onto a similar shifting of the popular impression of the Workshop's output. While the "mad scientist" label remains throughout the 1960s, the Workshop's connection to popular culture is growing stronger, and there is sympathetic treatment of these particular electronic composers, who, unlike the detached Continental composers, are participating in the continual scientification of secular popular culture as well. The year the press really started paying attention to this shift was 1965. For the first time, a reporter for the *Observer* calls the Workshop employees "composers" and proceeds to paint a picture of the Workshop as a hip, cutting-edge, Carnaby Street phenomenon, reporting how composition "is largely shared by three regulars—all under 30—Delia Derbyshire, modern, classically-slanted musician and mathematician; John Baker, composer of the more catchy tunes; Brian Hodgson, who handles the dramatic non-musical pieces."[72] Both reporter and composers must negotiate the tricky ground between the established role of the Workshop as "special sound" producer against its growing reputation as an exceptional studio producing more musical works. The mystifying terms often used to describe their craft, a dramatic move both reporters and composers are guilty of, place them on the tightrope wire of this discussion. Nearly every newspaper report includes fetishized lists of equipment, some real, some invented, as if the reporter had walked into a top-secret laboratory: "Hidden behind banks of tape recorders sit the white collar composers. No piano, no manuscript paper, not a single crochet. Just a lot of dials and thingummy-jigs.... A team of eight, including a secretary, are producing music from oscillators, noise simulators, a modulator, a wobbulator...and other highly technical equipment."[73]

Briscoe, as head of the Workshop, is cast in these articles as half mad scientist, half idiot savant, disconnected from culture but working toward the greater good. One can sense a real irony in the following *Punch* description of Briscoe and his "powers," as if the Workshop's output were controlling the thoughts of the general public. The writer begins by comparing him to a science fiction inventor, then menacingly suggests that he is planning to use his mysterious powers to measure actors' reactions, "their brain currents, pulse rates...and so on, converting the readings into equivalent electronic sounds, and using them to condition the responses of the audiences....But don't be alarmed. He has a sense of responsibility and he is moving ahead into the unknown outer silence with great care."[74]

Accompanying the emerging sense of the Workshop's output as music was a movement to claim individual authorship. When John Baker applied to the Performers Rights Society for the right to claim authorship over his compositions, he was battling not only against the Workshop's collective, professionalized identity, but also against the widespread representation of electronic music as a product of technology rather than an organizing intellect. As noted above, Delia Derbyshire didn't get credit for "Amor Dei," although Barry Bermange did. Baker was successful in his attempt, and after this point, Workshop composers retained the "intellectual" copyright over the material, while the BBC kept the mechanical (and financial) exploitation rights. It was a small victory, but shifting to a system of individual credit for compositions had a profound effect on morale within the studio.

Radio Nottingham (Radio, 1967): Baker

In the mid-1960s, the BBC began expanding its system of regional radio, giving each county its own station. These stations would specialize in programming for that region, including local news, weather, and individually produced programming, functioning similarly to an American local-access cable network. In the first years of their existence, these stations usually broadcast only a few hours a day, so each was anxious to make an impression on listeners. One effective way of making an impact is through a distinctive "sign-on" tune, announcing the beginning and end of each broadcast day. The main problem facing the stations, however, was the familiar one of very small budgets. A solution was to hire the Radiophonic Workshop, whose services, as an internal BBC organization, were quite cheap.

Radio Nottingham was first on the air, January 31, 1968. Broadcast on VHF 94.8 and Rediffusion Channel C, one of its initial call-signs was the sound of flying Sherwood arrows, reflecting the station's desire to maintain an individual sense of location.[75] Local sign-on tunes composed by the Workshop often depicted the distinctive trade of the region: as Sheffield was known for its steel industry, Workshop composer David Cain constructed the Radio Sheffield theme using sounds of Sheffield cutlery. The other primary call-sign for Radio Nottingham was specially composed by John Baker at the Workshop (see example 3.9).

"Radio Nottingham"'s sounds are not primarily electronic; rather, they are concrete, derived variously from the sound of air passing over the opening of an old bottle, a plucked ruler, and pouring water, with each note individually pitched on a variable-speed tape recorder to create the main melody.[76] The warmth of the tone produced by the bottle is almost flutelike and was one of Baker's favorites, used frequently for his elaborate tape-splicing compositions. Baker was equally well known for his unpitched complex rhythmic constructions, building on the techniques developed by Maddalena Fagandini. His syncopated patterns were

3.9. *Radio Nottingham*—(Radio, 1967)—Baker

More complex percussion begins

3.9. Continued

3.9. Continued

3.9. Continued

derived more from Baker's jazz training and popular music than any compositions had been before them, and the repetitious forward-moving motion in the
call-sign sounds, to early-twenty-first-century ears, remarkably similar to minimalist composer Steve Reich's process music of the 1980s. Baker's musical credentials were the most impressive of any Workshop composer to that point.
Trained in composition and piano at the Royal Academy of Music, he worked
primarily as a jazz pianist before coming to the BBC in 1960.

The form of "Radio Nottingham" is straightforward. Each sound element
enters at two-bar intervals: first, the "bottle" begins a treble ostinato pattern;
second, a bass line, constructed out of a bass guitar with plucked ruler added,

Figure 3.5. John Baker surrounded by tape loops. Copyright © BBC.

enters; third, the metallic percussion complex enters. Finally, the main melody, a bass tune, sounding slightly like a plucked electric guitar, enters. Its phrase structure is also regular: a series of four two–bar antecedent/consequent phrases, repeated three times, with a six-bar bridge between the second and third iteration of the main melody. The melody itself is a cute if banal tune; the "radiophonics" of the piece come in the intricate interaction of the different elements, and the quick tempo. As in a Bach Invention, the top, flutelike part moves in rapid arpeggiated triads with mechanical precision, each shift in harmony locking together as if assembled by computer; indeed, the primary impression of the piece is that it was realized by computer. The relentlessness of the rhythm and bass underpinning the signal tune, accompanied by the inevitability of its simple harmonic motion, sounds like a vision of a dynamic, efficient future, as efficient and machine-produced as any atonal composition by Stockhausen.

Baker's ability to craft solid, jazz-inflected tunes accompanied by scientifically precise rhythm tracks made him a popular choice for producers working on contemporary action programs like *Adam Adamant, Dial M for Murder*, and *Vendetta* (for which he wrote the music for seven episodes). More than this, though, Baker nudged the Workshop even further away from its origins as producer of abstract background noise and toward recognizably familiar harmonies. His tune "Musak" is a good example of this, surviving in two different forms, both of which betray their tonal origins. The initial version, originally written for the episode "Time in Advance" from the anthology series *Out of the Unknown*, is purely electronic, and strongly reminiscent of what Brian Eno would label "ambient music" seven years later on his album *Discreet Music*. Baker uses a slowly moving looped tonal bass line to ground a series of higher-frequency tape loops that recur in regular patterns. The soothing Muzak-like texture contains enough variety that it never bores, yet remains incongruous enough to function as background music, and indeed this is how it is used in the episode. Set "in the far future," one of the primary backdrops for the action is the bar at the elegant Hotel Capricorn Ritz. Baker's music plays nonstop during these scenes, and, while still recognizably futuristic, the harmonic progressions capture and reinforce contemporary stereotypes about the function of music in such a place. The second version uses this original as a foundation on which Baker plays a "cool" jazz improvisation on the piano. Here, his harmonization reconfigures the original bass loops into a much more interesting progression, and to my knowledge it is one of the first instances of jazz performed with a combination of acoustic and electronic instruments. A review of "Time in Advance" in the *Guardian* was absolutely scathing about every aspect of the production until this final sentence: "But the sound effects by the Radiophonic Workshop were very clever indeed."[77]

How, then, are we to hear these final productions at the Workshop before synthesizers changed forever both the way music was made and how that music sounded? As we have seen, composers at the Workshop had already moved past the early abstract textures of the first commissions, settling into a more tonal, tuneful framework for their compositions. For example, in January 1967, for the *Doctor Who* episode "The Underwater Menace," composer Dudley Simpson, collaborating with Brian Hodgson, had used the Multi-colour Tone Organ, treating the output in a way that resembles and anticipates the sounds of the synthesizer. Table 3.1 is taken directly from an inventory of the facilities available at the Workshop in April 1967.

Notice that the instruments hadn't changed substantially since the studio had opened seven years earlier; the equipment was now just of a higher quality. What had changed was the philosophical approach to composition. In the years immediately following the Workshop's opening, opposition from the Music Department was so fierce that radiophonic composers forged a path of their own, unconnected to the trends and fashions of the larger BBC music community. This path was derived largely from the musical inclinations of the composers themselves; Delia Derbyshire's love of mathematics encouraged abstract, timbrally complex

Table 3.1. Schedule of Equipment

Schedule of Equipment

BBC Standard

9 Tape recorders, Philips EL 3503, EL 3740, Trolley Mounted
1 Tape Recorder, EMI BTR/2 with aux. spool motor
1 Tape Recorder, EMI TR90, trolley mounted
4 Tape Recorders, Ferrograph, portable
1 Tape Recorder, Ferrograph, rack mounted. Stereo.
1 Disk Reproducer, TD/7
1 Disk Reproducer, RP/2
1 Disk Reproducer, DRD/5
3 Loudspeakers, LS/51A
1 Loudspeaker, LSU/10
2 Reverberation Plates, EMT, with remote control
3 Variable Correction Units, VCU 1/A
1 Quad Correction Unit
6 Microphones

BBC Non-Standard

1 Tape Recorder, Ampex, Trolley mounted
2 Tape Recorders, Leevers–Rich half-track, Velodyne Drive
2 Tape Recorders, RGD type 1550
1 Tape Recording Channel, Motosacoche. Two machines and Console
5 Mixer Units, MX18
8 Amplifiers, OBA/8 c/w power supplies
2 PA Stabilizers, MK1
5 Portable Effects Units, PEU/1
1 Portable Attenuator, AT18
4 Loudspeakers, LSU/7 with LSM/1 or MPA Amplifiers
1 White Noise Generator, bay mounted
1 Portable Amp. Det.
3 Ring-Modulators
1 Limiter, LIM/2

Commercial

1 Organ, Miller "Multicolortone"
1 Organ, Miller "Spinetta"
1 Signal Generator, Airmec 252
2 Wobbulators, Bruel & Kjoer, Type 1011 and No. 36
1 Decade Oscillator, Muirhead D/695/A
12 Oscillators, Jason
7 Oscillators, Advance

(*continued*)

Table 3.1. Continued

---

1 Square-wave Shaper, Muirhead D/783/A

1 1/3 Octave Filter, Albis Type 502/74

2 Octave Filters, AEE, Response Control Unit, Type A 1513

1 Octave Filter, Leevers Rich 46X 136

2 Disk Reproducers, Lenco

1 Frequency and Time measuring equipment, Venner TSA 3336

1 Film Viewing and Editing Desk, Prevost QC DT

1 Film Winder, 35mm

1 Film splicer, 35mm

1 Film splicer, 16mm

1 Leeraser

1 Time and Pitch Regulator, Eltro Tempophon

2 Solartron Stabilized 13v supply units

1 Portable Desk Recorder, EMI

1 Loudspeaker, Heathkit "Cotswold" and associated RDG Monitor Amplifier

1 Office Intercom

1 Microphone, Grampian DP/4

Locally Constructed

2 Guitars, with magnetic pick-up

1 Auto-harp with magnetic pick-up

3 Reverberation generators, using Hammond Units 4/F

3 Photo-electric 600Ohm faders, mains operated

1 Vibrato generator, using Hammond delay-line and variable speed scanner

1 Vibrato generator, using Hammond phase-shift amplifier per L/100 organ

1 8-way key unit with control amps

1 12-way key unit with control amps

2 Variable neon-operated metronome switch units

1 Audio-operated fader unit

3 Ring modulators, portable

Control desks and normal bay-mounted equipment are not included in this schedule.

"compositions"; Maddalena Fagandini's abilities to construct intricate rhythmic patterns led to her trademark interval signals; John Baker's jazz background encouraged rhythmically vital, harmonically rich tunes; and Brian Hodgson's interest in experimenting with tape treatments and dense textures led to atmospheric and moody backgrounds. Each of these would contribute to the Workshop's reputation, establishing in the public mind the nature of their work. With the incorporation of new methods of sound production by the end of the 1960s, however, many of the techniques perfected during these early years became quickly obsolete, and the composers had to adapt or face their own obsolescence.

4

The Coming of the Synthesizers

Good evening ladies and gentlemen, Hans Joachim speaking....
[Music] *The Daily Chronicle*, more strongly than most programs
reflects the face of the world, the state of our society....Our world
has altered since 1950. It has become more hectic, more materialistic, freer; quite simply, more modern whether we are happy about
it or not. We have, therefore, got the impression that our old signature tune has become rather old-fashioned, no longer up to date. It
is just a coincidence that this new tune, which you will soon hear,
has been composed by an English woman, Delia Derbyshire, but the
fact that you and I find nothing unusual in being in contact every
day with the rest of the world is for us also a symbol. Fifteen years
ago the world would have been astonished. This new melody is not
played by instruments. It has been made by artificially produced
tones in the Electronic Workshop of the BBC. Are the older ones
amongst us going to lament this fact? The world of 1966 is no longer
the world of 1950. We can only come to terms with it when we
accept this.

—undated *Daily Chronicle* transcript from BBC Written
Archives Centre

This transcript from the *Daily Chronicle*[1] goes some way toward defining for us
the issues and priorities affecting the West during the tumultuous 1960s. That
Joachim thought it was possible to represent "citizens of the modern era" by
using electronic music is clear. What isn't quite as clear is how he perceives the
music as accomplishing this. To be sure, electronic music emerges in the modern

era, if not the postmodern. If this is the case, how does electronic music represent this "more hectic, more materialistic, freer" society? Getting to the bottom of the way in which electronic music's meanings change in the 1960s from one primarily attached to the cultural avant-garde to a popular and populist appropriation of these sounds will require a close examination of the shifts as they occurred within the Workshop. In the 1960s, electronic music came into its own, developing in many directions, particularly with the emergence of voltage-control synthesis. As used in broadcasting, it still frightened, it still mystified and represented the psychologically off-kilter, as it had in its early days. But already by the early 1960s, radiophonic composers began to develop new techniques that allowed for more traditionally "beautiful" electronic and tape music. No longer could it *only* frighten; now it could also move audiences to tears. The remoteness from humanity that electronic music seemed in its early years to possess could now also represent a very human disjunction, melancholy, and wonder. At the Radiophonic Workshop this was done primarily by returning to tonally derived harmonies. In the case of the *Daily Chronicle* signature tune, it is significant that electronic music was being called upon to re-create a tune that already existed, but in a "modern" way. This use for electronic music, that of repositioning a musical world already in use, adapting and refashioning familiar melodies to configure them as now representing "modernity," would guide the Workshop's output throughout the next fifteen years. The reasons for this shift were built into the very mandate of the Workshop itself; it was a completely self-sustaining operation, closed off from overt influence from contemporary music trends due to its ban on allowing "outside" composers access to its equipment, and, ironically, shunned by the more mainstream "high" musical culture of the BBC as irrelevant to their interests. All these factors contributed to the hothouse environment wherein composers at the Workshop were allowed to develop a unique style for electronic music outside the control of traditional musical circles.

Behind the stylistic changes of the 1960s at the Workshop was a gradual shift away from exclusively tape-manipulated techniques toward the use of sounds produced electronically, first by simple oscillators and then, at the end of the decade, by voltage-control synthesizers. Therefore, to say that the synthesizers "arrived," heralding a new era, would be misleading. The philosophy behind the synthesizer as it would later be embodied had been established at the Workshop since the early 1960s, and their composers saw it only as another tool to create more easily what they were already doing. Presaged first by the keying units, then by the "multikey" unit, synthesizers such as the EMS VCS3 were all, fundamentally, just easier tools for producing the kind of music they were already making. The rest of popular culture simply caught up. Now, it is too much to say that the Radiophonic Workshop *caused* the synthesizer to develop the way it did, but the Workshop was the only institutionally supported studio to be producing electronic music that achieved such widespread distribution. There was sympathy with the projects of people like Raymond Scott, Andre Popp, and Tod Dockstader, but the department's operation was tailor-made to the development of the synthesizer as it would emerge by the 1970s. In this chapter, therefore, I will not be building up to some great moment at which the synthesizers arrive at the Workshop. Rather, I will approach their use of synthesizers much as the composers themselves did, as just another way to make the variety of sounds they wanted in the forms they wanted.

In the early 1960s the Workshop found its techniques shifting away from simple tape manipulation; with the proliferation of tape recording equipment in most studios, this kind of work was now being done by normal studio managers outside the Workshop facilities. With this shift came a more "musical" emphasis, a direction that promoted the hiring of musically trained staff, a move away from the traditional Drama Department studio managers (SMs) to ones that were "primarily musicians."[2] Although, according to Workshop composer Delia Derbyshire, "the BBC made it quite clear that they didn't employ composers and we weren't supposed to be doing music,"[3] this change was noted in an internal document from 1963, probably written by Desmond Briscoe. In it Briscoe explains that "it would seem that the work which the unit is called upon to create has steadily become more sophisticated, more precisely designed and shaped and above all more musical in nature."[4] This attitude contrasts sharply with the opinion expressed by the Radiophonic Effects committee as late as December 1961, when it was agreed that the Workshop staff (both SMs and engineers) should "confine their activities to the production of Radiophonic Effects. The production of background 'music,' signature tunes, etc., should be a combined effort between musician and Workshop staff."[5]

As earlier chapters have shown, this change to a more "musical" output was not received without some resistance from the musical establishment within the BBC. The drive for some to keep the Radiophonic Workshop as a "sound effects" studio was real, and Briscoe was forced to fight hard to keep the Workshop situated in the Maida Vale music studios after an attempt was made in 1963 to move it to Broadcasting House, the home of a new effects area.[6] In a letter explaining why this move would be a bad idea, Briscoe notes how the musical shift was brought about in part because the basic sound treatments the Workshop used to be relied on to supply were now within the abilities of normal radio and television studio managers to produce themselves. He cites the proximity of instruments such as, ironically, the Miller Multi-colour Tone Organ, now used frequently by Workshop musicians, acknowledging that the studio might be converted into an electronic composition studio, "where Music Department will invite composers to come and work, this would obviously be part of, and staffed by this unit; there is I think space for such a place here at Maida Vale."[7] Such a studio had been briefly discussed in 1961, and rejected, but Briscoe's purpose in reintroducing the subject two years later was clearly to align their product with that of Continental studios, at least in terms of the "musicality" of this output. He is clear, however, that one of the great differences between the Workshop and Continental studios is the sheer volume of material made at the Workshop; he observed, "It is perhaps the apparent psychological peace, apart from the freedom from casual visitors, and others to whom no doubt our very extensive facilities would be an attraction...which make it possible for the very considerable output of the unit, compared with similar studios on the continent."[8]

With staff increases and additional space came significant equipment increases. By 1963, although tape manipulation remained an essential component of the composer's arsenal and the Workshop had increased by nearly threefold their number of tape recorders, a gradual shift toward electronically generated sounds is apparent. Nearly every piece of equipment was geared toward producing or altering a sound or tone that could then be manipulated on tape. In particular, the two keying units listed on the equipment inventory in the previous chapter merit further discussion. These devices initially consisted of chained groups of Jason oscillators (in the form of the twelve notes of a piano, completing a chromatic octave), with each tuned to the regular notes of the scale. Soon after these oscillators had been joined to the keying units, it was felt that, in addition to an unwanted clicking noise that accompanied the tone each time the sound was switched on or off, the results were frustratingly "limited in their application."[9] Consequently, they were modified twice: first, the engineers at the Workshop added a simple decay to the pitch; then, still unsatisfied, they went on to construct a much more complex system offering three levels of attack and ten different steps of decay, but reduced the available pitches to just the white diatonic keys. These adaptations not only reflect that in the period *before* the keying units there was a regular effort to achieve pitches in a standard octave (as was the case in *Orpheus*), but that music using traditional Western chromatic and diatonic scales was in such great demand that it warranted using up banks of valuable oscillators for the device. And obviously, once such equipment is constructed, the kinds of works produced are affected by both its ease of use and its limitations. The closing off of all pitches not included in whatever scale is configured (a tempered scale, one assumes) returns electronic music to a type that potentially abandons the founding tenets of that field (as advocated by French and German composers such as Schaeffer and Stockhausen) for the traditional rules and functionality of tonal harmony. But of course, this was nothing new for the Workshop; its composers had done this throughout its existence, and this was merely the latest manifestation of that progression. To realize "normal" tunes *electronically* was the desire; to manufacture this aspect of British modernism, detached from the Continent but still with the power to express the feelings and attitudes of that movement, was the goal.

In 1968, the Radiophonic Workshop celebrated its ten-year anniversary with a party for all staff on December 5.[10] The milestone was also noted by the release of the first full-length album of Workshop music, *BBC Radiophonic Music*. Limited to the music of John Baker, Delia Derbyshire, and relative newcomer David Cain, the collection highlighted the shift to tonality seen at the Workshop during the first half of the 1960s, ignoring Brian Hodgson and Dick Mills's special sound and atmospheric backgrounds altogether. Perhaps assuming the audience for an album claiming to contain radiophonic "music" would have limited tolerance for abstraction, the compilers selected primarily signature tunes and short, melodic call-signs for local radio stations. While the commercial release of the album, dubbed "the Pink Album" because of its garish sleeve, was timed to coincide with the Workshop's anniversary, the collection itself had been internally circulating within the BBC for use as stock music for at least two years, making many of the tunes contained within already familiar to audiences. The album is a triumph of radiophonic tape techniques, an excellent summary of the type of work done during these "classic" years of the Radiophonic Workshop, demonstrating the three composers at their best, and the concluding attempt, before the arrival of synthesizers, to capture the essence of tape-derived music. Without the overly familiar *Doctor Who* theme here to distract the listener, one is left with tiny nuggets of musical ideas, often gone as quickly as they arrive, pausing occasionally to linger on a more extended, thoughtful track, such as Derbyshire's justly praised "Blue Veils and Golden Sands" or "The Delian Mode," both created as incidental music rather than as signature tunes. This approach also helps showcase the differences between the three composers: Baker's virtuosic ability to splice the tiniest pieces of tape to create elaborate rhythmic patterns; Cain's intricate counterpoint, such as on the beautiful and strange "Autumn and Winter"; and Derbyshire's complex timbral palettes, as on "Mattachin" and "Pot au Feu." The sales of the record were high enough for BBC Enterprises to commission another right away, "this time in Stereo," and reviews were positive.[11] The review in *Gramophone* compared Derbyshire to Iannis Xenakis in her ability to construct complex sound patterns, and praised Baker and Cain's tuneful contributions.[12]

However, the confidence of this collection belies the major changes that were occurring in the way electronic music was produced throughout the world, including the Workshop. Voltage-control synthesis, the first practical, flexible, and affordable form of electronic music synthesis, was being used in new ways and in new forms; "synthesizers" were coming onto the market. The Moog and, in Britain, the EMS range of synthesizers revolutionized electronic music with their ease of use and relative cheapness. Although they were not originally built with keyboards, these quickly became standard. Alongside the new "keyboard" instruments came the traditions associated with them, including melodic and harmonic ideas fundamentally based on Western tonal models, and more specifically in jazz and popular music. While these tendencies would express themselves most dramatically in the next generation of Workshop composers, in particular Paddy Kingsland, Peter Howell, and Roger Limb, their influence was certainly felt in the late 1960s as well. This was still a time of integration, however, and synthesizer works were often created in combination with the more familiar tape medium and, as I have shown, merely continued a trend toward greater melodicity away from electronic music's distinctly avant-garde roots. The diminishing relevance of radio drama was partly to blame, but the rising acceptance of electronic sounds, gradually becoming comfortably familiar to audiences, made their use just another aspect of popular music. This shift didn't occur overnight, however, and even with the arrival of the first synthesizers, there was still a marked tendency on the part of several composers to associate electronically generated sound with atonality. But before this can be explored, we must take a look at the first synthesizers used at the studio, and see how their technology affected composition.

The Mellotron

The keying units of the Workshop's resident engineer, David Young, were the studio's first "electronic keyboards," providing composers with a timbral palette limited to sine tones. But while pitch could be regulated with a great deal of control, the majority of sound manipulation was still achieved via traditional tape methods. In 1964, the idea of purchasing something called a "Multi-Tone Piano" with funds provided by the Music Department was broached, but ultimately, with the purchase of a normal piano, this request was abandoned.[13] A year earlier, the BBC invested a great deal of time and money exploring the possibilities of the Mellotron, a new form of electronic keyboard that was being aggressively marketed to them by Mellotronics. This company arranged a special demonstration of their new equipment in June 1963, and for the rest of that year and throughout 1964, BBC officials in Engineering and Finance thought of the Mellotron as one way to increase the speed of the Radiophonic Workshop's output. The Mellotron, like the Workshop's keying units, produced its sound through a traditional keyboard, but rather than linking each key to a separate oscillator, each key was connected to a tape playback unit—in effect, seventy-two small tape players that played up to eight seconds of prerecorded tape. Although their high cost prohibited their widespread use in each studio, it was thought by administrative figures outside the Workshop that by limiting their use to the reproduction of sounds effects, the Workshop could have a ready-made database of sounds.[14] This attitude shows a lack of understanding as to exactly how the Workshop operated; each sound effect there was created anew, and in general standard sound effects had no place either in the construction of tunes or in more abstract special sound. But given that for most people the Workshop had become synonymous with the creative exploitation of tape technology, it was perhaps understandable that to a layperson this new instrument might seem like a perfect fit for the constantly time-strapped composers at the Workshop.

Two Mellotrons were used at the BBC throughout 1963 and into 1964, one for importing sound effects during news broadcasts, and the other as a quick index of sound effects in the Effects Library.[15] The problem with the machines, as articulated in a six-page report by the Design Department on their potential widespread use within the BBC, largely boiled down to the low quality of playback from the rather cheap playback heads.[16] This was perfectly acceptable for "entertainment" purposes, but did not meet broadcast standards. The playback speed, meant to be 7.5 IPS, also fluctuated too much to be reliable: it took up to two hours for the Mellotron to work itself up to a consistent speed. The machine was also felt to be too limited, since the sounds were difficult to switch out, and, with individual tape playback limited to eight seconds, it was impossible to realize steady background sounds. Despite this, in July 1964 an additional Mellotron was purchased for £575 and installed in Sound Effects Centre, Western House. Here, the theory ran, a producer or director could find a sound effect quickly on the Mellotron and, after finding a suitable one, then get the proper original 78 rpm record and use it for broadcast. It seems incredible that the BBC saw in the Mellotron nothing more than an elaborate data storage device for the quick recall of sound effects, essentially a library in keyboard form. It is, of course, easy for us, with our knowledge of how the Mellotron would be used so creatively by artists such as the Beatles in songs like "Strawberry Fields Forever," to perceive the BBC's attitude toward the instrument as demonstrating a fundamental lack of foresight. While there seems to have been a profound misunderstanding on the part of the BBC as to the possible uses of this instrument, this limited vision ultimately has to be blamed on Mellotronics itself for designing a machine that didn't encourage the kind of flexibility early synthesizers offered only a few years later. The Mellotron was a cul-de-sac for precisely this reason. It was never exactly clear what the Mellotron was meant to be used for. The use of the Mellotron at the BBC continued largely because of a promised reengineered version of the machine, now called within the BBC a "Programme Effects Generator," and the BBC signed a "letter of intent" to Mellotron promising to buy a set number of these specially designed effects playback units. The BBC eventually reneged upon this deal when it found cheaper disc units that essentially did the same thing without all the engineering hassles and delays.[17]

Meanwhile, the difficulties facing the Workshop's composers had not gone away. Compositions lasting even a few seconds still took days to complete, with each sound specially recorded, treated, pitched, and assembled. In January 1967 it was suggested at the Radiophonic Technical Subcommittee meeting that the Engineering Department design and build a "Multi-Input Programmable Switch" that could select up to fifty sound sources, or tones, in sequence, with each individual sound having controllable attacks, decays, and level controls.[18] Ultimately this device was built by engineer David Young. An ingenious instrument, it used an old gramophone motor Young had found during his daily scavenging through the Portobello Road flea market. Operating like a Hammond organ, it was capable of producing a choruslike effect of pitches and was housed in a transparent Perspex case. Consequently, these units, of which Young built at least three with the help of assistant T. W. Tombs, were each dubbed a "Crystal Palace."

The Moog

The staff soon realized that keeping up with the latest developments in electronic sound production and engineering their own such devices, while not necessarily outside their ability, were beyond the scope of their resources. On the other hand, the staff at the Workshop knew the reality of their budget situation, and if a commercial purchase were to be made, along the lines of Robert Moog's new American synthesizer, such a piece of equipment might be subject to expensive import duties. In anticipation of such a device, either of their own construction or a commercially bought unit, a fourth composition area, Room 10, was envisioned, which would contain this equipment.[19] A new Workshop position was briefly discussed, exclusively for design and development of such devices, but the idea was quickly abandoned with the realization that such a position would be impossible to realize given the complexities of existing engineering conditions at the BBC at large.[20] The Moog was looking more and more appealing, especially since a distribution office for the company had recently been established in Dublin. Workshop organizer Desmond Briscoe planned to visit Manchester University, where a Moog synthesizer had been installed, but the death of that instrument's primary advocate there in early 1969 prevented this from occurring.

The Workshop wanted a synthesizer, however—particularly those composers who worked on regular programs like *Doctor Who*, for whom the turnaround was often no more than a matter of days. By the mid-1960s, the requirements for special sound for this program alone took the entire resources of Brian Hodgson for the duration of its season, as he created from scratch the science fiction sound effects for each episode. Anything that would make this job easier would have been regarded as a godsend. For the first time since the establishment of the Radiophonic Workshop, equipment specially designed for electronic music was now appearing on the commercial market, and it was noted in a technical committee meeting on February 4, 1969, that "even in its simplest forms it could save many hours and introduce new possibilities in the hands of the staff who now have a very considerable expertise using traditional equipment."[21]

How was voltage-control synthesis different to what had existed before? How was it able to speed up musical production to such a great extent? To answer these questions, I need to explain briefly how voltage-control synthesis works and how its invention not only changed the ease with which electronic music could be produced but also exponentially increased the options available to composers.[22] While basic electronic sound generators, or oscillators, had existed for a long time and had been in use at the Workshop since its earliest years, in the mid-1960s Robert Moog revolutionized their use as both audio sources and control sources. In other words, by introducing a control mechanism, so-called "voltage control," over the oscillators, Moog was able to more precisely manipulate aspects of an audio signal, including the application of carefully distributed voltages to generate specific pitches or effects. Out of this he designed in 1964 the voltage-control oscillator (VCO), the voltage-control amplifier (VCA), and the voltage-control filter (VCF). Part of the problem with using standard oscillators had been the pitch fluctuations composers encountered when trying to manually tune them; Moog's innovations simplified and stabilized the procedure for generating pitches and more complex waveforms, as well as allowing greater control over pitch and waveform generation. In addition, VCOs could be used interactively, controlling each other, or combinations of independent VCOs, VCAs, and VCFs could interact, creating a potentially unlimited combination of tone colors and tone effects, such as vibrato. Another exciting feature of voltage-control synthesis was the ability for VCOs to be "tracked" together, allowing complete polyphonic chords to be synchronized as they moved in pitch and to remain internally in tune. It is easy to see, then, that when combined with multitrack tape recorders, to the Radiophonic Workshop these new devices seemed the most exciting development since the advent of the studio, and represented a potentially limitless horizon of musical possibilities.

Briscoe wrote directly to Audiotek, the distributors for Moog, and a demonstration of the equipment was scheduled for May 13, 1969. After speaking to these distributors, he reported back to the committee that he believed that for around £5,000 he could get the new Room 10 ready with the synthesizers as well as the required tape recorders and loudspeakers to make the area a truly functional new studio.[23] The plan for funding this new expansion should, he felt, come primarily from television, since their commissions now accounted for 80 percent of all work undertaken by the Workshop. The demonstration was an overwhelming success, and the future of Moog at the Radiophonic Workshop seemed, at this point, all but secured. Briscoe realized that it was going to be hard convincing the radio and television divisions that what had been essentially a run-down, slightly downtrodden division of the BBC that seemed to thrive on its creative use of outdated, discarded equipment now needed a hugely expensive professional piece of equipment, almost the total of its annual budget. And in some ways, Briscoe himself was the source of this attitude. Hodgson, who succeeded Briscoe as organizer, once told me that Briscoe's attitude was that the idea was all, and the technology didn't matter. One reason he didn't work harder to acquire the latest technology for the Workshop was down to this philosophy: that if the idea was strong enough, the composer would find a way to achieve it despite technological limitations. Derbyshire in particular suffered under this attitude, constantly trying to create things beyond the means of the equipment available at the time.

Knowing this, Briscoe spent the summer and autumn preparing reports on the Workshop's need to acquire the Moog, at the same time explaining exactly what a "synthesizer" was and how it differed from existing equipment. A committee was formed to help acquire funding for this major purchase, as well as to deal with other development issues that had arisen over the previous few years. This committee was composed of members of all interested departments, such as Talks, Drama, TV Sound, and Programme Operations. Although their primary topic was the endlessly postponed new mixing desk (which had been on order, by January 1970, for four years!), the Moog occupied the second slot.[24] Stating that it was already being used by "elect" music studios throughout the world, particularly in the United States, he informed potential supporters that,

being self-contained, no separate mixing desk is required and "composition" can be performed directly on the machine without the laborious and time-consuming processes of tape manipulation which is the main feature of existing techniques. Furthermore, the device provides a whole new range of sounds which are just not available in any other form and its acquisition would stimulate the staff to experiment and extend the frontiers in what must always be a developing medium.[25]

Sometime early in 1970 Robert Moog and his wife visited London, where they met with Briscoe and discussed the potential purchase of the "Synthesizer 3," as it was now called in documents, as well as a new variable-speed tape recorder Moog had developed. On January 23, Briscoe assured Moog personally in a letter that he was working with the BBC to ensure the purchase of a synthesizer as soon as funding could be arranged. Another six weeks passed before Eddie Veale of Audiotek took the unusual step of writing directly to Briscoe, informing him that several members of the BBC had also inquired about the Moog synthesizer and that he had been dropping hints to them about the Workshop's desire to possess one as well, in the hopes that this might help Briscoe acquire funding.[26] Briscoe, also concerned by the chilly response he had received regarding funding, admitted a few months later that he was willing to accept the purchase of the synthesizer without the additional tape recorders if it would speed up the process, since it would allow the composers to get used to working with the new equipment in preparation for the opening of the new Room 10, when funding was actually made available.[27] For the Moog, however, the momentum had been lost. Over the next few months, attitudes toward the synthesizer began to cool, and one can sense a slight desperation in Audiotek's next letter to Briscoe in early July, some eighteen months after negotiations had begun, asking when they might hear something more concrete from the BBC.[28]

On July 16, Briscoe wrote to Moog himself, after having recently paid a visit to his home in Trumansburg, New York, breaking the news to him as gently as possible that circumstances had changed, but suggesting they might be interested in purchasing an as-yet-unavailable "mini-syser" (the Minimoog) that Moog had demonstrated to Briscoe during his visit.[29] The concession of this much more modest purchase prompted Audiotek to write four days later directly to Briscoe, lamenting, "I am sorry to learn that you may not be able to purchase a synth this year. Many people within the organization now know of your interest in obtaining one of these and may be able to help it if were made generally available within the org, have you explored this possibility or do you have other views on the subject?"[30] Moog himself wrote a polite letter a few days later, giving his regards specifically to Delia Derbyshire and advising them to let him know if he could do anything else for them.[31] And that was the end of the relationship between Moog and the Radiophonic Workshop.

To understand how that happened, we have to back up a bit and examine the Workshop's relationship with another company: Electronic Music Studios (EMS), a British firm that already had ties to composers at the Workshop. One of the two founders of EMS was Tristram Cary, who besides being a regular BBC composer and electronic music pioneer had worked with the Radiophonic Workshop, albeit sporadically, when assembling his electronic scores for the *Doctor Who* episodes "The Dead Planet," a fully electronic score, and "The Daleks' Master Plan," which combined electronics with conventional instruments. While his scores, including the electronic aspects, had been put together in his own studio, he worked closely with Workshop special sound designer Brian Hodgson on those stories to ensure continuity, and had a good working relationship with the staff of the Workshop. The eccentric Peter Zinovieff, the other founder of EMS, had his first official contact with the Workshop on October 28, 1964, when he was given a tour of the Workshop's facilities in his capacity as a Canadian Broadcasting Corporation employee.[32] Two years later he formed an independent electronic music studio, Unit Delta Plus, with two of the Workshop's composers, Delia Derbyshire and Brian Hodgson.

Thus, while the first mention of EMS in official BBC documents wasn't until January 1970, several composers at the Workshop were already quite familiar with the equipment being built there. Unit Delta Plus had been set up for the composition and encouragement of commercial, theatrical, and popular electronic music, and one EMS product in particular, the VCS3—or "Putney," as it was also known—had been used as a prototype model as early as 1967 by Derbyshire and Hodgson. Hodgson, in particular, knew what a boon it would be to his *Doctor Who* work if he could construct quick sound effects (electronic sliding doors, laser gun shots, etc.) with this simple, portable piece of equipment, and would occasionally bring his in to the Workshop to create these sounds, returning it in the evening to his Unit Delta Plus studio. In his words, eventually "we embarrassed the BBC into buying one for us." This wasn't until January 1970, when a demonstration was arranged for Desmond Briscoe of the equipment's usefulness. One gets a sense of Briscoe's notoriously officious side as well as the already close relationship between Derbyshire and Hodgson in the exchange between Zinovieff and Briscoe about this proposed demonstration. After the initial request was made, Zinovieff replied to Briscoe that since Brian and Delia already had one and were getting set to buy another, maybe they should just bring theirs in.[33] This was not satisfactory to Briscoe (or, for that matter, to Derbyshire and Hodgson, who at the time had theirs "plumbed in" to their studio), and an official demonstration was arranged in mid-February. In any event, the demonstration was a remarkable success. Briscoe noted that it was a useful source of treated electronic sounds and that "it can also be used for treating other sound sources, and the fluidity of control is most impressive. The construction and layout, together with the accessibility to the well designed printed circuit, are good and its technical performance would appear to be well up to standard."[34] In addition, the Workshop was being offered the VCS3 at the cut-rate price of only £300. So after some slight interdepartmental wrangling over who exactly was going to be paying for this equipment, in March 1970 the Workshop purchased its first VCS3. That this purchase was a success is borne out by the fact that only three months later, in the midst of the financial struggle over the Moog, an additional VCS3 was purchased, as well as a newly available keyboard unit for the existing instrument.[35] Considering its compact size, the VCS3 contained a remarkable amount of equipment: three VCOs, a white noise generator, a ring modulator, a VC Low Pass Filter, a reverb unit, a trapezoid envelope generator, a control joystick, and two input and two stereo output amplifiers. The voltage-control aspects were controlled through a unique pin matrix, whereas the Moog used bulky patch cords. The keyboard units also came with an additional VCO.

Briscoe seems to have become as enamored of the machines as his two younger composers, since during his spring 1970 trip to the United States (partially to check out Moog's studio) he worked for several days with students at the University of Wisconsin, using a VCS3 the university had recently purchased. While there he discussed radiophonics and directed three radio projects. One was Tom Stoppard's *Dissolution of Dominic Boot*, a production that was described in the local student paper. The article's discussion of the technology is confused; the author's interest is obviously in the sound treatments: "Briscoe is using WHA's new Putney (VCS3) synthesizer, also called a 'mini-moog,' to create the extra-verbal effects in the Stoppard play." The author goes on to describe the process: "Electronic music and sound effects are combined with experiments in stereo projection.... The final production was a collage on the subject of time, made from sounds and words recorded by students of Wisconsin's radio workshop."[36]

It was against this background that Zinovieff and Cary unveiled their latest synthesizer, recently installed at Radio Belgrade. This synthesizer, known as the Synthi 100, was essentially a group of several VCS3s with a 256-event sequencer and other effects built in. This new, much larger machine had several advantages over the Moog. First, the learning curve for this instrument at the Workshop would be considerably lower, since the basic features of the synthesizer—such as the pin mechanism by which all EMS synths operated, as well as the VCFs and other sound treatment options—were already familiar through the VCS3s. Second, the sequencer allowed complicated patterns to be recalled and played back, a feature not available on the Moog. The third and possibly most important thing the Synthi 100 had in its favor was its Britishness. The BBC was keen to be seen supporting British industry, and this synthesizer seemed to exemplify the power, real or imagined, Britain still maintained over music and technology.

At the July 7, 1970, meeting of the Technical Committee, Briscoe reported on his trip to Moog's factory in America, also discussing the ARP Odyssey synthesizer as a possible purchase for the Workshop.[37] He mentions the new "electronic studio" from EMS specifically as a "British substitute" for the Moog.[38] The specs arrived a few days later, and that seemed to have sealed the deal; the larger Moog wasn't mentioned again. Now all the Workshop had to do was secure the slightly larger amount of £5,400 for the "Delaware," as the Synthi 100 would be renamed, in honor of the road outside the Maida Vale studios that were to house the synthesizer. This they were able to do by the autumn, through another complicated set of development reports, and they secured a delivery date of mid-February.[39] One significant practical issue concerned the doorway leading into Room 10: it wasn't wide enough, and Engineering had to come in and widen it to 4 feet 6 inches, adding a second door before it could accommodate the Delaware, which measured 38 inches long, 33 inches wide, and 80 inches high.[40] While they waited, a keyboard for the second VCS3 was ordered, and these synths, with keyboards, were used by Dudley Simpson, Brian Hodgson, and Dick Mills for the incidental music and special sound for *Doctor Who*'s seventh season, the first season in which that program used the Workshop's equipment almost exclusively for both its music and its sound effects.[41]

By April, the Delaware synthesizer was fully installed and had been used for some basic program work. From the start there were unanticipated problems. In particular, two major issues clouded those initial months. First, without the multitrack recorder installed in Room 10, it was very difficult to realize the full potential of the machine. To help with this, engineer Richard Yeoman-Clark designed an "Interconnection Reduction Interface," which was based on a successful machine that he had created earlier and that acted as a primitive portable stereo mixer between the Delaware and existing Telefunken recorders but would also work to link the synthesizer to the eight-track recorder hopefully to be ordered soon.[42] The second problem was that the Delaware arrived with no operation manual! While it was similar to the VCS3s, it was made exponentially more complex by the addition of the interaction between them and the sequencer. Brian Hodgson and Dick Mills immediately set about creating one; this project lasted several weeks, but the result was ultimately used by EMS itself.[43]

The Delaware caused an instant sensation, the impact of which was felt in ways that could not have been anticipated. Most positively, it gave the Workshop an influx of publicity on a level not seen since the success of the *Doctor Who* signature tune back in 1963, despite the constant efforts of its composers to raise the studio's profile over the years. This was primarily achieved through a concert presented before the queen on May 19, 1971, at the Royal Albert Hall, which prominently featured six VCS3s and a Synthi 100, all loaned to the Workshop by Zinovieff (since the Delaware itself couldn't be removed from Maida Vale). The concert, directed by Brian Hodgson and organized by the entire Workshop staff, was a multimedia extravaganza, with lasers, light show, and an extremely powerful PA system, and highlighted the popular direction in which the Workshop had been moving in recent years. In his description of the desired audience for "The Radiophonic Workshop in Concert," Briscoe indicated during the preparations that "the caliber of the audience is such that while there is a natural interest in music, electronics, and the arts, the social nature of the event and the presence of the ladies, requires that the program is non-technical, entertaining, aesthetically pleasing and as visually interesting as possible."[44]

Ostensibly the concert, which was performed twice that evening, at 9:00 and again at 10:45, was in honor of the hundredth anniversary of the Institute of Electrical Engineers (IEE), but the occasion was used by the Workshop as an excuse for the debut a new composition by Delia Derbyshire, "IEE 100," which was intended to show off the capabilities of the new Synthi 100. Imitating a Victorian playbill, the program's hyperbolic tone ironically contrasted the cutting-edge technology on display with archaic descriptions: "A popular programme of Electronic Music supported by: The Electric Incandescent Lamp, The Electric Cinematograph Projector, The Electric Magic Lantern, The Magnetic Tape Reproducer, and introducing The Electric Voltage Controlled Synthesizer." Speaking before Derbyshire's piece, Briscoe introduced the synthesizer as "a triumph of collaboration between the scientist and the artist, between the electrical engineer and the composer," a notion borne out by the composition itself, which was "based on a chronological history of the use of electricity in communications. Every note you hear is derived from IEE in one form or another."[45]

In reality, the premiere of Derbyshire's work very nearly didn't happen. Typical of her method of working, she had developed numerous ideas and written detailed notes about the piece, but put off working these ideas out until the last minute. The night before the concert, as Derbyshire was still putting the finishing touches on the piece, concert director Hodgson started to get a bad feeling about her mood. He instructed Workshop engineer Richard Yeoman-Clark to secretly make two copies of the tape she was having him run of the final version of the work and to give Hodgson the second copy that night. He recalls: "I said to Richard, 'Run another set in Room 12, don't tell Delia you're doing it, and that copy bring to me in the morning, because I have an awful feeling she was going to destroy the tape.' And he did that. And she came in the next morning in tears, around 11 o'clock. And said, 'I've destroyed the tape, what are we going to do?' I don't think she ever forgave me for that."[46]

This story hints at the pressure these composers were under to produce works with tight deadlines and also demonstrates the changing dynamics of the Workshop: the technological introductions of the late 1960s permanently altered the methods composers used to produce their music. For Derbyshire, these changes weren't entirely welcome, and the frustration both she and John Baker, as well as those who had to deal with them, felt is notable in much of their music around the turn of the decade. As Hodgson remembers,

> That piece of Delia's was thrown together with a whole pile of stuff we'd
> been farting around with for weeks. She had no real concept of any sort
> of form of what she wanted to do. I came up with this idea of putting
> together a program of stuff we can find in the archives, about the IEE
> together, and I just went in to the archives to find all sorts of things that
> made a sort of vague sense, threw it together as a sort of framework, and
> we grafted a lot of Delia's nicer bits on top of it. And all the time I
> would say probably half the composition, if it could even be described as
> a composition, was me. But somebody had to produce something, the
> fucking queen was going to be there, for Christ's sake, in the Festival
> Hall! It wasn't brilliant, but it was there, it sounded loud, and if it's loud
> it sounds impressive.

In some ways the seven-minute piece resembles much of Derbyshire's earlier works, particularly in the use of complex, drawn-out tape pedal points, in this case, layering on top of these excerpts of famous events in scientific and broadcasting history, such as the Apollo moon landing and the opening and closing of the BBC's Savoy Hill studios. Her use of the Delaware is not particularly adventurous, however, and the piece could quite easily have been performed on one of the VCS3s. She seems to have limited its use to the multilayered fanfare that opens and closes the piece, occasionally interjecting the main melody between a line of dialogue. Figure 4.1 shows her initial notes for the piece.

The concert received largely favorable reviews in many of the major newspapers, including the *Times*. The positive attention continued throughout the year, and one can sense the feeling of promise and excitement in all of these articles, not least from Workshop head Briscoe himself. He discussed in the *Guardian* how "for ten years...we worked without any equipment specifically designed for us. Now the new equipment has altered the whole conception of how you can produce sound and change it."[47] He went on to promise a new

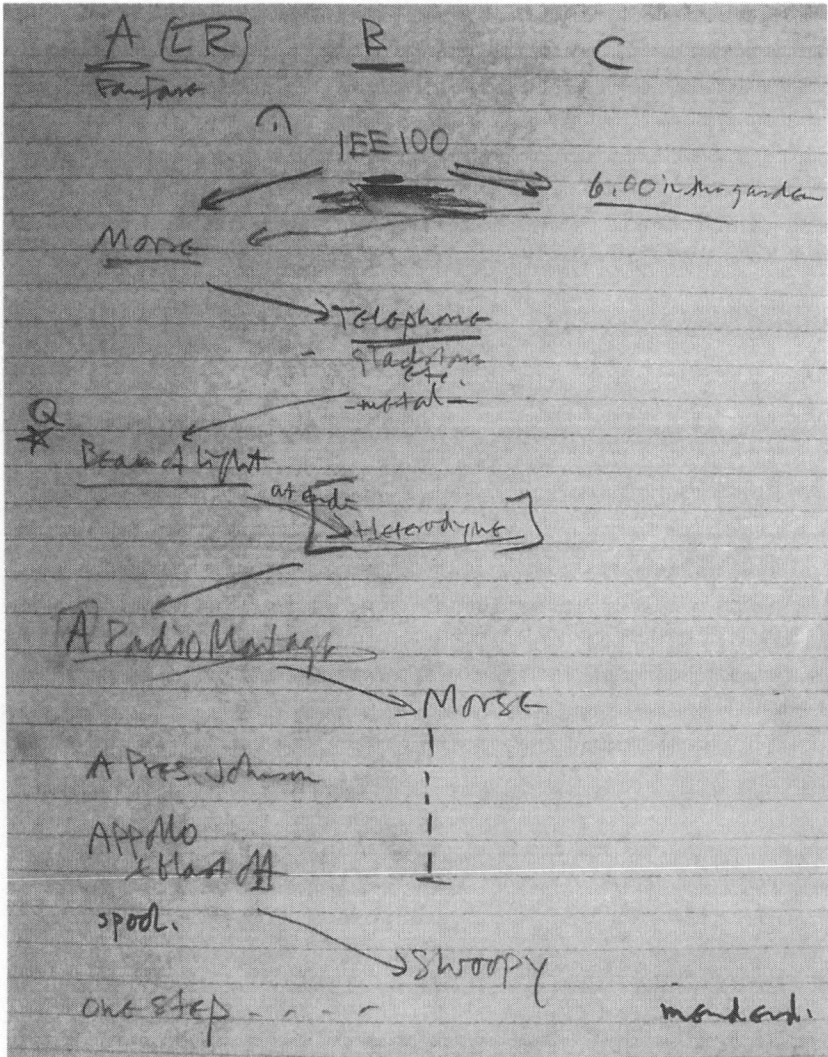

Figure 4.1. Delia Derbyshire's initial sketch for her composition *IEE 100*, written to show off the capabilities of the Delaware synthesizer. She began by sampling recordings of historic engineering breakthroughs, from Morse code to the Apollo moon landings.

arrangement of that most venerable tune to emerge from the Workshop, the *Doctor Who* theme. "It's been altered, when Doctor Who [the actor] changed, and when the program went into color, and soon it's going to be re-done on the big synthesizer."[48]

The honeymoon was relatively short-lived, however, as the instrument's quirky characteristics became quickly apparent. Although it was absolutely state-of-the-art for the time, it had certain frustrating limitations. Primarily, the 256-event sequencer barely allowed for a single melody to be recalled once all of the programmed aspects had been taken into account. This was a severe drawback, although one that was just about tolerable if the Workshop's composers were to acquire the multitrack recorder to use with it. Despite these problems, the Delaware changed music making to a remarkable extent in the first few months of its use. According to a memo from Hodgson to Briscoe, "One music cue for Dr. Who would have taken at least a day to realize by conventional methods. With a mini synthesizer the fastest time was 1 hr. 15 mins. With the Delaware, after only a few weeks, realizations, more ambitious than ever before, were being completed in 34 minutes."[49] In September, Zinovieff offered, for £150, an updating kit that would change the "maximum number of clock pulses from 1000 to 10,000." While this didn't solve the problem of the sequencer, it would make its practical efficiency that much greater, a fact Hodgson spelled out to Briscoe: "Desmond, this is *essential!* Especially this year. I don't care if we all have to chip in to pay for it, I will make an incredible difference to the value of the sequencer by extending the time available per sequence."[50] Briscoe agreed, and rushed the modifications forward so that they would be completed by the time the work on the new season of *Doctor Who* began on October 25, 1971.[51] Other modifications done in-house at the Workshop in the first few months included a spin wheel designed by Richard Yeoman-Clark, assisted by Dave Young, that gave manual control of the memory, in either direction.[52] It's likely that the positive publicity for the Workshop helped secure the funding for the £5,400 Studer eight-track recorder, because by March 1972, both it and the long-delayed stereo mixing desk had finally arrived and were in use at the Workshop.

Stereo had been a long time coming to the Workshop. In 1968, a watershed year, most of the new local stations switched to stereo broadcast with David Cain's *RUS*, a history of Russian culture, labeled a "Total Radio Stereophonic Experiment," the most ambitious stereo program the Workshop had ever attempted. Like Derbyshire, Cain studied mathematics before joining the BBC as a studio manager in 1963. He became a full-time Workshop employee in 1967, which was, as we have already seen, a key year in the Workshop's shift from pure tape techniques to more electronic sound production. One can trace this evolution in his music—from his earliest commission, *War of the Worlds* (1967), with its largely tape-manipulated score, through *RUS*, which uses musical material also derived from concrete sources, to his later scores for *The Hobbit, The Day of the Triffids*, and, in 1973, his music for Isaac Asimov's *Foundation Trilogy*.

The Delaware brought about more institutional changes that weren't originally envisioned. With the efficiency of music composition so much greater, Briscoe took this opportunity to reevaluate the overall structure of the Workshop. Primarily, he saw the problem this way: the old-fashioned engineering staff (referred to as "programme operations assistants," or "POAs") was no longer required to do the kind of work they had always done, that is, fixing broken mechanical and electric equipment and creating and designing new equipment. Most of the musical instruments now came from commercial retailers who were also largely responsible for servicing them. Some of the engineering staff had therefore become quite experienced composers, such as Dick Mills, who took over *Doctor Who's* special sound from Brian Hodgson in 1972. Others from the engineering staff, such as Richard Yeoman-Clark, would also be called on to do composition work, particularly when the work required more technical skill than musical. Briscoe set out these musical divisions in a document in 1971:

> There are now quite clearly 2 principal levels of creative work for the assistants...
>
> Level a:
>   A. Long and/or complex pieces, involving the interpretation of abstract concepts or original creative composition and using the most detailed and advanced techniques.
>   B. Composition and arrangement of musical or non-musical sequences, requiring detailed construction and interpretation and using complex treatments.
>
> Level b:
>   C. Straightforward, using fairly complex treatments, for background use, but not requiring very detailed construction or difficult interp.
>   D. Re-issue or very simple treatment, involving a minimum of creativity or interpretation.[53]

Briscoe recommended that the number of "creative assistants," as he wished the studio managers to now be called, be increased to five, with one additional post just under this in rank; this request was ultimately approved.[54] The second draft of this document, probably written by Briscoe's boss, Geoffrey Manuel, head of program operations for Radio, expanded on the role played at present by the POAs: "With the advent of new equipment, especially the synthesizers, the need for operational support has disappeared. The two POA posts are in fact occupied in the production of electronic sounds. One of these post holders is engaged on the composition of electronic music of the same caliber as the assistants. The second is allocated to less demanding requirements, namely to the production of sounds rather than music."[55]

One can also sense in Briscoe's report the effect all of the recent purchases must have had on his frustrated creative side. He recommended the creation of an entirely new post, that of "deputy," which he hoped would enable him to return to work in a more musical capacity. He was concerned that since he was out at least 40 percent of the time doing promotion work, he was losing touch with electronic music production methods. This was true: given the levels of publicity work the Workshop now faced, the organizer position had essentially become an administrative one. The request for a new post was denied. Instead, Richard Yeoman-Clark was given the additional responsibility of acting as "facilities organizer," evaluating new technology and equipment and relaying his findings to the organizer and composers. Helping the composers with the new stereo technology was to be a prominent component of the new position as well.[56] This was perhaps a more logical notion: Yeoman-Clark was in a better position than Briscoe to understand the composers' needs.

All these organizational changes within the Workshop can be linked to the acquisition of the Delaware synthesizer, and the gradual substitution of traditional tape techniques by voltage-control synthesis. But there were equally profound changes occurring on a personal level at the Workshop. Within two years of the Delaware's arrival, most of the "Classic Workshop" team—Delia Derbyshire, John Baker, and Brian Hodgson—had left. While these three had different relationships to voltage control, it was still an important factor behind each person's departure. In 1972 Hodgson started his own commercial studio, Electrophon, with his friend John Lewis. After the failure of Unit Delta Plus, largely because of the conflicting artistic goals of the three members, the more commercially minded Hodgson felt confident he could interest companies outside the BBC in using electronic sounds for advertising. He was primarily motivated by a desire to improve the existing technology, working outside the bureaucracy of the BBC. The Workshop's acquisition of the Delaware, and his weeks spent writing its manual, proved to Hodgson that the technology still had a long way to go. For one thing, the Delaware was notoriously unreliable in the area of tuning. In particular, it was incredibly sensitive to changes in temperature and required very high heat, so that not only was Room 10 stiflingly hot, but also if someone opened the door, exposing the machine to outside air, it would go out of tune. Also, many sounds, once achieved, could never be recaptured. In 1971, Hodgson collaborated with Dudley Simpson on the signature tune for the prestigious *Ascent of Man* series, using the Delaware. After hours of programming, they discovered a wonderful reedy brass sound for the opening fanfare. They quickly recorded Simpson's melody, and, as they feared, were never able to recover the sound again! Hodgson's work with Simpson, incidentally, would find a new home at Electrophon, where they collaborated on many projects, including an album of popular classical compositions arranged for electronic instruments, "In a Covent Garden," and most important the music library for *The Tomorrow People*, for Thames Television. In 1973, when Hodgson was interviewed about his studio and his work for this program, he raved about voltage control. One can sense the excitement in his voice as he discusses the future of electronic music, practically dismissing everything he had done before: "Although people have been experimenting for years, nothing much happened until voltage control became possible. Before that, if you wanted to play a scale you had to have 12 oscillators to do it, but with a voltage control oscillator, you simply alter the voltage going through."[57]

As for Derbyshire, while she had embraced the VCS3, she never warmed to the more complex Delaware. As her Albert Hall meltdown showed, she was growing more frustrated at the lack of purely musical opportunities available to her at the Workshop. Indeed, she could excel at music written with the synthesizer, as her highly regarded score and voice treatments for the drama "O Fat White Woman" demonstrate. This episode of the highbrow *Play for Today* series told the story of a beaten-down wife of a sadistic boarding school headmaster, and the already tense narrative was, according to the critic in the *Guardian*, "sharpened with Delia Derbyshire's radiophonic raw-nerve noises."[58] These instances were exceptions, however, and she rarely worked with the instrument, preferring the more abstract options offered by traditional tape techniques. One hearing of the promised Delaware version of the *Doctor Who* theme, arranged by Delia on the instrument, can serve to demonstrate her lack of faith. For this arrangement, Delia simply replaced all of her original lines, bass pulses, and melody, her "wind bubbles and clouds," with electronic substitutes, in the process removing all the warmth of the original. The regularity of the bass rhythm, which had been smoothed over in the original by its organic fuzziness, is, in the Delaware version, front and center, precise, and utterly dull in its monotonous four-squareness. The bizarre whooshing of the wind is replaced by computer blips with the same level of precision as the melody, altering this signifier from "mystery" to a more datable and much less interesting "technology." One can hear the effort that went into this remake, and the logic behind it, but one can also hear the frustration in Derbyshire's music as she is constantly restricted by the infinitely fewer options available to her with this technology.

After leaving the BBC in 1973, she worked for a time with Hodgson at Electrophon, helping to produce a series of radio commercials and music for

Figure 4.2. This is the only known photo of Derbyshire and Oram together, at a party celebrating the Workshop's twentieth anniversary. Photographer unknown.

theatrical productions, but as Hodgson had also been converted almost entirely to voltage-control techniques, with the equivalent of the Delaware installed in his personal studio, by the mid-1970s she had completely retired from music. According to Hodgson, Derbyshire's primary frustration had always been with inflexible equipment, and the consequent inability to see a vision through. "She always felt the limitations of the technology. It was so difficult, you were wrestling with it the whole time, and the deadline would be creeping up and there was no time if you had an idea and it wasn't working. There would come a point where you couldn't go back and try new idea because the deadline was going to be there. It just took so long to do anything."

John Baker's departure in 1974 was also down to the changes brought about by the arrival of the synthesizers. His heavy drinking had been gradually getting worse throughout the early 1970s, and he clearly disliked much of the work he was being asked to do. He wasn't overly fond of the Delaware but was perfectly capable of using it when he needed to. As we have seen, his forte was carefully and rapidly splicing tape, then using it in a rhythmic, jazz-derived context. While he liked the keyboard aspect of the Delaware and VCS3s, he felt held back by the lack of immediacy of the synthesizers, the sheer amount of time it took to get a good sound out of them.

All three of them felt the limitations of the Workshop for artistic expression. They were never under the delusion that they were there to provide anything but a service, and realized that theirs was only a single aspect of a larger production, but this didn't stop most composers from suffering under the frustrations of the BBC bureaucracy. They all worked long but eccentric hours, usually to avoid Briscoe's interference. As Hodgson remembers, "John was such an amazing talent, but the strain of the Workshop and Desmond became a great bogeyman at some point in the 1960s. He [Briscoe] was seen as an obstacle rather than anything else."

The divided nature of much of Baker's later work can be heard in his excellent score for the episode "Welcome Home" from the series *Out of the Unknown*. It combines his traditional rhythmically complex tape patterns, as in "Radio Nottingham," with synthesizer sounds taken from the Delaware. After starting out with a short pattern and some atonal music, both realized on the Delaware and reminiscent of Glynis Jones and Desmond Briscoe's score two years later for *The Stone Tape*, Baker then uses Delaware sounds as basic source material for a chase sequence. After returning to the atonal "theme" for a few more brief cues, he then uses his rhythmic pattern as a motif in its own right, allowing it to fuse with the abstract synth theme, moving organically between the two ideas for an extended two-minute cue. These two techniques sit side by side, uncomfortably but logically, in an episode about a conflicted personality, a mind torn between two worlds, as seen in video example 4.1.🔊

Baker's "Welcome Home" score is a tour de force of electronic music, and one of his most successful scores, but serves to introduce one of the most problematic issues for the early composers of music on the synthesizer: now that the sounds themselves were relatively easy to create (compared to the labor-intensive process of tape manipulation), what sorts of music should these new instruments be playing? What style of music should they be performing? Walter Carlos offered one perspective in 1969 with the release of *Switched-On Bach*, a collection of J. S. Bach's works realized on the Moog synthesizer. Perhaps surprisingly, with the exception of a few compositions, the composers at the Workshop initially rejected this approach, favoring an atonal direction. Perhaps Baker, Derbyshire, Hodgson, and Briscoe found it too easy to play the synthesizer like a piano.

Don Buchla, an American synthesizer developer in the 1960s, faced the same dilemma when designing his influential equipment:

> I saw no reason to borrow from a keyboard which is a device invented to throw hammers at strings....I tried once to put a keyboard on my system...and I found myself overwhelmed by the psychological aspect of looking at this very familiar twelve tone structure and wanting to do music that was very much against what I was conditioned to do.[59]

Doctor Who: "The Sea Devils" (TV, 1971): Clarke

The arrival in 1969 of a new composer may have influenced the compositional styles of the older composers as well, without their knowing it. Malcolm Clarke had come to the Workshop before the arrival of the synthesizer, but his style really developed once the Delaware was installed. In his first year, he produced a huge amount of music, mostly signature tunes, and basic sound effects, collaborating with Desmond Briscoe and Delia Derbyshire as he found his footing. He worked on a series of radio dramas with producer Betty Davies, and with former radiophonic composer–turned–children's producer Jenyth Worsley on two episodes of the popular radio series *Springboard*, among dozens of other commissions. Already in 1970, though, he was giving demonstrations of voltage-control equipment, including an installment of the television series *Music Now*, where he produced the music for the episode "Moog" and later that year delivered a talk on the VCS3 for an episode of the program *Music Club*. His affinity for synthesizers really showed itself in his first big attention-grabbing commission: in 1971, he wrote the score for the six-part *Doctor Who* serial "The Sea Devils," thus cementing his

Figure 4.3. Malcolm Clarke twiddling knobs on the Delaware synthesizer. Copyright © BBC.

dual reputation as either the mad genius of the 1970s Workshop or the incompetent hack who tried to shock audiences rather than placate them.

Clarke's "Sea Devils" score is notorious in both *Doctor Who* and Radiophonic Workshop history for its sheer anarchic craziness. For some, it is an example of the newfound freedom voltage control offered composers: Clarke really lets his imagination loose, ignoring almost entirely the basic traditions of film scoring technique. While themes do exist here to a certain extent, and primary characters like the Sea Devils, the Master, and the Doctor to some degree have identifiable music that recurs throughout the six episodes, Clarke's music often seems to have a mind of its own, bleeping, oscillating, and screaming throughout in arbitrary places, apparently oblivious to the action on screen and to the basic laws of tonality. The sounds blurt out with a remarkable degree of variety in tone quality and timbre, but it can be difficult to understand how the score is meant to convey the action on screen. Is it an attempt to expand the traditional nondiegetic palette to include greater atonality? The 1960s and early 1970s were the heyday of the mainstream dissonant score, as composers tried to do just this, challenging audiences' expectations in the same way avant-garde classical composers were doing in art music. Whether they use preexistent contemporary music, such as *The Exorcist's* (1973) borrowing of Penderecki and Crumb, or specially composed music, such as Workshop veteran Roberto Gerhard's *This Sporting Life* (1963), or Jerry Goldsmith's *Planet of the Apes* (1968), these films don't necessarily challenge traditional notions of the meaning of dissonance; as horror, Angry Young Man, and science fiction films, respectively, they all are concerned to a greater or lesser degree with the portrayal of alienation, isolation, and the uncanny. It is the degree to which they expand the traditional levels of dissonance that made these films challenging, and Clarke's score fits this definition. The problem with this reading of "The Sea Devils," though, is that Clarke's music is almost always dissonant, and always timbrally challenging. Even the most tender, emotional moments, such as the Doctor's description of "having been to school with the Master," has its relatively tonal melody, a variation on the signature tune, defamiliarized by its harsh timbre. His music doesn't seem to be interested in telling the audience how to feel about specific scenes through the careful use of controlled discomfort; instead, it uses the same language of abrasive timbre and dissonance uniformly throughout, even for those scenes that could conceivably call for less intrusive cues.

Perhaps the score can be interpreted as an overarching symbolic representation of the universe this episode inhabits, describing the slightly surreal, non-quite-contemporary Britain depicted in these episodes. On the commentary for the DVD release of these episodes, director Michael Briant describes how subtle choices made throughout the production, such as the removal of the doors on the cars, were meant to show that the story takes place not in the reality of "now" but in some slightly futuristic version of today, in which case the music can be taken to represent some possible future music that the audience of that future would be used to hearing. In other words, the music is perhaps meant not for "us" but for "them," those individuals in the audience of the imaginary "future Britain," and we, in our mundane version of today, simply have to roll with the slightly askew version of the future we are presented with.

Working against this interpretation, of course, is the director's own displeasure with Clarke's score. His primary concern was the score's ambiguity between music and special sound, the diegetic and nondiegetic worlds. To the director, the music sounded too similar to the sound effects, and he felt the audience would have trouble distinguishing between these two aspects of the program. This was always going to be a potential problem for Clarke when he abandoned the organizing principle of tonality: there is no way a recognizable melody could be mistaken for a gunshot. But as Clarke knew that Brian Hodgson, in charge of special sound, would be representing the diegetic world of the Sea Devils through VCS3 VCOs while Clarke simultaneously punctuated that world with nondiegetic scattershot commentary, also realized on VCOs, he was asking for trouble. Briant ended up cutting quite a bit of Clarke's music in the most confusing places, but even so, it can be difficult to tell, particularly during battle scenes, what is meant to be music and what is meant to be sound effects.[60]

Adding to the confusion, Clarke also peppers his music with stings and Mickey Mousing, imitating the sounds of the Doctor's golf ball, the handing over of money to the motorbike owner, as well as more traditional stings, such as the Sea Devils' shriek when their hands reach up from the water to destroy the Doctor's rowboat. Moments like this have the problematic effect of making the score feel as if he was writing as he went along—spot-scoring, essentially, without any larger sense of form or direction. An example of this can be seen in video example 4.2.◗

For all this criticism, however, there is no denying the effectiveness of much of this score. Its audacity and sheer in-your-face quality is frequently stunning and transforms what was potentially a mediocre story into an atmospheric, disturbing, and memorable series of episodes. Almost entirely because of the disorienting nature of Clarke's music, these six episodes generate an astounding amount of suspense. By removing the coziness and familiarity of the traditional Doctor Who sound, the story stands as a scary, dystopian vision of the future, in much the same way that A Clockwork Orange's score by Walter Carlos a year later would do, in that case by replacing the comforting sounds of traditional music by an electronic replacement, or simulation. In "The Sea Devils" Clarke removes even the familiar element of tonality, leaving us with just the threatening alienness of the Sea Devils, as if they had already won, already replaced our music with theirs.

Doctor Who's audience was already familiar with the sound of the VCO as music, since the scores for the whole prior year had been written entirely on EMS equipment, but, like Carlos's score, Dudley Simpson's music for the Doctor Who episodes "The Mind of Evil" and "The Claws of Axos" in that season demonstrate what happens when the synthesizer is treated as just another orchestral instrument. Simpson's musical language was essentially classical, in the style of traditional film music; harmonies and melodies were derived from this training, and this music was written out as if for a conventional ensemble. Brian Hodgson worked with Simpson to arrange this music for the EMS synthesizers. It was a novel approach that matched the more "action-adventure" tone of Doctor Who in the early 1970s, combining John Barry–like harmonies with a space-age sound. Simpson was to become the primary composer for the program throughout the 1970s, and by 1972, Simpson started composing for traditional instruments in combination with electronics and special sound provided by Brian Hodgson and Dick Mills, an arrangement that lasted nearly seven more years.

Paddy Kingsland and the Arrival of Pop Music

Simpson's use of the Delaware can be effectively contrasted with that of new-comer Paddy Kingsland. Kingsland was hired in 1970, in some ways as a supple-ment and replacement for the ailing John Baker, who though still employed by the Workshop was increasingly out sick. Kingsland was initially sent on the usual six-week attachment to the Workshop, where he wrote a short bagpipe tune on the Delaware for the Radio Aberdeen program *Highland Morning*, among a few other signature tunes. These were well received, and he was hired in 1971 as an "assistant," as Workshop composers were now to be called.

At this time, commissions for the Workshop came when a BBC producer approached Desmond Briscoe, who decided whether it was the kind of program for which the Workshop would be appropriate. Briscoe then made the decision as to which assistant would best suit the particular program. These commis-sions—or "hot potatoes," as later composer Peter Howell called them—seldom stayed on Briscoe's desk long, and with Baker's regular absences, many of the increasingly frequent popular music jobs went to Kingsland, and he rapidly developed a large catalog of work. In the early 1970s, Briscoe was especially eager to encourage a broader use of the Workshop than had been traditionally done, primarily seeking to update the image of the Workshop and expand its appeal. Although purely electronic pop music hadn't exactly taken off in the charts, with the creation of the regional radio networks, there was greater demand to provide them with the kinds of catchy tunes John Baker had previ-ously written, like his call-sign for Radio Nottingham, but with the new sounds of the synthesizer. Kingsland, who was only in his early twenties when he started at the Workshop, had always been interested in the technical side of music, building radios and other electrical gadgets as a child, but also had a closer con-nection and interest in the current trends in popular music than the other, older composers at the studio. After starting as an editor with the BBC, he quickly moved to a producing position at Radio 1, and from there, fresh from working with the latest pop musicians, to the Workshop. His youth gave him an advantage over other Workshop composers that would pay off during his first year there, resulting in the first solo album by a Workshop composer, *Fourth Dimension*.

In 1971, Briscoe was approached by Jack Aistrop of BBC Records, who had the idea of commissioning a set of short, catchy pop songs for playing against the backdrop of the BBC test card. These tracks would then be assembled onto an album to be released by BBC Records. The idea appealed to Briscoe, since it would show a more "with it" side of the Workshop. His initial idea was to high-light the works of the more popular-music-minded composers, which would have included David Cain, Baker, and Kingsland. Cain had shown a real aptitude, while at the Workshop, for writing catchy melodies in a popular style, including his fantastic signature tune for the arts program *Artbeat* and the call-up sign for Radio Sheffield. But by the early 1970s, his output had shifted: he was now working almost exclusively on serious radio drama and was increasingly interested in pursuing an integration of radiophonics and early music, with programs such as "Pre-Bach." Also, for nearly all of 1971, Cain was occupied by the massive twenty-six-hour project *The History of Everyman,* a prestigious commission that required him to essentially convert Room 36 to a personal studio, leaving him with little time for much else.

Briscoe approached the other two "pop" composers, Baker and Kingsland, with the notion of the test card album, offering them each one side of the record. They began working on songs, mostly expanding already-existing signature tunes, giving them middle eights, and generally converting what had been brief themes into proper pop songs. Within a few weeks, however, it became apparent to Briscoe that Baker's tunes weren't going to be finished by the deadline Aistrop had indicated, and following his "hot potato" philosophy, he approached Kingsland with the idea of composing the entire album himself, and dropped the Baker side altogether. Although Kingsland had only been at the Workshop a short time, he already had quite a back catalog of compositions, and quickly expanded an additional set of pieces, and composed one new tune, "Flashback," for the album's closing track. While the idea of using these songs as test card music was eventually abandoned, BBC Records went ahead and released the record on its own, highlighting the stereo and Radiophonic aspects of the collection; as a result, the album is credited to "BBC Radiophonic Workshop" rather than Kingsland (although his name is listed as composer in small print on the back of the record).

When listening to the record, one is immediately struck by two things. First, it's shockingly unashamed of its electronic grooviness. Although other, conventional, instruments are present, particularly the trappings of rock music—that is, electric guitars, bass, and drum kit—what really stands out is the prominent use of the EMS synthesizers as melodic instruments. Kingsland is keen to incorporate them completely within the instrumental ensemble, the synthesizers filling the vocal role in the ensemble. Second, one is struck by the absolute contemporaneity of the pop songs. Formally, they resemble the then-current progressive rock inclinations of other British musicians in the way Kingsland takes simple Tin Pan Alley AABA structures and traditional rock ensembles and then varies them slightly, by using irregular meters, adding extra bars, incorporating extra countermelodies, and so on. These aren't self-conscious additions, however, merely suggestions, and they rarely make themselves noticed. The primary mood is one of an overwhelming lack of uncomfortable dissonance. Kingsland spent his youth playing in rock bands in his local village hall, imitating the instrumental tracks of bands like the Ventures and the Shadows, and it is probably this influence that is felt the most on these songs. A steady rhythm guitar is present on most tracks, as is a combination of electronic and electric bass. The more bluesy approaches of Chuck Berry and the Rolling Stones were also primary influences, not so much on the melodic or formal outline of these tracks, but in inspiring a melodic sensibility that prioritized interesting timbres over complex chord structures.

Probably the clearest example of this on the album is "The Space Between." It was originally prepared as one element of a radio program highlighting the output of the Radiophonic Workshop, also called "The Space Between," which was part of *Stereo Week*, a series dedicated to cutting-edge recording. The hour-long installment, dubbed "A Stereo Miscellany from the BBC Radiophonic Workshop," had been specially commissioned by the controller of Radio 3 and featured works by Workshop composers of the past and present, but showcased new compositions created on the Delaware and the Studer eight-track.[61] This review of this program from the *Radio Times* shows how firmly Kingsland controlled his niche: Desmond Briscoe comments, "We've moved into the pop field in a very successful and sophisticated way with the work of Paddy Kingsland. He's a writer of beautiful tunes—something you don't always find in the pop world." In the same review, Kingsland marketed his pop credentials as well, noting that "my background is technical rather than academic. I'm still learning to sight-read now."[62]

For "A Space Between" and most of the other songs on the album, Kingsland avoided using the Delaware's sequencer, feeling that the 256 events it allowed were too limited for his extended melodies, but he took full advantage of the Studer eight-track recorder. He recorded the drum backing track in Maida Vale Studio 4 (one floor below the Workshop) with a session musician, but played all the other instruments—rhythm guitar, electric bass, VCS3, and Delaware—himself. Like all of the songs on the second side of the record, the side assembled after Kingsland discovered he was to take over the whole album, "A Space Between" contains an additional countermelody created on the Delaware—a countermelody filled with portamento, a technique that was not easily achieved on that instrument and required much more time to realize.

The song is a waltz with a simple form based on an AABA structure. Bookended by a four-bar introduction and coda, the A theme is ten measures long, followed by a modified version of this theme extended to twelve measures. This A/A1 segment repeats exactly with additional countermelodies before an eight-bar B theme, also repeated, introduces new melodic ideas. Finally, the double A/A1 theme is repeated, concluding with a four-bar coda. The outline of the form, then, is:

Table 4.1. The Space Between

mm.	1	2	3	4	5	6	7	8	9	10	11	12
A	C	G	C	G	A	E	A	G	F	F	G	
A1	C	G	C	G	A	E	A	G	G	G♯	F	FG

> Intro (4 bars) A (10 bars) A1 (12 bars) A–A1–B (8 bars) B–A–A1–Coda (4 bars).

The four-bar opening introduces the basic rocking motion that will guide the entire waltz, alternating slowly between C major and G major with added second. When the ten-bar A theme enters, the diatonic harmony, combined with a complete lack of abrasive or dissonant timbres, other than the gentle warmth of a major second against the G, fills the piece with a sense of absolute purity and joyful simplicity, as table 4.1 demonstrates.

The effectiveness of the track is down to the comfort with which the electronic melody sits alongside its more traditional strummed folklike background. As Kingsland would do on other commissions of the early 1970s, he relies on the audience's familiarity with a genre (in this case, folk rock) to allow for more challenging timbres and complex song forms. The gentle, innocuous acoustic guitar strumming, particularly the comforting harmonies it plays, in fact prepares the audience for the warm, round tones of the Delaware when the primary melody enters after the introduction, and the countermelody's portamento lends a "human" touch to the potentially "science fiction" effect electronic music's reputation had acquired, as the excerpt in music example 4.1 demonstrates.🔊

The album was reviewed in several journals and newspapers, and these reviews were almost all positive. Internally, the album was praised as a successful example of one direction the Workshop should take in the future, and as an example of the high musical quality of the work produced there.[63] Despite the confusing credit on the album's cover, Kingsland is always referred to as the songwriter in external reviews, and, as to be expected, the synthesizers are given equal attention in them. This was, according to reviewers, a "really exciting album"[64] for which Kingsland "produces some remarkable music."[65]

Not all of the reviews were this enthusiastic, and some of the criticism of the record draw attention to the ephemeral nature of the tracks' creation. By participating, albeit only by suggestion, in some of his tracks, in the current vogue of progressive and folk rock, Kingsland opened himself up to the burgeoning world of rock criticism and its standards, inherited from classical music, prioritizing "originality," "individual genius," "authenticity," and "ineffability." Where the first Radiophonic Workshop album, the "Pink Album," had been successful precisely because it knew its place as an effective sampling of electronic music produced for radio and television, Kingsland's album is difficult to place, generically. It is neither fully a collection of instrumental rock songs, nor a soundtrack album. It isn't even strictly electronic music, and is certainly not academic electronic music. By the criteria used to evaluate each of these genres, the album would fail, unless one appreciated the album's hybridization of all of them. The following review seems to regard the generic confusion as a conflict not reconciled here: "The trouble with *Fourth Dimension* . . . is that it falls midway between the two [clever and exciting]—a sort of electronic muzak. The synthesizer doesn't really add to the tracks—all radio and TV show titles. But if you like the music that packages the programs, this one will please."[66]

"Easy Chords and Interesting Timbres"

By 1972, the Workshop had largely abandoned the older techniques of tape manipulation and focused its attention on the acquisition of additional synthesizers. The Dutch Organino, which had been requested the previous year, was abandoned in favor of the new ARP Odyssey, which was seen as providing more flexible and original sounds: in particular, it could easily bend pitches with a simple rotary knob. On the advice of his composers, especially the technological liaison Richard Yeoman-Clark, Briscoe informed the Radiophonic Technical Committee of this decision:

> The ARP Odyssey Electronic Music Synthesizer should be substituted
> in the scheme in place of the Piano Organino. We have had the ARP
> on loan from Bauch for some weeks, and it has proved to be a most
> useful device; complete with its own keyboard it will provide the
> sounds of the Organino, with a much sharper attack, together with a
> variety of sounds which hitherto have been unobtainable at the
> Radiophonic Workshop. It is, in fact, a much more advanced device
> than the Organino, in that while the latter is essentially a performance
> instrument, the ARP is designed as a performance and sound source
> device. The difference in cost is £145 above the amount included in
> the Scheme for the Organino, and after considerable discussion it was
> considered a worthwhile additional expense.[67]

At the bottom of the memo, Yeoman-Clark scribbled, "We must get rid of the Organino!"[68]

Why might the Workshop's composers prefer "original" sounds over those of the Organino? It reflects the belief that while they made "music," that music was to be defined by its timbre rather than its tonal organization. This idea wasn't new, but what that music symbolized was. When the synthesizers first arrived at the Workshop, they tended to be used to re-create the uncanny, the mysterious, the unknowable. Now, with their use in popular musical forms, this meaning had shifted. But the composers wanted the flexibility to create music that didn't sound like it was made on familiar instruments. In the words of Paddy Kingsland, the initial proponent of this new philosophy, "It was about easy chords, and interesting timbres." This meant two things: it was the sound of the future, and the sound of the progressive current. For this new generation of composers didn't find electronic music frightening, or the portent of a dangerous and threatening future; rather, they saw in technology the promise of a new generation, believed that technology could make life better and, more simply, that it was a ubiquitous aspect of modern life, as integrated into the musical fabric as any guitar. It was also another way of fulfilling the initial role of the Workshop—to produce special sound using noises that would not be perceived as typical of traditional musical instruments. By this philosophy, the ARP's waveform generators, particularly the Pulse Width Modulation waveform, created sounds that no other instrument could create and generated sounds that imbued electronic music with timbres as complex as any traditional instrument while confounding the listener's ability to identify the sound source.

In early 1973, signifying the obsolescence of much of their equipment, Briscoe proposed a reconfiguration of Room 36, which had recently been used by David Cain for *The Long March of Everyman* and which housed the Miller Spinetta and the "white elephant," as Brian Hodgson called the Multi-colour Tone Organ.[69] The plan was to remove it and the other old organ, creating a replacement for the editing area that had been in Room 10 before the Delaware arrived. This new space could be used with its neighbor—Room 37, the piano room—to comprise a studio and recording room suite where both words and instrumental music could be recorded "without interfering with the electronic composition work being undertaken in the fully equipped rooms."[70]

In a significant moment that underscores the important place special sound still held as an equally important aspect of the musical output of the Workshop, Dick Mills was finally appointed equal rank to the other assistants. While he had been originally hired as an engineer, this role had diminished as commercial products took over from improvised ones and the engineering aspects of his job became less time-consuming. His aptitude for the creation of unique sound effects, particularly on the VCS3, had led to a growing demand for his input, and his new title acknowledged this change. It also signaled a lessening, at least within

the BBC, of the class distinctions so important a decade earlier—the divide between the "working-class" engineers and "middle-class" creative types, such as
the studio managers. On October 20, 1972, at a special meeting (from which
only John Baker was absent), Briscoe announced the new designations: there
were now to be six full-time composer/assistants, and one liaison (Yeoman-
Clark).[71]

Aware, though, that the designation "assistant" didn't credit the amount of
creative work that went into the composition of electronic music, Briscoe
continued searching for a label for his composers. On the one hand, the assistants
wanted to be acknowledged for the musical and compositional effort that went
into their work. On the other, the term "composer" seemed limiting and
old-fashioned and didn't acknowledge the ways in which their work differed
from a traditional composer's. At the beginning of November, he suggested the
following ideas and jotted down the collective responses to these suggestions:

"Radiophonic Composer"—acceptable to all staff concerned.
"Producer, Radiophonic Workshop"—accepted with some reservation by
some of the more conventional "musician composers" at the RW.
"Composer/Producer, RW"—this seems an effective compromise, which
would distinguish the staff here from other producers, and yet give recognition to the composition element; this is a major factor in the "job
description."[72]

This question would dog the composers at the Workshop until the 1980s, and
really only affected their job titles internally at the BBC, as in the actual credits
for programs the generic labels "Special Sound" and "Incidental Music" would
be used, depending on the circumstances.

Look and Read: "Joe and the Sheep Rustlers" (TV, 1973): Kingsland, Baker

A final example of Paddy Kingsland's early style will perhaps better demonstrate
his working methods at the time. It will also show how the changing techniques
introduced primarily by Kingsland fundamentally altered the musical output of
much of the Workshop. The *Look and Read* series for BBC Schools consistently
used the Radiophonic Workshop, initially because they were a cheap source of
music, but ultimately because in addition to delivering their music on time, they
produced a distinctive sound for the various installments of the series. Each year
the series offered a multipart independent story, essentially a children's serial,

utilizing location filming and a full budget. This story bookended the internal portion of each episode, an educational, studio-bound segment, which contained songs and other material based on the main story, each on a different topic related to reading. For *Look and Read*'s fourth story, and the first to be made in entirely in color, "Joe and the Sheep Rustlers" (1973), Kingsland was given the responsibility of scoring the incidental music and titles to the dramatic bookends for all ten parts, and John Baker was commissioned to write the songs for the educational portions.

Kingsland's music is arranged in much the same way as his *Fourth Dimension* album, with electric bass, Delaware, VCS3, electric guitar, and rhythm guitar, but now also with the new ARP Odyssey providing a buzzy timbre to the more tension-filled cues. No drum kit was used; the bass and rhythm guitar supplied the percussive background. Almost all of the musical material used in the serial comes from two pop tunes, the first introduced as the opening and closing signature tune, and the second making its first appearance in episode 4. The signature tune has a catchy, folk-tune-like quality, perfect for suggesting our main character, Joe, a shepherd, as seen in video example 4.3.◉

The rocking motion in the bass over a modal chord progression captures the rustic background on screen during the opening credits, as Joe is shown herding his sheep down a country road, a jangly rhythm guitar accompanying it. As always, the main melody is played by the synthesizer, slightly buzzy and reedy, which, following traditional semiotic codes for reed instruments, suggests the rural and rustic. Behind it another synth weaves a countermelody, warmer and more flutey. This signature tune remains unchanged despite the various crises throughout the serial and despite changes to the opening credit's visuals. For example, when Joe's sheep are kidnapped halfway though the series, the opening sequence shows Joe and his faithful dog looking forlornly around an empty field to the same jaunty signature tune. All in all, the signature tune suggests security and warmth through consonance, while still evoking the folky atmosphere behind the story. At the same time, the deliberately electronic nature of the melody encourages an understanding of the program as "modern" and "of today" in a way traditional instruments couldn't do. While managing to avoid directly referencing any specific genre—that is, rock, country, progressive rock, classical, or jazz—Kingsland's music remains familiar and unthreatening through its careful incorporation and blending of the least aggressive elements of contemporary music. The picture and story, naturally, serve as a vital component of this music's success; it reconciles these disparate elements by adding an additional level of unity. The character of Joe, in particular, is an amalgamation of these various cultures, musical and otherwise, all side-by-side in post-1960s Britain. He is good-looking, with a stylish haircut, and alternates between fashionable clothes and work clothes. Although he speaks in a broad Yorkshire accent, he acknowledges that "many of us sound different, even though we speak the same language." Kingsland's new musical "genre," an amalgamation of current trends in contemporary music, is a fictional construction, like Joe himself, that presents within the confines of children's television a vision of Britain, and British music, that blurs difference while making consonance out of the similarities.

For the first several episodes, most of the incidental cues are based on the signature tune, as seen in video example 4.4.◑

Exceptions include a few dramatic stings, which consist of a pleasing major seventh strummed on an electric guitar, given added strength with a single bass note on the ARP Odyssey underneath. In episode 4, "One in Three," Kingsland's second song is introduced, and it's used throughout the rest of the story in several variations, after initially being sung diegetically by our main characters. Like the signature tune, it has a folky melody, full of Scotch snaps and modal harmonies, with flattened leading tones. The first time it's heard, Joe and his friend Jill sing it to try and brighten their mood. Jill begins by saying, "Come on, Joe, cheer up," and proceeds to whistle the melody before starting to sing verse 1 by herself, Joe injecting comments. As video example 4.5 shows, by the time she's halfway through the first chorus, Joe has joined her, singing verse 2 with her, and they conclude with a double chorus, ending in laughter.◑

In the next episode, it's sung during the internal, educational portion of the program, usually musically entirely separate from the main story, but here used as a challenge to the children watching at home. They begin by singing the tune straight through together, but rather than have the music emerge nondiegetically from nowhere, as it had in the prior episode, here they turn on a reel-to-reel tape recording that contains Kingsland's accompaniment, and sing along with it. Afterward Jill suggests to the audience that they send in their own words to the song: "I'll tell you what, you send your words in to Joe, and he'll try and sing them!" Throughout the next five episodes both this song and the signature tune are repeated nondiegetically in a number of different ways, in varying forms. In the final chase sequence, seen in video example 4.6, a greater rhythmic drive is added to a rising chromatic figure in the signature tune, filling the scene with a climactic propulsion.◑

The importance of the *Look and Read* series for fostering an appreciation for the sound of electronic music cannot be overstated. More than any other program, with the possible exception of *Doctor Who*, this series exposed multiple generations of children, but particularly those in the early 1970s, to a kind of music they would normally hear nowhere else. This introduction, brought largely about by the twin forces of Paddy Kingsland and the Delaware synthesizer, would herald a new era in electronic music by the late 1970s, with the Radiophonic Workshop again at the forefront, Kingsland leading the way, surrounded by a new, younger generation of electronic composers raised on the synthesizer. These mavericks would lift the Workshop to greater success than it had ever known, before the revolution caused by MIDI brought their achievements within the range of ordinary people.

5

The Second Golden Age

Throughout the 1970s, synthesizers continually dropped in price while improving in design and ease of use; consequently, electronic music was no longer only within the financial and technical range of universities and government-funded institutions such as the BBC. In particular, the successful use of synthesizers by popular artists and film composers like Pink Floyd, Tangerine Dream, and Vangelis forced the composers at the Radiophonic Workshop to adapt their compositional style. As we saw in the last chapter, with the addition of pop musician Paddy Kingsland the general tone of the Workshop's output changed, combining a distinctly commercial sound with a tech-heavy emphasis on electronic production. By the 1980s, the Workshop was responsible for hundreds of pop electronic incidental scores for successful, influential television programs—both science fiction, like *Doctor Who* and *The Hitchhiker's Guide to the Galaxy*, and more mainstream commissions, of which David Attenborough's *Living Planet* is among the best-known.

The 1970s opened with a similar spirit of optimism, with the introduction of voltage-control synthesis and stereo radio, which allowed for the development of all sorts of exciting, innovative techniques, such as complex phasing and panning, as well as the ability to "place" characters and sounds in the sonic field. This excitement was damped only slightly by the decline of the radio play; as technology was opening up exciting new possibilities for radiophonic composers and producers, audiences (and BBC critics) were losing interest in the kinds of experimental works commissioned in earlier decades, exemplified by the transformation of the Third Programme in April 1970 into Radio 3, which would primarily broadcast classical music. This is not to say that serious, innovative programs didn't continue to be made, only that venues for their broadcast were reduced, and, with them, much of the motivation to produce these kinds of esoteric experimental works. Notable exceptions include David Cain's stereo production of Isaac Asimov's *Foundation*, adapted in eight parts in 1973. Like many early stereo works, Cain shifts dramatically throughout the extremes of the stereo field, for both his music and special sound. As producer of the series, Cain had much more control over the sounds used and took full advantage of the Delaware synthesizer's flexibility to imagine the sounds and music of a distant culture. His interpretation is largely atonal, not really "musical"—more like a sonic impression of the sound of technology. The sounds blend into the background, standing out only when functionally serving as a bridge between scenes, but are still a symbolic representation of the Foundation's ideas (and the technology it believes in). While the entire production is exceptional, there are a few moments that stand out musically, and these tend to happen when the music shifts to the diegetic plane. In episode 2, diegetic music of the future is represented in music example 5.1.◉

But the most fundamental shift that occurred in the 1970s was a change in the BBC's attitude toward experimentation. In belt-tightening times, the old notion that experimentation was worthwhile even if there were no immediate results was abandoned. One of the consequences for the Workshop was a move away from the elaborate tape constructions of John Baker, Delia Derbyshire, and Brian Hodgson; the favored musical style shifted to something more immediate and accessible, quick and popular, suiting the new "music factory" quality of the work produced there. This change didn't occur overnight: it took nearly the entire decade for the Workshop to acquire technology that made a true factory approach feasible.

That the Workshop had largely abandoned its founding mandate—to create sounds unattainable through other sources—is apparent in an internal 1973 document by Desmond Briscoe, the studio's director. He was anxious to encourage the use of the Workshop as just another musical option for producers, not musically coded as either "alien" or "mysterious," and worked hard to dismiss the stereotype of the studio as the "BBC's Bleep Factory," as Humphrey Littleton had labeled it only a year earlier. Briscoe's document credits the synthesizer for revitalizing and indeed changing the nature and capabilities of electronic music. He wrote: "The work tends to become more musical; in the case of radiophonic music the dehumanization which started with the absence of a performer is beginning to disappear as techniques develop. In the field of electronic music some people feel that whatever humanity is not already inherent in a musical work cannot be revealed by interpretation."[1]

This last statement reflects Briscoe's new faith in the ability of electronic music, particularly music produced on the synthesizer, to express emotion and "humanity" just as well as traditional instruments—indeed, to be powerful enough to eliminate the necessity of a human mediator. It also conveys Briscoe's belief that the Workshop now had the capability to compete fully with any other music studio, whether producing special sound, traditional incidental music and signature tunes, pop singles, or advertising jingles. He also seems to feel the need to placate the more reactionary elements of the BBC, going so far as to offer the possibility of legal action if his employees overstep their ethical boundaries: "In fact legislation should, perhaps, be introduced to impose heavy penalties on those who invite the electronic computer to usurp any of man's more pleasurable and satisfying functions."[2]

Computer paranoia aside, Briscoe recognized some of the limits of new equipment, and the potential still residing in traditional tape techniques. It was perhaps a bit naive of him to suggest that synthesizers will "never *supersede* tape as a medium for creativity."[3] But it is true that in the special sound area, Dick Mills, who took over composing *Doctor Who's* special sound effects after Brian Hodgson left the Workshop in 1973, largely continued to use tape effects derived from concrete sound sources, occasionally but not always in combination with the VCS3, whereas Hodgson had constructed his special sound almost entirely on the synthesizers since their arrival. This was partially due to the difficulty in obtaining the Delaware for such a lowly job as *Doctor Who* special sound, but also to Mills's own predilection for the traditional methods of electronic music production, the evolution of which he had witnessed since the Workshop's opening in 1958.

It's also true that in the early 1970s, very little commercial equipment was on the market. In 1972, besides the ARP Odyssey, a new variety of VCS3 that fit in a portable suitcase was purchased. However, the £575 "Organino," made by Lowthor Manufacturing Company, was rejected as of too limited an application. It had originally been described as a Dutch machine that "provided a type of sound which was not readily available in any other form, and fulfilled a long standing need at the Radiophonic Workshop" and as "a polyphonic variable tone color keyboard instrument also capable of producing percussion effects," but this was not enough to warrant the expense in increasingly difficult financial times.[4] Over the next few years the studio's ability to acquire new equipment would be hampered by severe budget problems affecting the entire BBC—indeed, the entire country. An inventory of the Workshop in 1974 highlights the essential nature of the synthesizer as an integrated element of the working studio, present in three of the four working areas:

> Studio 1. three mono tape machines, mixer, two synthesizers; EMS
> Synthi A and ARP Odyssey, variable tape machine, video

Studio 2. Three mono tape machines, one variable speed tape machine,
   VCS3 synth, mixer, third octave filter, tempophone
Studio 3. Studer A-80 8 track, Synthi 100
Studio 4. Glen sound mixer desk, three stereo tape machines, Studer
   A-80 8 track, variable speed tape machine, film viewer[5]

In June 1974, while the Workshop was given an approved budget of £8,000, divided equally between radio and television, the administration ordered them to freeze their spending for the entire year.[6] Nevertheless, they went ahead with a master plan to convert the organ room (containing the old Multi-colour Tone Organ and Miller Spinetta) to an additional working studio, and ordered desperately needed Studer B62 and Leevers-Rich Mark VI tape recorders on the slim chance that the financial situation would improve. One money-saving idea floated at the time was the suggestion to cobble together an eighteen-track mixer out of three six-track Glen Sound mixers.[7] This thrift-shop mentality pervades the internal documents of the mid-1970s; for example, one item the Workshop purchased then was a "shop soiled" compressor limiter.[8]

A fascinating struggle later in 1974 concerning equipment can bring the lack of a secure equipment budget into relief. When, after several years of continuous use, the Studer A-80 eight-track recorder permanently attached to the Delaware began to show signs of stress and wear, Briscoe wrote an extended letter to the head of Engineering with a request to purchase another, putting the blame for the equipment's deterioration firmly on the shoulders of their most prominent commission, *Doctor Who*:

   The Dr. Who requirement—the original music recording is made using
   8-track tape to facilitate further treatment and composition at the
   Workshop—which is almost always at comparatively short notice, for the
   time between the studio music recording and the final dub, is always
   limited, makes use of a combination of the Workshop's large synthesizer
   in association with an 8-track tape machine. In previous years it has only
   been possible to complete the Radiophonic Workshop contribution at
   the cost of disrupting work on other people's programmes and/or the
   staff concerned having to work outside normal hours.[9]

The brief reply was short and to the point: "I hardly feel that the requirements for one television program would be sufficient justification for the provision of an additional multitrack recorder."[10] While Briscoe acknowledged at the next meeting of the Radiophonic Technical Committee that "it was possibly unfortunate that the memo had pushed the Dr Who series so hard,"[11] it tells of the tenuous economic situation at the Workshop that one program could have such an effect on the functionality of the whole studio. It also demonstrates the degree to which the Workshop was at the mercy of other departments for their equipment.

If anything, 1975 was an even worse budget year for the Workshop. EMS had designed a new computer interface for the Synthi 100, at a cost of £7,500, which would increase the Delaware's sequence length to about 25,000 events.[12] When Peter Zinovieff wrote to Desmond asking if the Workshop might be interested, he replied, "Unfortunately, whatever our interest in the device, the present financial situation precludes us from even considering your offer, as I have been informed that there is no development money available whatsoever for the Radiophonic Workshop for the coming financial year."[13] Zinovieff followed this reply by offering a special discount, lasting for the next two months.[14] Again Briscoe responded by noting, "I regret that the financial position has not changed since I last wrote and, therefore, I regretfully have to decline your offer."[15] The demand for a new eight-track had not gone away, and Richard Yeoman-Clark suggested possibly purchasing a used Studer.[16] For some time, this budget situation was to remain unchanged, and it severely strained the kinds of innovations possible at the studio.

Roger Limb

Paddy Kingsland's arrival at the Workshop had a profound influence on the types of productions realized there in the early 1970s, furthering the "popular" aspects of their output in the direction John Baker had advocated rather than the more abstract, concrete tendencies of both Brian Hodgson and Delia Derbyshire's music in the 1960s. The hire of two composers, Roger Limb and Peter Howell, in the first half of the decade pulled the Workshop even further in the direction of both popular music and traditional television scoring, and closer to the realization of the Workshop as a music factory rather than a place of experimentation. Radio announcer Roger Limb came to the Workshop in 1972, and like Kingsland, he found his primary musical influences in the pop and jazz worlds, although he had classical training as well.

With an eye to these sympathies, and to the inventory list of 1974, it will be useful to examine one of the prolific Limb's earliest contributions to the *Look and Read* series, a program on which he would later serve as unspoken "house composer." Whereas in "Joe and the Sheep Rustlers" the work was divided between the educational songs composed by John Baker, and the internal story's incidental music composed by Paddy Kingsland, for 1974's "Cloud Burst," Limb alone was responsible for all the music, including the signature tune, incidental music, and educational songs. His selection for the songs as well as the incidental music wasn't that surprising, since Limb already had a great deal of experience writing songs. While he was on his initial three-month attachment to the Workshop, Delia Derbyshire had heard some of his songs, liked them, and recommended him for some initial songwriting commissions, so he already had something of a reputation as a songwriter; in addition, the traditional songwriter, John Baker, was no longer available. Limb's music for these eight episodes closely resembles Dudley Simpson's scores for *Doctor Who*'s seventh season: very traditional, slightly old-fashioned music that was realized electronically on the EMS equipment. Performed almost entirely on the ARP Odyssey and EMS VCS3 and Delaware, Limb's music has a more sentimental, easy-listening style and less of a rock-and-roll feel than Kingsland's; this is apparent from the mellow signature tune and the traditional use of "orchestral" vibrato transposed directly onto the synths. Like Malcolm Clarke's entirely electronic score for "The Sea Devils," Limb's music reflects a growing comfort with electronic sound production: acoustic drums, used for the signature tune and sparingly throughout the rest of the production, are the only acoustic instruments included. Still, the influence of Kingsland is everywhere; the very notion of composing "tunes" as opposed to "incidental music" betrays that direct influence, something Limb acknowledges today: "He set the style in 1970, '71, '72. So it wasn't surprising that my first commission was in his style."[17] It is also apparent in the modal quality of the melody, in particular the use of the flat-seven, something of a trademark for Kingsland, as demonstrated in his folklike music for "Joe and the Sheep Rustlers."

While Limb uses the VCS3 for effective stings, most of his music is in the form of short bouncy jingles, as in video example 5.1⬤, from episode 1.

As the story progresses, Limb justifies his use of the VCS3 with his creation of several suspense cues that take advantage of the timbral uniqueness of the synth's sounds, emphasizing their uncanniness, but unlike earlier generations, who would use these sounds to represent the "alien" or "bizarre," here Limb has naturalized the sounds to represent a standard evocation of a generalized "suspense." Video example 5.2⬤ demonstrates this.

This use is different, and possibly more effective, than Clarke's use of unfamiliar timbres throughout his score for *Doctor Who*'s "Sea Devils," since Limb has already naturalized the synth's tones through "normal music" in earlier episodes. He draws the exceptional sounds into relief as representing suspense through the contrast from earlier sounds. In fact, it's the banality of Limb's "happy" music that is perhaps the most revolutionary aspect of his scoring. The comfort with which his conventional melodies have adopted their new electronic clothes mirrors a growing comfort on the part of British audiences to accept these sounds as normal. This is not to say that Limb's music here is "better" than Clarke's for *Doctor Who*; actually, when Limb attempts a similar "dissonant" effect, his timbres are almost always less interesting than those earlier sounds devised and deployed so anarchically in the earlier serial. See video example 5.3.◐

Limb is well known for his ability to write quickly and efficiently, a facility already apparent in this early *Look and Read* story. He manages to reuse most of his cues several times throughout the series, confounding any attempt to construct anything but the most basic mutual implication between the image and the music. Usually, Limb falls back on simple relationships, such as dissonance equaling suspense and villainy, and consonance and diatonic melodies paralleling our heroes' action. In Limb's eye, though, these kinds of basic relationships mirror his own workaday approach to scoring; these commissions were not art, they were jobs:

> I learned a lot about what you shouldn't do. During "Cloudburst"
> I invented my own motto, which was "If two notes will do the job, why
> write 12?" When it comes to film music, the simpler, the better. Once
> you start getting too complicated, while it may work, it takes such a long
> time to do, and quite often it interferes with the action.

His reliability and facility with this material led to his rehire on most of the future *Look and Read* programs, demonstrating an aspect of commissioning that isn't always apparent from just the paperwork. Many of the commissions for Workshop composers came unofficially through prior contacts. These producers would get in touch directly with the composers they had already worked with, and request their services. After a quick look at their schedules, confirming their availability, the composer would only then run the project by either Desmond Briscoe or Brian Hodgson and secure the job. The program's producer, Sue Weeks, worked closely with Limb, and while not musically educated, she knew what worked for children. It was generally agreed that Limb's songs for *Cloudburst* were too long, and in later *Look and Read* stories, their length would be reduced to a minute at most. Given that the point of the songs was to teach children aspects of grammar or spelling, the lyrical content was extremely important. Consequently, on each program, Limb worked in collaboration with the producer, the lyricist, and a "language consultant"; such writing by committee required a willingness to compromise and a flexibility encouraged in Workshop composers by the mid-1970s.

Although it did not appeal to traditional artistic notions of autonomy and inspiration, the newer "music factory" mentality nevertheless prevailed in this decade. More than anything, completing a commission on time and to the satisfaction of the producer or director trumped any artistic considerations. As discussed in chapter 4, the growing emphasis on productivity stifled composers such as Delia Derbyshire and John Baker, who were used to the leisurely pace tape compositions allowed and required. An obsessive perfectionist, Derbyshire in particular hated turning over any of her work before she felt it was exactly right. Paddy Kingsland recalls working with her during her final years at the Workshop:

> The BBC changed so much around 1970, and in the 1960s the BBC was
> a place that would employ somebody like Delia Derbyshire, but it was
> quite obvious that she could no longer work in an environment that
> was a music factory.... She was very much a researcher, somebody who
> would spend perhaps weeks looking for the right sounds. I worked with
> her a few times and found she was a wonderful person to be with, and
> I would try chiding her, saying, "That's a very good cue, why don't we
> put some leader on it," "Oh, I'm not sure," and I'd go home, and she'd
> stay until three in the morning. I was kind of her amanuensis a little bit,
> because she did need somebody like me to make sure she got to the dubs
> on time, but part of that was finishing the music done on time.

Exactly when and why this occurred is debated among the composers themselves. Limb believes that there was a pragmatic shift in corporate policies within the BBC in the early 1970s that encouraged a more "productive" culture at the Workshop. Incidentally, he particularly enjoyed this culture, since it meant he never had to spend too much time on any one project and instead could continuously move on to new things.

Richard Yeoman-Clark sees the shift as occurring slightly later in the 1970s and locates much of the change in the switch in engineering staff:

> Until that time the Workshop had its own dedicated engineering staff in
> Dave Young and some of the younger engineering assistants. So we
> could all collaborate very easily between the artistic and engineering
> sides of the Radiophonic Workshop. Once Dave Young retired the
> maintenance side of things came under the general BBC maintenance
> engineers so the special pioneering and experimental relationship was
> lost on the technical side.

Regardless of when the change was instituted, it had a profound effect on the musical style of the studio, perhaps more than any other in the Workshop's history, resulting in a more accessible and consequently more popular, and populist, output.

To observe this stylistic shift at work, I will focus on one of the most prominent commissions of 1974: a big-budget adaptation of the popular children's novel *The Changes*. The story concerns the mysterious "rebellion" of technology against humanity in modern Britain; the use of machinery or high technology by people begins affecting their minds, making them aggressive and antisocial. After citizens violently smash the machines they relied on, "civilized" society is forced to turn quasi-feudal, returning to a more primitive state. The story is told through the eyes of a teenage girl, who, after being separated from her parents, joins up with a large family of Sikhs and learns how other cultures have operated without "advanced" technology.

As usual, it was Briscoe's job to choose a composer for the project, deciding on Paddy Kingsland for this prestigious multipart production, among his first high-profile commissions. Anna Hume, the producer, considered music of primary importance and felt strongly that a program about the place of technology in society should sound "modern." For example, she worked closely with Kingsland to ensure that the signature tune demonstrated the reaction of technology against humanity. After beginning with a straightforward modern pop/funk sound, complete with ARP Odyssey and Delaware synthesizers but also with more traditional, familiar instruments, such as the electric guitar, drums, and brass, the "changes" suddenly are reflected by a distortion of these familiar and "advanced" sounds with a dissonant electronic clang. Just as important, though, Hume wanted the closing credits to reflect a traditional "tune in next week" sensibility, which Kingsland realized through straightforward pop music with a brass-heavy ensemble. One of the benefits of using the Radiophonic Workshop was that with Kingsland composing both the music and special sound, he could define the "changes" as they occur in society through nontraditional electronic means, and then incorporate those sounds into his more traditional musical score. His use of the synthesizers for the incidental music in most of the series is fairly straightforward, and the ARP and Delaware tend to double traditional instruments, or play simple diatonic pop melodies throughout. "Naturalizing" electronic sounds in this way—using them as ordinary instruments, with warm, soft timbres—puts the similarly produced but much more dissonant "changes" sound into sharp relief, representing a different side of technology. Here, the "changes" symbolize the threat, the danger of relying too heavily on technology. Ironically, of course, this image of technological sound is a retrogression to an earlier era of electronic music, when all that was available to composers of electronic music were abrasive timbres, with the new technology capable of representing only the alien, disturbing, or threatening. It was this new use of the technology to create more "human"-sounding music that was truly cutting-edge, and the music that more accurately symbolizes the future of electronic music, particularly at the Radiophonic Workshop.

In total, though, three musical elements compete in this program. Traditional Western pop/funk music sits alongside the electronic special sound, in particular the "changes" effect. But given that the program incorporated to a significant extent the cultural world of the Sikh family, Kingsland felt it was important to sonically represent aspects of this non-Western music world, primarily through the choice of the sitar and tabla. Kingsland's orientalized "Indian music" is meant merely to suggest Sikh culture rather than incorporate actual Sikh melodies into the score, for while the tabla is an important part of Sikh music, the sitar is generally not used; the baja (or harmonium) is much more common. But this is irrelevant to Kingsland's point. Like a reverse *Lord of the Flies*, the story riffs strongly on the long-standing Romantic pastoral, primitivist tradition, whereby the "other," in this case a mythic India, is held to possess a "pure" or "natural" way of life, unlike the corrupted West, with its soul-destroying technology. This simple notion, intended for Western viewers, doesn't require anything more authentic than the stereotyped suggestion of otherness already familiar to audiences.

Film music scholar Jeff Smith usefully discusses the way Henry Mancini incorporated elements of jazz into his film and television scores of the 1950s and 1960s in a primarily dramatic way. He notes how Mancini distinguished between his style of film composition, which he called "dramatic jazz," and more "authentic" versions of jazz music. In particular, Mancini acknowledged using certain aspects of jazz, such as harmonic vocabulary and instrumentation, while combining them with the more traditional instruments of the symphony orchestra familiar to film music scoring.[18] Similarly, Kingsland wasn't interested in actually writing "funk" or "Indian music" for *The Changes*; rather, he uses familiar signs denoting "funkiness" or "Indianness," such as tabla, sitar, or electric bass. These signs can then be manipulated in fairly complex ways. For example, the synthesizer often doubles the sitar against an acoustic guitar and electric bass, particularly at moments where our heroine is working closely with her adopted Sikh community, implying an integration of Eastern and Western traditions. Occasionally the sitar acts as a drone against a synthesizer melody, again demonstrating the underlying influence of both cultures. Video example 5.4⬤ demonstrates this.

Kingsland recalls how he was able to incorporate such a large contingent of both Indian and traditional orchestral instruments in his score:

I had done Christmas jingles for BBC1, using players because they wanted it to have a bit of an impact. I'd got french horn players, trumpets, from the symphony orchestra, in the canteen. They came in as freelance. That worked well, so I got them in for *The Changes*. The percussion in *The Changes* was played by the orchestra's timpani player, Terry Emery, which also gave us access to bronze plates for three stories. In those days there was a musicians union, and if you came in to play for a session fee, you couldn't switch tracks, but Terry and I got into it and putting all sorts of instruments alongside everything else. That takes us to the Indian bit. There was an Indian family, and we used a tabla. It gave it more color than you could get out of a VCS3.

Ironically, the "advanced technology" represented by the synthesizers in *The Changes* belied the increasingly tatty situation of the Workshop's equipment in the mid-1970s. This meant real technological advancement was impossible, and the next big change came about through a purchase made by Radio 2, a Yamaha SY2 synthesizer, with the agreement that if the Workshop would store the bulky instrument, their composers could have access to it when it wasn't being used by the radio station. Given the budget constraints imposed on the Workshop, the instrument was a lifesaver for composers like Kingsland, who relied on using up-to-date sounds for his pop music, and in one important respect it anticipated the synthesizers that were to follow. One of the first commercial synthesizers to be designed around the shape of a piano (rather than having an "attachable" keyboard, like the Delaware and VCS3), with an internal solid-state construction requiring no patch cords or bays, the SY2 also abandoned the notion of "anything goes" tuning. In other words, it did not simply produce "sounds": its output was inevitably broken into a twelve-note chromatic scale. It also possessed an "aftertouch" feature, allowing for the careful release and decay of a note after its initial attack. Although the SY2 was monophonic, it was extremely versatile. It had no patch cords or (as in EMS machines) "pin patch boards"; instead, its preset sounds could be chosen from colored switches above the keyboard, and there were controls to the left of the keyboard that allowed considerable modification. The oscillator could utilize separate low- and high-pass filters as well as a low-frequency oscillator for modifying the sound, giving various forms of vibrato or modulation.

Peter Howell

The next new hire to influence the direction the Workshop would take in the 1980s was Peter Howell. He had had a relatively successful career as a performer with John Ferdinando on a series of psychedelic folk albums in the late 1960s, including a version of *Alice in Wonderland*, playing guitar and keyboards. He had also worked extensively in theater, providing folk, rock, and traditional music for stage productions. Howell, working at the BBC as a studio manager and doing voice-over work for programs like *Top Gear*, recalls how he first heard about the Workshop:

> I was composing stuff for the BBC's own internal theater group, called Ariel Theatre Group, and we performed in London. And upstairs they had some electronic gear, some VCS3s, which I'd never seen before, and I was fiddling around on them, and I quite enjoyed it, and I just added some synthesizer stuff to the music I'd written for the play, and someone said, "You ought to work at the Radiophonic Workshop," and I'd never really thought about it.

After taking the studio up on the option to work there on a three-month attachment as a visiting composer, he was given basic radio signature tunes and call-signals, mostly for Radio 4, and within a few weeks he was assigned incidental music for radio and television drama. Howell believes he was hired primarily to supplement the pop music Kingsland had been doing, as these commissions had been consistently increasing, and to a certain extent he considered himself in competition with Kingsland for work, especially at the beginning. If anything, his experience with the electric guitar was more valued than his keyboard and synthesizer abilities. This is not to say that Kingsland or Howell felt threatened by one another; in fact, it was Kingsland who first took Howell under his wing, teaching him the ropes in the idiosyncratic studio: "I remember being very green, and Paddy explaining very basic things to me."

After two three-month attachments, he took a short break before returning to the Workshop full-time in October 1974 to compose additional music for the *Doctor Who* story "Revenge of the Cybermen." It was a potentially delicate situation for the rookie composer, as the music had already been written by veteran composer Carey Blyton. This was the third and final time Blyton's distinctive music had been used in the series. The request came from *Who* producer Philip Hinchcliffe, who felt Blyton's music was inadequate. Only a year earlier, Blyton had worked with Dick Mills to help realize his score for "Death to the Daleks": Mills helped him navigate his way around the Delaware, what Blyton called "The Beast in Room 10."[19] This time around, Blyton attempted a purely acoustic soundtrack, and it displeased Hinchcliffe. Howell's supplemental music is easy to spot, since Blyton's traditional instruments, including saxophones, marimbas, and brass, sound a million miles from Howell's entirely synthesized contribution. The distinctive sounds of the Delaware occasionally ape Blyton's trademark melodic style, but more often, Howell just supplies stings in dramatic situations, providing a total of seven or eight cues.

During his first year, he also provided the special sound for Lawrence Gordon Bowen's high-profile *Ghost Story for Christmas* adaptation of M. R. James's *The Treasure of Abbott Thomas*, creating squelchy sounds for the emergence of a demonic long-entombed monk from his burying place. One of Howell's earliest original incidental music scores was for an episode of the six-episode BBC2 *Playhouse* fantasy-horror anthology program *The Mind Beyond*, "The Daedalus Equations." For this score, composed in March 1976, Howell combined traditional instruments such as piano and strings with the reedy timbre of the Yamaha SY2 and the rich bass lines of the ARP Odyssey to construct elaborate polyphonic counterpoint. Harmonically, Howell harks back to late-nineteenth-century techniques, an approach amplified by the chamber music quality the piano and solo violin impart, heard in video example 5.5.◉ What makes scores like this stand out from incidental music produced by a "normal" composer, of course, is the way he blends special sound with traditional music.

Fag-Ends and Lollipops

While Howell claims that his decision to use traditional instruments in programs like *The Mind Beyond* was purely artistic, the truth remains that he had very little choice: if he had wanted to write cutting-edge electronic music, his options were severely limited. He had the EMS synths, which by 1976 were already starting to sound dated, with their "noisy" rather than "musical" qualities. He had the ARP Odyssey and the (borrowed) SY2 as his two other options, and very little else with which to manipulate sound. Traditional tape techniques and manipulation had by this point been largely abandoned by all Workshop composers with the exception of veteran Dick Mills for his special sound work on *Doctor Who*. The reality was that Workshop composers were expected either to write traditional incidental music without legitimate access to union musicians, or to produce cutting-edge electronic music on rapidly aging and overtaxed equipment. The perception within the Workshop was that while Briscoe and Yeoman-Clark, in his capacity as technology liaison, were adequately researching the latest commercial technology, the department was unable to follow through with actual regular equipment purchases without a proper guaranteed budget. Conversely, the Workshop was occasionally given seemingly extravagant "gifts" from the powers that be, when what they really needed was a more secure operating budget.

The purchase of the EMS vocoder can serve as a demonstration of this phenomenon. In the mid-1970s what the Workshop really needed were new tape recorders. Any multitrack work done had to be produced on the one Studer recorder in Room 10, but it was usually connected to the Delaware and unavailable for use. The other tape recorders, in particular the 1960s-era Philips recorders, were in constant use by Dick Mills for *Doctor Who*. Briscoe noted the dire situation in a Technical Committee meeting: "At present Studio H (room 11) was being used as an office as no tape machines were available to put the area to its correct use."[20] Given that a major new science fiction commission, *Blake's Seven*, was soon to begin, he said, the future ability of the Workshop to fulfill its requirements was in jeopardy. But without a regular budget there was no way to meet this need, and the Workshop faced the real possibility of having to refuse commissions. Another urgent need at the Workshop was for picture synchronization assistance. Until the mid-1970s, this was achieved through a complex system of measurements on the Workshop's Prevost film-viewing desk (which measured in feet per second) and tape (which was measured in inches). This machine was prone to breaking down, and replacement parts, such as "film horses," for such antiquated equipment was getting more and more difficult to acquire. One thing the studio desperately needed was a VCR to help time music cues, but without a fixed budget for such things, Briscoe was reduced to begging his bosses:

> During recent months, we have been involved in a number of programs for Open University, when the only source of video material has been on Philips cassette; on each occasion the Production Office have arranged to loan us "their" machine for a very limited length of time. This arrangement is satisfactory neither for us nor to the Production Office and of course involves the machine being transported between Alexandra Palace and Maida Vale.[21]

Into this situation came the offer of the purchase of a new £8,000 EMS Vocoder 5000. The vocoder is an instrument that modulates the human voice through a complex process, reproducing sounds electronically through a series of filters that imitate an unprocessed vocal input, resulting in an "electronic" version of the human voice. While the technology for the instrument had been around for decades, only in the mid-1970s did such technology become compact and affordable enough (relatively speaking) to allow for companies like EMS to begin producing them commercially.

Ordinarily, an instrument like this would obviously have been financially out of bounds for the Workshop, given its budget situation in the mid-1970s. Richard Yeoman-Clark, in his capacity as Workshop technology liaison, had visited the EMS shop in Wareham to take a look at this new piece of equipment and reported back in March 1976 that it was a useful device with a great deal of potential for Workshop composers. Before EMS developed their vocoder, both Peter Howell and Paddy Kingsland had shown interest in instruments that could modulate the human voice. Yeoman-Clark had already pieced together a primitive version for them from the driver transducer of a PA horn speaker he had at home and an assortment of PVC tubing. The end of the tube had to be inserted into the mouth at the corner of the lips. He recalls:

> It was therefore tricky and uncomfortable to use and needed some
> practice and expertise. Also, of course, it wasn't very hygienic. So when
> the idea of an electronic device to do this type of job came up I was
> very interested. We had had some practice using the peaking filters in
> other EMS synths for various forms of simple modulation so we could
> see how a multiple filter device could be very useful.

At the initial meeting in March, Briscoe revealed that he knew of a potential source of funding in a new "Creative Radio" allocation, for which the vocoder might qualify.[22] A few months later, at the next Technical Committee meeting, it was reported that although the Radiophonic Workshop had no money of its own to purchase the vocoder, Martin Esslin in the Drama Department was "putting together a special case for buying one."[23] This money eventually materialized, and the instrument was delivered in November 1976. This strange situation—that while basic operating costs were not being met, there were occasional extravagant purchases out of all proportion—characterized the Workshop's financial circumstances for most of the 1970s.

This was to change, however, when Brian Hodgson was brought back to the Workshop in 1977 to serve as the studio's "organizer." In another reconfiguration of the administrative setup of the studio, Briscoe was promoted to "head of Radiophonic Workshop," responsible for publicity, commissions, and overseeing the division's general health. Hodgson's duties included day-to-day management, including budget allocation, and one of his first tasks was to try to fix the studio's ongoing money problems. He saw the situation up to that point as one of mixed-up priorities, as well as a difference of philosophy between Briscoe and himself: "Desmond had this idea, that if the idea was sacred, we didn't need all this equipment. That was what frustrated Delia, she had these incredible ideas, but the technology wouldn't let her bring them to fruition. You were pushing the equipment beyond its ability to give you what you wanted, so everything was a compromise." The only reason equipment came to the Workshop, in Hodgson's eyes, was through a policy of "fag ends and lollipops": that is, because other departments had a budget that had to be used by the end of the year or they would lose it, the powers that be would appease the Workshop's call for equipment by shifting the money around to the Workshop, "stuffing a lollipop into Desmond's mouth to shut him up."

Hodgson envisaged creating a studio for each composer and filling each studio with the latest equipment, tailoring each area to the composer's own needs. He approached the new head of resources for Radio, John Dutot, describing the untenable situation as it stood. He complained about the impossibility of bringing the studio up to date and speeding up the production process, and eventually convinced him of the problem's urgency. To create an independent budget, though, Hodgson would need the approval of Dutot's colleague in Television, Michael Checkland (later to be made director general). He produced a paper and action plan for Checkland, who accepted the budget Hodgson recommended. According to this plan, one studio per year, starting with the oldest, would be individually updated. "We had perfect freedom, we were able to exploit the technology that was coming on the scene, and we were able to talk to manufacturers, and we came up with what Yamaha research engineers called the most sophisticated MIDI setup in Europe, probably the world." Along with the decision to allocate each studio to an individual composer came a reclassifying of the studios themselves, changing from numbers to letters.

The Second Golden Age

The new budget revived the Workshop, giving its composers a renewed energy and spirit and a new sensibility. Finally, the musical desires of the composers began to match the capabilities of the equipment. Institutionalized support enabled the "music factory" to soar to a new level of prolific composition, for the first time combining the commercial- and pop-minded sensibilities of the late 1970s with the technological ability to realize them in an efficient manner. This wouldn't be the only result of the influx of new technology, however. Also emerging around this time was a new, much more optimistic conception of "the future," as manifested through Kingsland, Howell, Limb, and newcomer Liz Parker's overwhelmingly confident vision of technology. The acquisition of new synthesizers and other cutting-edge electronic equipment over the next several years would result in a distinctively utopian sound, finding a parallel in contemporary British culture at large as a nihilistic punk attitude morphed into the colorful, blissful new wave movement.

That this new era was regarded as such was demonstrated in a documentary by TV Science director John Mansfield, broadcast on BBC1 in early 1979. Roger Limb composed the theme for this feature, and one topic was this theme's realization, with Limb demonstrating the new synthesizers and their capabilities. Malcolm Clarke was interviewed discussing his adaptation of Ray Bradbury's *2026: There Will Come Soft Rains,* and Peter Howell described his recently completed music for *The Body in Question.* The program also featured interviews with external composers like EMS founder Peter Zinovieff. A few months later, a special episode of *Nationwide* celebrated the twenty-first anniversary of the Workshop, tied to the release of a new collection of Workshop music, *Radiophonic Workshop—21,* with one side given over to "greatest hits" of the past and the other containing works taken from recent commissions, using the newer equipment.

For the first time in years Desmond Briscoe was freed up from many of his most time-consuming obligations and was able to pursue his love of radio in a series of old-fashioned radio features, using Workshop staff as his production crew. Several of these projects went on to win major radio awards and contributed to the growing reputation of the Workshop as a place where serious commissions could sit beside more mainstream, commercial productions. Chief among Briscoe's successes during this time was *A Wall Walks Slowly,* capturing the Cumbrian landscape in the words of poet Norman Nicholson and the people who live there. Briscoe's inspiration was the musicality of the Cumbrian people's speech. Armed with tapes of poetry and conversations with locals, Briscoe worked closely with Peter Howell, who also wrote the music to accompany the *concrète* construction. The resulting program won three awards from the Society for Radio Authors and received some of the best reviews in the studio's history.[24]

The Body in Question, "Breathless" (TV, 1978): Howell

Evidence that the new technology had a direct influence on the quality of music produced at the Workshop can be seen in Peter Howell's extensive thirteen-episode score for *The Body in Question.* The ambitious spirit of the revitalized studio combined with the efficiency of new production techniques gave Howell the confidence to compose an epic amount of music on a scale unimaginable in earlier years. I will focus on one episode, "Breathless," to demonstrate his working methods and philosophy. The score uses synthesizers, and technology in general, with such enthusiasm and to such a degree that it is difficult not to hear in this renewed energy a larger feeling of euphoria over the possibilities of this technology. *The Body in Question* anticipates by two years Vangelis's music for Carl Sagan's American-made *Cosmos,* a program that owes a lot to Howell's earlier effort. Howell himself finds real inspiration in a much earlier representative of an optimistic Enlightenment-era rationality and logic, Walter Carlos's smash 1968 hit *Switched-On Bach*. Like Carlos's album, Howell's work uses an "antique" musical language, realized in an electronic way that ignores contemporary pop harmonies. Carlos's pioneering Moog-based record imagined a world where computers could realize Bach's meticulously logical and teleological music with a precision impossible in human performers, maintaining an illusion of automated performance. Much of Howell's score uses the language of the eighteenth century to evoke memories of those earlier periods of optimism (both the eighteenth century and the late 1960s), but for this new album, unlike the earlier one, Howell composed all original music, reinforcing its "classicalness" by occasionally supplementing the electronics with traditional instruments. Despite this, one is never in doubt as to who the stars are here: the Yamaha CS-80 and the new vocoder. The results represent the concept "science" not only through their semiotics but also through their very technological origins. Here we see the opposite reaction to C. P. Snow's fear twenty years earlier that the sciences and the arts were moving in profoundly different directions.

The Body in Question was a major undertaking for Howell and was conceived in close collaboration with Jonathan Miller, the program's writer and producer, who regarded music as essential to the project. For example, the Workshop didn't own a Yamaha CS-80 synthesizer, but Howell was able to rent one on a weekly basis, charging it not to the Workshop but to Miller's production.[25] Of the many hours of music Howell wrote for the anatomy series, perhaps the most memorable cue was for a sequence in episode 4, "Breathless," demonstrating the historical discovery of the operation of the lungs brought about by the systematic application of the scientific method. Dubbed "Greenwich Chorus," the cue mimics the Enlightenment-era belief in the regularity of the universe, re-creating the clockwork nature of the rhythm of the body in a mechanistic way. How better to demonstrate that mechanism, in the mid-1970s, than by evoking the spirit of cybernetics through "mechanized" voices via the vocoder? Given an almost unique prominence at the time in television, the music was used to guide the images shown, with Miller and Howell working carefully to align the rhythm of the music with the images, as medieval clocks, gears, and seventeenth-century scientists flash by, timed to the beat, juxtaposed against the sounds of cybernetic human voices in lush diatonic harmony. Howell produced the track by combining an obviously synthetic melody with multitracked vocals processed through the EMS vocoder, making the striking and beautiful sequence a stunning example of two visions of the future. First, the musical style is reminiscent of an eighteenth-century overture, complete with basso continuo and filled with common harmonic progressions and careful dissonance preparation. Equally important is the timbre of the sounds, however, for they imply not the seventeenth or eighteenth century, but the contemporary audience's future, and this particular brand of optimistic faith in science and progress. This can be seen in video example 5.6.◉

Once Howell had introduced the piece in this episode, he continued to use its melody throughout the remaining episodes, often in different arrangements. Particularly if the music was meant to provide a subtle backdrop for a scene, he relied on a less prominent arrangement without the distinctive vocoder. For example, in the final episode the theme is used when the discussion of postmortems returns the subject to the eighteenth century. As Miller speaks, the "Greenwich" melody quietly plays in the background, as a reminder of its earlier use, and also as a standard "period" piece evoking the era, as heard in video example 5.7.◉

The order of the actual thirteen episodes was fluid until quite late in the day, and "Breathless" was originally going to be episode 2. Howell met first with Miller to discuss the music for this particular episode in June 1978, but didn't edit the completed music into the program until September 15. In his initial meeting and viewing of the "silent" episode with Miller, it was agreed that there should be eight total cues, including the opening and closing credits. This is slightly fewer than the other episodes, but the length of "Greenwich Chorus" (over five minutes) in some way makes up for this. Figure 5.1 shows his initial episode plan.

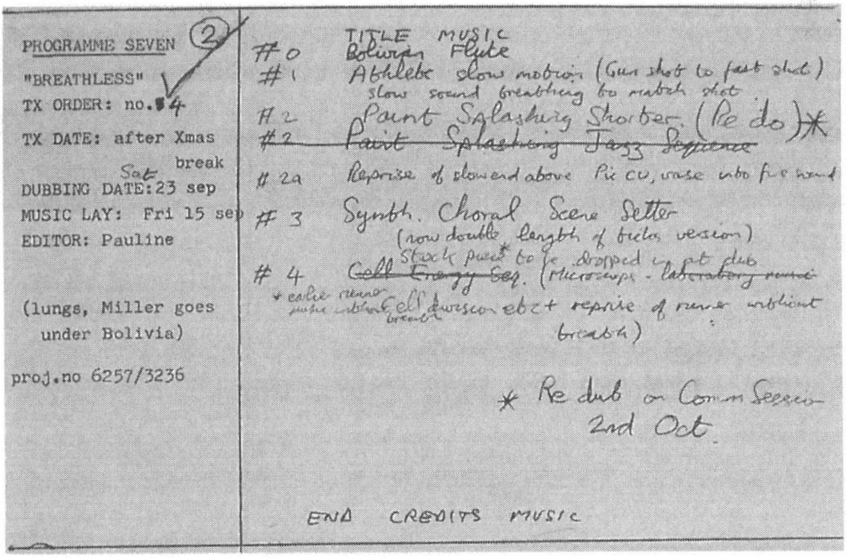

Figure 5.1. Peter Howell's initial music breakdown for *The Body in Question*, episode 7, "Breathless." Photograph by the author.

After the opening credits, Miller wanted authentic Bolivian music to accompany images of the Andes, perhaps with flute and guitar. Howell suggested a possible shift from a flute and guitar duet fading in to a solo guitar as the image of the Andes gives way to the episode title and a shot of Miller in front of a Bolivian church. Ultimately this 1:30 cue would use stock solo Bolivian flute music, without the guitar, fading just as the title appears, giving way to the sound of the church's bell.

The second cue was meant to imitate the slow-motion sound of a runner's heartbeat, which Howell realized on the ARP with white noise "swoops." He carefully noted that the cue is to begin exactly with the shot of a pistol going off, and abruptly end with a shift back into normal speed.

The third cue was to parallel images of Miller randomly splashing paint onto a white wall. At this point Howell envisioned a humorous jazz percussion sequence, which he dubbed "Quite a Splash." The two-part cue he wrote carefully Mickey Moused the action, punctuating paint splashes with stabs and alternating jazz rides with rock rhythms and fills, cymbal crashes and bells. At some point this fully realized cue was rejected and replaced with a much more surreal but equally humorous electronic cue consisting of a heavily vocoded human voice and atonal electronic blips and bleeps, also Mickey Mousing the individual splashes of paint. The second part of the original percussive paint cue was to enter thirty seconds after the end of the first, accompanying a shot of an ancient Greek vase. In the newly revised cue, this second half is entirely unrelated to the vocoded silly cue and consists of a warm synth melody backed by spacey upward-rising filigree lasting just fourteen seconds.

The next cue, "Greenwich Chorus," was originally dubbed both "Synth Choral Scene Setter" and "Seventeenth-Century Sequence" and had a running time of 2:55, later increased by simply repeating the cue three and a half times. The scene largely consists of a montage, with Miller's voice-over frequently giving way to the tune, allowing music to take center stage for the only time in this episode. One isn't immediately aware of the multiple repetitions, given the amount of variety embedded in the counterpoint, and the cue is carefully timed to begin at key moments in the montage, giving an added emphasis to those instances. To guide himself as he controlled each aspect of the cue, Howell wrote out a basic score on music paper, indicating first the four-beat clock-tick intro followed by the harmonic chord progressions throughout the entire twenty-one-bar length of the piece. Also indicated on this score are alternate voicings for the melody, as heard in the final episode, for example, with flute, trumpet, and voice suggested at various points instead of vocoder. Such scores aren't "performance" scores as such; rather, they served as guides during the complex synchronizing process, helping the composer orient himself during the multitrack recording sessions.

Finally, the last cue before the closing credits was originally called "Cell Energy Sequence Microscope" and was meant to accompany images of cells dividing as viewed through a microscope. This laboratory music was eventually dropped, either because of time constraints or because Miller was unhappy with Howell's cue. The cue was replaced with a "stock piece to be dropped in at dub," on October 2, two weeks after the final music-laying session in September, demonstrating the constant flexibility and fluidity Workshop composers had to have. Ultimately, musical choices were made at the discretion of the director, and the composer served to satisfy them and not primarily their own artistic ideas. Hopefully the two could be reconciled, but in the event of a disagreement, the composer always had to relinquish artistic control. In all, eleven minutes and fourteen seconds of music were used in the episode, or a little more than one-fifth of its total running time. While this doesn't sound like a great deal of music, remember that Howell was always working on multiple episodes at the same time, each at various stages of completion.

While deep into *The Body in Question*, Howell was also hard at work on the Workshop's first solo record since Paddy Kingsland's *Fourth Dimension* seven years earlier. In fact, it was Howell's suspicion that he was in competition for the same commissions as Kingsland, which ultimately resulted in the second solo album released by a Workshop composer. *Through a Glass Darkly* was Howell's attempt to showcase his keyboard abilities rather than his guitar skills. The first side of the album is one long synthesizer "concept" track, in the style of Jean-Michel Jarre or Tangerine Dream, while the second side contains, like Kingsland's earlier album, selections from Howell's radio and television work extended to include middle eights and given a more traditional "pop" structure. He remembers:

> I did the album to prove I was a keyboard player. When I arrived, I was treated as Paddy's protégé, because I had been a guitarist. I tended to use acoustic a bit more, but it became clear that I was not being considered for some work that came in because it was assumed I was another Paddy. I was in the guitar-based tuney bit, and consequently, I felt there wasn't enough of that work to go around, and I felt I needed to prove myself as a keyboard player. I had been playing keyboards as well. That was the entire notion behind the long piece.

He was able to interest BBC Music in releasing the album largely on the strength of the idea of a "concept album," which according to the composer the label liked because it "was what the big boys were doing," meaning big-concept albums along the lines of *Tubular Bells*, *Lamb Lies Down on Broadway*, and Pete Townshend's ill-fated Lighthouse project. The prior successful track record of

Workshop recordings also helped Howell sell the project. Of the tunes on the B side, "Caches of Gold" in particular displays a new ease with which electronic music can sit alongside traditional instruments. This tune creates a relentlessly major-mode technological utopia, built out of the SY2 and the ARP Odyssey as well as a slew of other instruments, such as the Eventide Harmonizer, a clever piece of equipment popular with contemporary recording artists like David Bowie and Led Zeppelin that took small samples of sound and reproduced them at various pitch levels. "Magenta Court" is possibly the Workshop's first true "rock" tune, reinterpreted in an electronic idiom, using vocoder technology in a sea of synth-driven rhythms alongside a rock-infused electric guitar and drum pattern. This is contrasted dramatically by "Wind in the Wires," which harks back to Howell's days in folk-rock bands, pairing the SY2 with a Simon and Garfunkel–esque acoustic guitar riff. Again, though, all this music is relentlessly optimistic and in no way sees the use of technology as a threat, or even a benign "accompaniment"; rather, the synths are so prominent that they can only be interpreted as a driver of the optimism, as if technology is responsible for creating this bright new future. Probably the most successful track on the album is "The Astronauts," derived from two *Horizon* episodes, "The Case of the Ancient Astronauts" and "Space for Man." "The Astronauts" begins quietly, with dramatic and slow-moving synth pedals gradually generating tension through the accretion of new elements. Eventually, this tension reaches a breaking point, triggered by a stirring timpani roll and the entrance of a fanfare-like synthesizer melody against a driving rock beat. Again, Terry Emery (used in Kingsland's score for *The Changes*) was recruited to play timpani, recorded in the hall outside the Workshop. The composer recalls:

> The timpani were being stored outside my studio by the symphony orchestra, so I didn't have to book the instruments. Apart from the timpani, the entire "Astronauts" was all the ARP Odyssey, multitracked to kingdom come. It's a very multilayered sound, it was all done monophonically. There really was no chord played at one time in the whole thing, so that meant... because it was all done monophonically, all those chords, all the notes done separately, it's very similar to what happens live with players in an orchestra, you've got discrepancies, really.

The Hitchhiker's Guide to the Galaxy (Radio, 1978–1980): Kingsland

By the time Howell was constructing his solo album, Paddy Kingsland had already received the commission that would probably define his time at the Workshop more than any other, *The Hitchhiker's Guide to the Galaxy*. For the first series, broadcast in early 1978 but recorded in late 1977, Kingsland was hired only to provide special sound—the music was to come from preexisting sources, such as Terry Riley's *A Rainbow in Curved Air* and György Ligeti's *Lontano*—but for the pilot he did compose several cues that operate much like music. For the interior of the Vogon Constructor Fleet ship, for example, Kingsland composed a soothing electronic drone that is an effective contrast to the decibel-smashing destruction of the Earth immediately preceding it. Other notable examples of his special sound include the electronic noises made by the Guide itself and the use of the Eventide Harmonizer for the voices of the Vogons.

After working on the pilot episode, Kingsland briefly left the Workshop on attachment as a producer for Further Education, where he produced a series of programs called "Music and Principles," the point of which was that music fundamentals were the same regardless of genre. Each episode focused on one element of music: melody, harmony, and so on. One episode, on the topic of music in films, featured onetime Workshop collaborator and three-time Academy Award–nominated film composer Richard Rodney Bennett. During Kingsland's absence, the rest of the first series of *Hitchhiker*'s special sounds (or "sound effects," as they were credited in the *Radio Times*) were provided by science fiction special sound veteran Dick Mills and, visiting on attachment, Harry Parker, with special mice sound effects provided by Liz Parker.

After the initial six-episode series was a critical and ratings success, producer Geoffrey Perkins asked Kingsland to contribute both special sound and music for the inevitable sequel. The first series was rebroadcast several times over 1978, and, continuing where the first series left off, episode 7 (known as "Fit the Seventh" or "the Christmas Special") was broadcast on Christmas Eve 1978 as a way to tide listeners over until the second series, which was broadcast over the course of five nights, January 21–25, 1980. Kingsland remembers:

> Since the scripts didn't arrive until the last minute, I found myself
> working day and night. By the Monday we had only two programs
> ready for broadcasting. I actually enjoy working like that, but there's no
> denying it was a chore. When the scripts demanded robots talking to
> humans, the treatments needed just the right balance, otherwise Ford
> Prefect would talk like a robot and the robots like people. We put all the
> voice-lines onto multitrack and had the whole thing to bits more than
> once in order to get it right.

One hears in Kingsland's attitude the perception that *finally* the Workshop was beginning to live up to its potential, and it is easy to hear in these works of the late 1970s a reinvigoration. With the generous new equipment budget came more prestigious commitments, brought about largely because with Desmond Briscoe as head and Brian Hodgson as organizer, both had more time to recruit for work, and these new high-profile success stories fed into the impression that the Workshop had again the ability to musically depict the contemporary and modern. In other words, in an era when the "modern" and the "technological" were trendy again, the Workshop was at the forefront of representing them—indeed, fashionable. Kingsland insightfully summarized the attitudes within the Workshop at the time, recalling:

> When I started in 1970, there were three rooms, 11, 12, 13, plus the piano room and organ room that housed a great big electronic organ that someone thought might be useful. It wasn't. John Baker was in Room 11: he had three Philips tape machines and the room was lined with hooks that had hundreds of tape loops hanging from them....Next door in Room 12 were Brian Hodgson and Delia Derbyshire with a VCS3. They had Electrophon Studios and a connection with EMS, so they'd persuaded the Beeb to buy some VCS3s. Then in Room 10 there was the Delaware. Composer Dudley Simpson used the Delaware a lot for Dr Who....I enjoyed it but as I wasn't really into "weird" I didn't feel I was doing anything that couldn't have been done anywhere else. Not until I started on Hitchhiker's Guide to the Galaxy, that is! Then suddenly I thought the Radiophonic Workshop came into its full potential: it was using the place properly.[26]

One popular strategy Briscoe had for marketing the twenty-year-old studio was to emphasize the genre changes brought about since its last huge public relations success with the acquisition of the Delaware. He liked to emphasize how the studio's equipment now equaled or surpassed that of the pop world. Discussing the studio with Briscoe for a piece about Hitchhiker's second series, one reporter commented that the program

> taxes to the full the Workshop's sophisticated electronic battery of synthesizers and multitracked tape decks. "All we had then was an ex-wartime sound mixer salvaged from the Albert Hall and an couple of tape machines," he [Briscoe] says, "Now, with the world of pop music fixing the pace technology has almost overtaken us."[27]

These prescient words foreshadow the eventual end of the Workshop nearly twenty years later, but at the time the studio could more than compete with the best popular studios. Indeed, by the early 1980s no other studio in the world could approach the volume of equipment, or the quantity and quality of the electronic music produced there. The scene was set for the acquisition of the studio's biggest commission yet, but outside pressure was building on the Workshop to face directly the competition growing all around it. For while Workshop composers had succeeded in demystifying electronic music, the price of their success was their ultimate downfall in a culture that learned to copy their successes more efficiently.

6

The Price of Success

Ironically, as the technical and financial conditions at the Workshop improved throughout the 1970s and 1980s, those same economic conditions helped fuel competition outside the BBC for the kinds of services that had once been unique to the studio. By the mid-1980s, understanding that it no longer held the virtual monopoly on electronic music in Britain, the Radiophonic Workshop sensibly reconfigured its priorities to reflect what it could do better than any home studio: capitalizing on its reputation, it consolidated, developed, and pioneered the use of cutting-edge technology, such as the Macintosh computer, in music programming and sequencing. For a while the studio was considered the greatest Mac-driven MIDI studio in Europe, and this helped keep it competitive in an environment that increasingly tended to devalue the importance of music in media productions. Ultimately, however, as popular musicians and composers for television and film continued to adopt electronic techniques, it became impossible for the Workshop to provide their services as cheaply as these freelance composers did, and the BBC's decision that all departments must be self-sufficient merely provided the final nail in the coffin for the studio, which closed in 1998.

One sign that the Workshop's confidence had reached new heights is apparent in a plan launched by Workshop organizer Brian Hodgson to prioritize electronic music within the BBC. In a July 1981 memo, Hodgson suggested a course of action involving monthly or fortnightly programs of electronic music from across the spectrum, "from Stockhausen to Kraftwerk, and news of Electronic Music events around the country."[1] He also recommended that the BBC sponsor a national competition for British electronic music composers, culminating in a public concert of the best pieces. But the centerpiece of his proposal was the establishment of a new electronic music studio dedicated exclusively to the production of electronic music in its own right, the first time such a thing had been suggested seriously at the BBC since the early 1960s. Perhaps Hodgson was inspired by a Workshop collaboration with composer Michael Tippett in June 1978, where for his Symphony No. 4, Tippett and his publisher, Schott, consulted the Workshop for help designing an artificial breathing sound effect for use in the piece. Richard Yeoman-Clark constructed the effect using the VCS3, which made it, according to Tippett, "virtually impossible to tell which is the live breathing, unless one knows in which order they were recorded."[2] For Hodgson's plan, the "artistic policy [would be] decided by Music Division, but the day-to-day running of the department left to Radiophonic Workshop." He envisioned a studio adjacent but separate from the Workshop, with as much contact as possible between visiting composers and Workshop staff. As the Workshop already contained state-of-the-art equipment, the only new facility envisioned would have been an acoustic performance space for the recording of electroacoustic music. The goal of the studio would have been to wrest some of the control over electronic music from the hands of universities, and Hodgson proposed a tour of the major existing facilities, first in Britain, then abroad to Stanford, the Institut de Recherche et Coordination Acoustique/Musique (IRCAM,) Utrecht, and Cologne.

Doctor Who

While this proposal never went further than an initial planning stage, it demonstrates the progressive thinking behind many of the Workshop's undertakings in the early 1980s. Undoubtedly the most ambitious decision to reach fruition was the commission to score all-new episodes of the *Doctor Who* series starting in 1980. Bringing international attention to the Workshop and its new, more polished and commercial sound on a scale never before seen, this commission, beginning with *Doctor Who*'s eighteenth season, was in addition to its ongoing commitment to provide its special sound.

Incoming producer John Nathan-Turner wanted to revamp the program, which he and much of the public felt was becoming a bit stale and complacent. He had worked on the show since 1968 in the capacity of production assistant and believed that the production values had fallen and that the show was failing to address the serious problem facing all television science fiction: how to successfully compete for an audience against such sensational challenges as theatrical blockbusters like *Star Wars*, loaded down with spectacular effects, and the luxury of months of filming and endless expense. American television's response to this interest in science fiction was to emulate the big screen's high budgets with programs like *Buck Rogers* and *Battlestar Galactica*. At the financially ill-equipped and government-regulated BBC, however, it was impossible for *Doctor Who* to compete with the financial and technological superiority of Hollywood's science fiction films, which saturated the British market in the late 1970s and early 1980s. Nathan Turner wanted to boost the realism and the level of sophistication in the program's writing and, indeed, all other aspects of the program. He also "wanted a change of emphasis away from the over-dominant humor toward stylish, intelligent, sophisticated scripts."[3]

The audience for *Doctor Who* had over the previous ten years matured from mostly children to young adults in their late teens and early twenties. The audience had, in effect, grown up with the program. Media studies scholar John Tulloch noted that "a long-running series like *Doctor Who* or *Star Trek* tries to target and access different 'streams' of SF audiences at different times."[4] This is indeed what the program did in 1980. As a part of this new sophistication, Nathan-Turner felt the program should also refer to more "high-art" elements. One example of this was to allude to classical or respected literature in the stories, or to hire literary science fiction writers, rather than established television writers who had written for many different types of programs, as had been done in the past. A significance percentage of the program's audience were college-educated and middle-class, exactly the group who would be receptive to the use of "serious" science fiction writers and these sorts of high-art references.[5] In this endeavor, though, Nathan-Turner faced several major obstacles. First, the program had to find a balance between popular entertainment and high art. Science fiction as a genre has traditionally challenged the dual notion of popular and serious, both in literature and in other media. Science fiction writers are not taken as seriously as writers of more "legitimate" genres. In the visual media, viewers are offered such conflicting images of science fiction (*Alien vs. Predator / 2001*, pulp/intellectual) as to make a simple genre designation of "popular" or "serious" impossible. Second, Nathan-Turner's production team would still be faced with the same budgetary and time restrictions that had plagued all previous teams. To deal with this, he tended to use younger, fresher, less expensive but respected up-and-coming talent behind the scenes.

Along with these production changes, Nathan-Turner had very specific ideas about how music should function within *Doctor Who*. First, he felt that Dudley Simpson had to be replaced. Simpson had worked as the show's de facto composer for nearly ten years, and had been using almost exclusively traditional instruments for several of those years, a situation largely out of the composer's control. He had felt an ever-growing sense of coldness from the BBC about his use of the Delaware to supplement his conventional scores, and, according to him, since Hodgson's revamping, the management of the Workshop told *Doctor Who*'s producer he was forbidden access to the studio's equipment. This, in the end, seriously hampered his work on the program, and he was forced to use smaller, rented synthesizers to complete his soundtracks. He remembers how this hampered his collaboration with special sound composer Dick Mills: "It made it much more difficult. But in the end Leslie Pearson, my top keyboard player, bought his own synthesizer. It cost about four thousand quid, but it paid for itself in the end."[6] Simpson acknowledges that his later scores just weren't as good as they had been when he'd been allowed access to the equipment at the studio: "All of a sudden I had to do *Doctor Who* with all music, simple music, and it wasn't as good. You know, I needed those effects, just that little bit, to lift and make it gel as science fiction, rather than as pure drama."[7]

Indeed, Nathan-Turner believed strongly in the use of electronic music as the most appropriate vehicle for portraying the sound world of *Doctor Who*: "With all respect to Dudley Simpson, he was financially restricted with the number of musicians he could use.... There was a certain sameness, whether the story was set on Earth or another planet. With electronic music, there are so many different sounds and musical noises that can be made. There's a distinctly alien feel."[8] In his view, electronic music in *Doctor Who* worked on two levels: first, it conveyed a sense of "alienness" as exemplified by earlier Workshop contributions to the program; second, it complemented the new more sophisticated style of the program, especially the kind popularized by such "intelligent" electronic musicians as Jean-Michel Jarre (whose music Nathan-Turner played to the head of BBC Drama, TV, as an example of the kind of music the new *Who* should pursue). This opinion, however, obviously conflicted with Simpson's impression that "electronic music and electronic effects didn't contrast as well."[9] Nathan-Turner also believed that Simpson's simultaneous work as composer on *Blake's Seven* and *Doctor Who* prevented *Who* from establishing its own distinctive sound, and at a long lunch, the new producer told Simpson of his plans.[10]

It was financially impossible, of course, to replace Simpson with high-profile musicians of Jarre's caliber, so the decision was made to commission all of *Doctor Who*'s music from the Radiophonic Workshop, whose composers felt confident that they could reproduce the desired sound. Nathan-Turner recounts his initial approach to the Workshop: "Brian Hodgson at the Radiophonic Workshop was delighted with my proposal...and I asked if I could have as many different composers as possible during the season so that, hopefully, every story would have a different musical feel."[11] Before they were given the job, however, Nathan-Turner asked the Workshop in December 1979 to produce a brief demonstration of the kind of thing they were capable of providing. Peter Howell and Paddy Kingsland composed several short cues for the previous season's story

"The Horns of Nimon," incorporating elements of the program's signature tune into the atmospheric, arpeggiator-heavy synth texture. It proved to the producer that it was possible for the studio to offer the precise mixture of up-to-date pop sensibility and "futuristic" space music he had been looking for, and the two composers, as well as Roger Limb, were engaged to provide the music for the entire season. The Workshop was also commissioned to "revamp" the signature tune to bring it up to date. Limb remembers how he became involved in that first season:

> He [Nathan-Turner] asked Paddy Kingsland and Peter Howell to initially provide the music for the first seven stories in that particular season. Halfway through the season it became apparent that Paddy was going to be involved with *The Hitchhiker's Guide to the Galaxy* television show...and so Brian Hodgson suggested to John Nathan-Turner that I would do one of the stories and Brian gave me a glowing report, I presume (I wasn't there), but I could have probably done it from the start, it's just that it so happened that John had heard of Paddy and Peter.[12]

Incidental music was one thing. Messing with the *Doctor Who* signature tune was something entirely different, and had always been taboo within the Workshop. As we have seen, the one earlier serious attempt to remake it (the so-called "Delaware version") had been quickly rejected, and over the years only cosmetic changes had been allowed. It had been, and continued to be, "both a milestone and a millstone" within the Workshop, according to Desmond Briscoe.[13] So any attempt to redesign it was politically very tricky, something Peter Howell was realistic about when he was given the job:

> I realized how dangerous an area I was entering because the tune was so very well established and in a way had helped make the Workshop's name for all of us.... I didn't want to throw the baby out with the bathwater; didn't want to do something so ridiculously new that nobody would know it was the same tune. As far as I was concerned I was trying to prove that you could use all the techniques that we have learned over the years and still make something fresh with all this new equipment.[14]

He was given carte blanche by Brian Hodgson to use anything and everything the studio had to offer, and in February 1980 he began work on the theme, spending five and a half weeks on nothing else. After closely analyzing the original version, he decided to focus on three primary elements: the bass, the melody, and incidental sounds. For the bass, he updated its fundamental rhythm, giving it more forward motion. Howell used the ARP Odyssey but combined it with a prominent Yamaha CS80, adapting the preset "Funky 1" and "Bass" sounds with a "touch response initial pitchbend," and his original intention was to incorporate a "constant throb on C bass disco bass drum beat."[15] The slight scoop in the lowest voice was achieved by preceding each bass note with a brief, eighth-note anticipation on the pitch directly below the fundamental note.

For the melody he envisioned an "unworded vocoder 'voice' gushed in deep space echo."[16] This was realized by manipulating square wave chords from the ARP through the vocoder by mouthing vowels into a microphone to shape the sounds, giving it "a 'swirly,' almost backwards quality."[17] This electric-guitarlike sound was then passed through the EMT Stereo Plate. And finally, to fill in the background texture, he wanted to incorporate "close passing dry sounds."[18] Driving him were the potentially contradictory impulses to remain faithful to the original while generating the same spirit of mystery that earlier version had evoked, only updated for a new era, stating that he "didn't want anyone to listen to it and know how it had been done.... There is no easy way to explain how the theme tune was reperformed. The sounds were generated from so many different things—it was an amalgam of all sorts of different techniques."[19]

Giving him particular trouble was Grainer's original middle eight, the ethereal quality of which didn't necessarily match the rhythmic vibrancy of the new version, and Howell drafted several alternate versions, seen in figure 6.1, changing the rhythms slightly to give it more of a sense of forward motion.[20]

Howell mixed the completed theme on a sixteen-track recorder, reserving each track for specific elements. Table 6.1 shows how he identified each of the separate tracks.

When both the mono and stereo mixdowns were complete, he sent three versions on to producer Nathan-Turner and Sid Sutton (head of Drama Group,

Figure 6.1. Peter Howell working out the revamped *Doctor Who* signature tune's middle eight section. Photograph by the author.

Table 6.1. *Doctor Who* Signature Tune Track Designation

Track 1: Opening sting (FX) middle 8 line 1
Track 2: Opening sting (FX) middle 8 line 2
Track 3: Opening sting (FX) middle 8 line 3
Track 4: Bass
Track 5: General stereo reverse echo (predominantly bass)
Track 6: General stereo reverse echo (predominantly bass)
Track 7: Top line original 1
Track 8: Stereo FX
Track 9: Stereo FX
Track 10: Top line original 2
Track 11: Vocoder 1
Track 12: Vocoder V. trigger 1
Track 13: Vocoder excitation 2
Track 14: Vocoder speech trigger 2
Track 15: ISG Voc final
Track 16: Bass gulps

TV), each with a different-length opening sting, asking the producer to select one, and recommending his favorite.[21]

Howell didn't take any time off, however; he immediately set to work on the incidental music for the first story of *Doctor Who*'s new season, "The Leisure Hive." In this score, Howell attempted to realize Nathan-Turner's high-art goal, evoking rhythmic and melodic elements of various popular classical music works, such as Holst's "Mars, Bringer of War" from *The Planets*, and Ravel's *Bolero*, and synthesizing them. The resulting effect propelled these familiar works into the future.

Over the next six years the Workshop would score thirty-one complete multi-episode stories of *Doctor Who*, occupying up to 25 percent of the annual output of the studio in any given year. Although it was never possible to completely realize his plans for a high-art soundtrack for a high-art program, Nathan-Turner continued to encourage Workshop composers to aspire to this goal. For example, in the soundtrack to "Earthshock," broadcast March 8–16, 1982, Malcolm Clarke directly quotes from the classical music canon. At one point in the story, the Doctor's companions are exploring a cave. As one of them notices dinosaur fossils on the walls, Clarke plays Camille Saint-Saëns's melody "Fossiles," realized with an electronic xylophone sound.

Nathan-Turner was particularly successful at marketing the program abroad, frequently visiting Doctor Who conventions, and emphasizing the Radiophonic Workshop's contribution, so that the studio consequently became well known for the first time outside the United Kingdom. Nathan-Turner worked closely with public television stations in the United States to make sure the program had as wide a distribution as possible, and made merchandise available outside the United Kingdom as well. In particular, the stereo single of the Howell *Doctor Who* theme sold well, as did a new album of music covering the Workshop's first two years scoring the show, *Doctor Who: The Music*, and its subsequent follow-up, *Doctor Who: The Music II.*[22]

Back at the Workshop, however, the "music factory" was facing the reality of producing an enormous amount of new music each week. For a major commission such as *Doctor Who*, deadlines were usually incredibly tight. Howell was given an unusually large amount of time by the director Lovett Bickford for the music on "The Leisure Hive," since it was important that the music of this first "new team" episode was successful. But the music on other episodes was nearly always composed after the finished episode had already been edited, and if there were production delays, the deadlines would be even closer. On *Doctor Who*, usually the first contact for a composer with a director after the initial request would occur at a meeting between the incidental music composer, special sound composer Dick Mills, and the episode's director. The incidental music composer, in collaboration with these two, would view a timecoded VHS copy of the episode, noting those moments where music might be effective, along with a one- or two-word description of the general tone of the cue, such as "scary" or "tension." Regular *Who* composer Roger Limb recalls the delicate balancing act between the two branches of radiophonics in each episode of *Doctor Who*:

> The phrase "horse trading" comes to mind. Dick would say that he was going to do something and I would nod, and agree to bear it in mind. Sometimes we still had trouble. On "Revelation of the Daleks" there was a very big Dalek bust-up scene at the end. I was zapping my music in as hard as I could and Dick was zapping his sounds in—it was a tricky situation."[23]

Occasionally the composition of actual musical themes for specific characters would be requested by the director or suggested by the composer, also a matter settled at this initial meeting. It was important for the composer to get a solid feel for what the director wanted, since given the time constraints, this meeting was usually the only contact with the director until after the music had been inserted.

Doctor Who: "Logopolis" (TV, 1981): Kingsland

A closer look at Paddy Kingsland's score for actor Tom Baker's final story, "Logopolis," will demonstrate the compositional procedure typical for *Doctor Who*'s incidental scores in the early 1980s. We are lucky in that most of Kingsland's behind-the-scenes material survives, offering a unique insight into his compositional practices. When one compares the finished score with his initial notes, a picture of the studio emerges that both reinforces the notion of a "music factory" mentality and demonstrates just how much careful planning went into each episode's score. The story, written by script editor Christopher H. Bidmead, takes the opportunity offered by the departure of the show's long-serving lead actor to explore aspects of the program's own history, particularly the fact that the Doctor's time machine, theoretically able to appear in any form, has been stuck in the shape of a police telephone box since 1963.

Traveling with his young companion, Adric, the Doctor decides to finally fix the Tardis's external appearance by first measuring a real police box in contemporary England, then traveling to the mathematics-obsessed culture of Logopolis, who will be able to repair the Tardis's appearance. Unbeknownst to the Doctor, his nemesis, the Master, has already materialized his own time machine around the same police telephone box on Earth. After gratuitously killing a policeman and new companion Tegan's aunt, the Master eventually reveals his plans to exploit the Logopolitans' ability to create matter out of mathematics, otherwise known as Block Transfer Computation. The Master is unaware, however, that Logopolis is using their mathematics to artificially hold at bay the overwhelming effects of entropy, which threatens to overtake the universe. When he realizes this, the Master attempts to blackmail the people of the universe by unleashing the entropic field, killing billions of people in the process. The Doctor defeats the Master, but only at the cost of his own current incarnation, falling from a radio tower and regenerating into a new form (played by Peter Davison) at the conclusion of the fourth and final episode.

In Kingsland's initial meeting, director Peter Grimwade expressed his concern that viewers might be upset over the departure of Tom Baker, and suggested that Kingsland compose a theme for the mysterious character of the Watcher, who appears throughout the story as a way of preparing viewers for the change of lead actor. The composer had already composed a theme for the introduction of Adric in his debut, two stories earlier, "Full Circle." Kingsland remembers, "I went along to the studio to see Adric in action, so that I could create his theme, before I began working on the score. I think Matthew Waterhouse was rather unsure of himself, and Adric's theme sort of reflects that."[24] From this

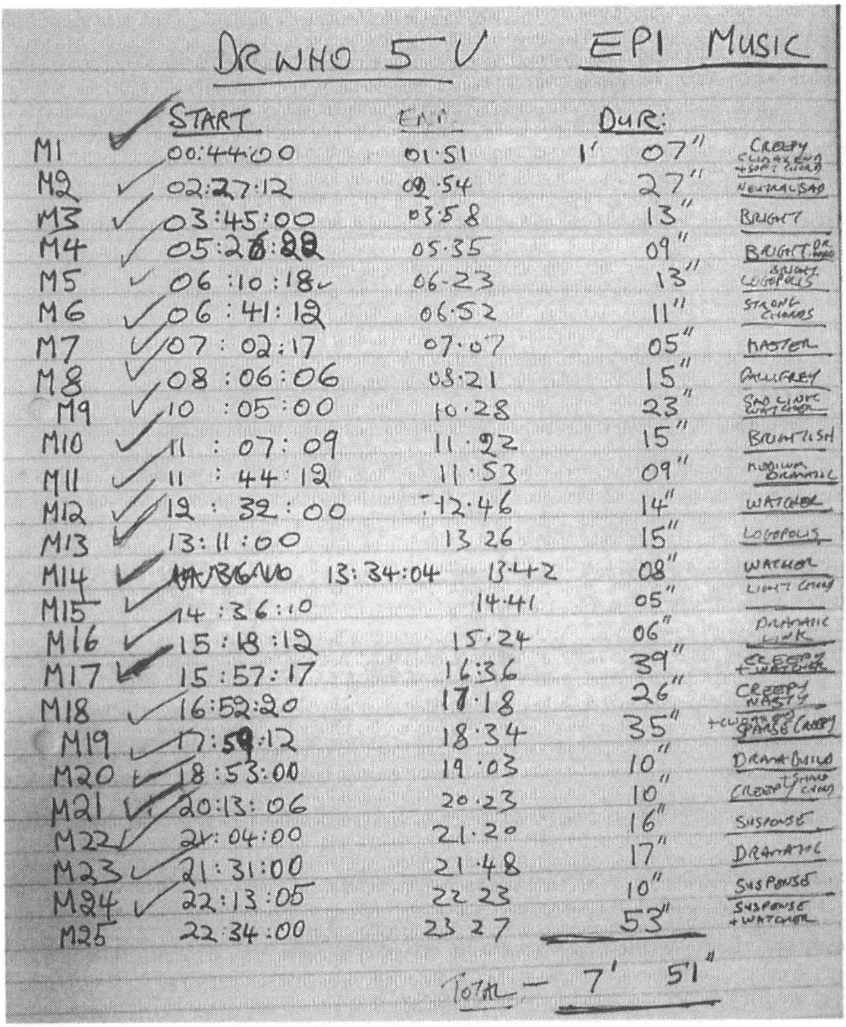

Figure 6.2. Paddy Kingsland's breakdown of the twenty-five music cues for episode 1 of *Doctor Who*'s "Logopolis." Photograph by the author.

meeting and initial viewing in the director's office, Kingsland produced his cue sheet for episode 1, twenty-five cues, from five seconds long to well over a minute. He wrote these down over several pages, loosely notating starting times and durations, as seen in figure 6.2, with brief suggestions for the tone, before carefully printing the list on a single sheet for the entire episode, a process repeated for each of the story's four episodes.

Kingsland returned to the Workshop and began working on the episodes individually, taking careful notes detailing the exact entrance and exits of the specific cues. For "Logopolis" he used a collection of three synthesizers: melodies were primarily produced on the monophonic Yamaha SY2 for its flexible portamento and rich flutey sound; the Oberheim OBX, a polyphonic synthesizer, provided a thick harmonic string texture underneath Kingsland's SY2 melodies; and the Jupiter 4, famous for its arpeggiator, was used to add a "spacey" quality to his trademark consonant sound, as well as supplementing short stings. With such continuity between cue instrumentation, he rarely indicated instrument or sound choices for specific cues, instead relying largely on generalized descriptions of tone or mood at this stage.

Every week, after Kingsland had worked out the music for each episode, he faced the challenging task of actually incorporating the music correctly into the drama. Today, working with a computer, you can simply insert a cue digitally into its exact spot, enabling a careful interaction with the action on screen. But in the early 1980s, a composer at the Workshop still had to go through an elaborate process to time cues so they would fit exactly. Peter Howell had prepared a 120 bpm click-track tape of himself counting off the minutes and seconds, and this would be recorded onto one of the eight available tracks on the standard eight-track recorder. But this gave composers only a very restricted sense of time, since the composer is inevitably and unconsciously driven to follow the 120 bpm beat, so the next step would be to choose a tempo for the specific cue and lay a track at this tempo on another track. It was then possible to synchronize the picture to the tape by pausing the video player on a frame and releasing while listening to the counting track. To facilitate this rather complex process, for each cue Kingsland wrote out notes on a separate page, with landmarks indicating important shifts in the music during a cue, or the entrance of specific themes. Kingsland recalls:

> It had to be set up way before the start of the cue, enough to allow time to mute the counting track, switch on the preferred click track and grab a pencil to watch the sequence through while marking up cuts, lines of dialogue et cetera on the bar chart. Sometimes I put the sound track from the video on another track as an additional reference. From then on I was able to play the parts without watching the video, using the crude score as a reference for synch points. I used to do simple lines or pads for all cues and then fill them out later, all the bass parts all the percussion and so on. It made me feel better about the deadlines to have a basic version of everything done early on.[25]

In this way, all four episodes of "Logopolis" were scored. In episode 1, all of the major themes for the entire story are introduced, including a new theme for the Master, which consists of a simple three-note descending pattern, D♯, D, G♯. When we first hear this theme it is accompanied by an image not of the Master himself, but rather of the Master's Tardis, also disguised as a police box. The scene (and episode) opens with a shot of a policeman attempting to use the police box's telephone. He is forcefully dragged inside by an out-of-shot acousmatic Master, represented only at the scene's conclusion by a sinister laugh. Throughout the scene the melody is repeated several times, but is buried within an overall musical evocation of "menace," and is heard clearly only at the end underneath the Master's laughter, identifying this acousmatic threat with the three-note motive. While not melodic in the same sense as Dudley Simpson's famous "Master" theme used for Roger Delgado's portrayal of the character in the early 1970s, this theme exemplifies Roger Limb's motto—"Why use twelve notes when two will do?" Unlike earlier radiophonic composers, Kingsland doesn't rely on dissonant or abrasive timbres to inform his audiences; instead he uses the same timbre for good as for evil, relying on the harmonic and melodic content to underscore the mood of the scene. The "Master theme" contains within its brief duration three important markers of "danger" or "threat." First, the very fact that the theme moves downward evinces a notion of "badness." Linguists George Lakoff and Mark Johnson have detailed the all-pervasive influence of metaphor in language, and their observations can often be applied to musical language as well. They observe that the metaphor "happy is up" is one of the basic orientational metaphors that guide the way Westerners interpret their sur-roundings. "Such metaphorical orientations are not arbitrary. They have a basis in our physical and cultural experience. Though the polar oppositions up–down, in–out, etc., are physical in nature, the orientational metaphors based on them can vary from culture to culture."[26] From such a simple metaphor they are able to identify all sorts of binary oppositions, such as "more is up; less is down, high status is up; low status is down" and, in the case of the "Master theme," "virtue is up; depravity is down," as in the expressions, "He is high-minded. She has high standards. That was a low trick. I wouldn't stoop to that. That would be beneath me. He fell into the abyss of depravity." Translating this linguistic metaphor to music requires another metaphor—"high pitch is up; low pitch is down"—but as listeners we are taught from an early age to hear this. For example, in tonality, we hear the third in a minor triad as "lowered" and in major triads as "raised," with the implication that the raised version is somehow happier. In Renaissance modality, however, the modes that contained so-called "softened" hexachords (the equivalent of our minor) were thought to be "sweet," as opposed to the "hardness" of the raised third. That we hear and interpret these culturally determined metaphors, and their semiotic implications, without noticing them only attests to their ubiquity. So Kingsland's use of this simple metaphor takes advantage of very powerful, unconscious impulse in us to hear music, seemingly inevitably, a certain way.

The first descending interval in the "Master theme," a minor second, is considered the second most dissonant interval in tonality (as used in John Williams's *Jaws* theme,) surpassed in its instability only by the next interval in the "Master" theme: the tritone, the legendary "devil in music," an interval that in the West has symbolized tension and pain since the Middle Ages. So, Kingsland is able in three notes to define this largely unseen character (indeed, unseen throughout most of the first two episodes) musically in a way that strongly informs the audience as to his nature.

One of the primary defining features of a Kingsland score is the frequent use of consonant chords constructed out of major or minor triads with an added major second, giving the chords a pleasant and gentle dissonance. This harmony is also the basic material out of which melodic material is generated. Kingsland himself cites his experience as a guitar player as an influence behind his particular method of working:

> I'm a dreadful player of keyboards so I don't play in the same way that a keyboard player would. You can often hear keyboard players doing electronic music and it sounds very different from people who aren't trained in that particular way. It means that I write in straight lines, as you would for the clarinet and the flute and those single note type instruments.[27]

In particular, one repeated melodic idea that seems to symbolize an opposition to the tension in the "Master theme" is used throughout "Logopolis": the notes G, A, and D. In several ways this theme represents a neutral emotion, settling a sonic backdrop that can be offset by the sudden inclusion and tension of the "Master theme" in a scene. Melodically and semiotically it is essentially the opposite of the "Master theme"; it rises, while the "Master theme" descends; its first interval is the much more pleasant major second, as opposed to the Master's minor; and the leap consists of the rational fourth instead of the tritone.

Two other consonant themes operate throughout the episodes, "The Watcher" and "Logopolis," both of which carefully follow traditional semiotic patterns as well. The "Watcher" theme uses the SY2's distinctive flute sound, giving it a comforting warmth more electronic-sounding themes occasionally lack. Like the first occurrence of the "Master theme," "The Watcher" is initially overlaid by a thick string texture suggesting tension. Here, a dense F-minor harmony foregrounds the melody, largely owing to the mysterious nature of the Watcher's white form, but unlike the "Master theme," "The Watcher" consists of a rocking bass motion implying a traditional dominant-tonic relationship between C and F. The melody for the Watcher does move along the troubling minor third, but consistently resolves itself on the tonic, suggesting resolution, and (ultimately by the final episode) contented resignation. The careful use of dominant-tonic relationships in *Doctor Who* scores of this period as cadential figures is relatively rare, however, and tend to be deployed in this abstract, suggestive way rather than in larger, more straightforwardly "functional" ways. One notable exception is the conclusion of Roger Limb's score for the first episode of "The Keeper of Traken," the story immediately preceding "Logopolis." Here, in a dramatic build to the cliffhanger ending, Limb concludes his suspense cue on an agonizing dominant chord, resolved only by the complementary tonic of the closing theme tune.

The "Logopolis theme," as befits a "logical" race, is composed of a relatively complex fugue, and as such is the most self-contained theme of the story. However, the main theme of the fugue is deployed melodically whenever Kingsland wants to suggest the planet, its people, or even simply the concepts behind their science. Like the "Watcher theme," it is in a minor mode, perhaps symbolizing the severity of Logopolis's role as safekeepers of the universe, or the seriousness with which they carry out their work. Indeed, the "Logopolis theme" is used in its longest iteration during a montage sequence showing the inhabitants working through a series of mathematical figures.

Another thematic idea introduced during the serial is a short theme for "Gallifrey," named after the Doctor's home planet and standing in for both that world and the Doctor's former Gallifreyan companion Romana. The brief, slightly melancholy melody resembles the "Watcher theme" in timbre, but is used only twice in the episodes. The theme occurs first when the Doctor opens Romana's now-empty bedroom door in the Tardis, and it recurs when he mentions jettisoning the room. Like an old-fashioned 1930s Hollywood leitmotif by Max Steiner, the theme emerges organically out of the musical texture as a kind of shorthand. It also rewards attentive viewers, since the theme was first introduced in Kingsland's score several stories earlier, "Full Circle," to represent Gallifrey.

Building on Nathan-Turner's desire to reference high-art signifiers, Kingsland also includes two improbable references to Richard Wagner. One humorous example occurs twice in episode 2, first as the Doctor suggests they open the Tardis doors underwater, in an attempt to "flush the Master out." As he speaks, the opening rising triadic "Rhein" melody from Wagner's *Das Rheingold* is heard. This music returns later when the Doctor and Adric realize they missed materializing under the Thames and walk out onto a dock in the middle of the river.

The most prominent preexisting musical reference, however, is the use of the *Doctor Who* theme itself, incorporated into the program's incidental music in episode 1 of "Logopolis." Kingsland had already done this in his earlier score, "Full Circle," and Peter Howell would do again in the twentieth-anniversary special "The Five Doctors" three years later. Here, however, Kingsland's use of the theme comes at the end of a scene between new companion (and first-time air stewardess) Tegan and her aunt, as Tegan recites aloud her stewardess spiel. Indeed, without the Doctor, Tardis, or any other markers of the program itself, the inclusion of the *Doctor Who* melody seems to be reminding viewers that they are in fact still watching *Doctor Who*, stamping the mark of the program on the scene, as it were. The continual presence and functional, structural nature of *Doctor Who*'s incidental music since 1980 did not allow for the wholesale reuse of older music in new serials. Therefore, the composers frequently used the only musical material they had at their disposal that was discreet and memorable: the signature tune. While it was perhaps a bit much to expect audiences to remember specific incidental music motifs (such as "Adric's theme," or the "Gallifrey theme"), they could be counted on to at least remember the theme tune.

Composers of the program's incidental music began inserting fragments of the tune into the score around this time, usually just the distinctive three-note opening melody, but occasionally the bass pattern as well. Although composers had occasionally incorporated the theme into their scores since the early 1970s, the early 1980s was the first time that this practice began to appear frequently. Roger Limb tended to use the signature tune as a quick-and-dirty way to reference the character of the Doctor himself, since the show didn't allow space for extensive themes: "The thing about doing music for *Doctor Who* is there's not often a lot of time for musical development, it's quite a fast-moving, pacey program and there's a cut from one scene to another and get on with the dialog straight away."[28] Limb is referring here to the most common use of the theme as a signifier within the program; but as a reference to the program's past, this quoting perhaps becomes a bit confusing. Occasionally the signature-tune melody is heard in a whimsical way when a character is referring to the Doctor. It is also used on occasion when the Tardis is shown, with or without the Doctor; or can also be used whenever any general mention is made of the show's past. It is not always clear what composers mean when they insert the fragment, and again, this lack of clarity probably results from a lack of any other distinctive musical motifs in the program's history.

Figure 6.3 shows Kingsland's timing cue page for episode 1's thirty-nine-second cue M17, labeled "creepy and Watcher" on his original cue sheet. At the top of the page he has written out its precise timing, indicating key moments for the cue. Below this is a chart showing how he is to time each entrance of these musical ideas according to Howell's 4/4 click track on track 8 of the multitrack recorder. He begins the cue at precisely 15:57:15, easy to time visually since the scene breaks between the interior of the Tardis to the exterior as the Doctor moves outside. Nine seconds later, Kingsland notes "car," not an indication to do anything different musically, but only as a visual landmark to time the rest of the scene, as the Doctor looks around and notices Tegan and her aunt attempting to repair their car's flat tire near the Tardis. The music throughout this section remains "creepy," gently rocking back and forth between a minor second in the bass and the flute SY2 sound. Again, Kingsland notes a cut back to the Doctor's face at 16:11:12. But the following note, "sees Watcher," indicates a shift in music. At this point, while the camera remains on the Doctor, motionless, the composer inserts a sting that implies he sees the Watcher off-camera. This is a purely musical indicator, and a great example of the metadiegetic: a musical cue that seems to be mirroring a character's internal thoughts rather than an external reaction to the diegesis. After this sting, as the Doctor is shown pondering the significance of the Watcher's presence, at 16:22:20 Kingsland shifts to the "Watcher theme" rhythm, and the SY2's flute melody that had been rocking back and forth with the earlier "creepy" music suddenly rises in prominence. He concludes the scene by converting that half-step motion to a suggestion of the signature tune by swooping up an octave and completing the half-note descent, using the iconic three note tune (C$\sharp$, c$\sharp$, c) to suggest the character of the Doctor himself. The Watcher's rhythm, and the security it offers, continues a few seconds longer, providing its cadential fulfillment on a bright C-major chord before cutting off at 16:35:16 with a return to the inside of the Tardis, and a "cut to Adric." Video example 6.1 ♦ contains this scene.

The ambition Kingsland, Limb, Clarke and Howell display in their *Doctor Who* scores of the early 1980s demonstrates just how much attitudes had moved on from the 1970s at the Workshop. These are not just musically effective scores, but commercially savvy ones as well, informed partly by the techniques and priorities of contemporary popular music, but equally by the world of advertising and its requirement to efficiently convey an impression. Kingsland in particular felt comfortable in this milieu and was interested in acquiring outside advertising work, an activity discouraged by his BBC bosses. It is important to remember that Workshop composers were on salary at the BBC, and moonlighting was frowned upon but not expressly forbidden. Kingsland had had some success outside the BBC while employed at the Workshop; one tune in particular, his 1973 theme for introducing rugby, was heard by jazz flutist Herbie Mann, who was staying in the Dorchester Hotel in London recording his album *The London Underground*. He contacted the BBC and ultimately tracked down Kingsland, who wrote Mann a middle eight for the tune, which subsequently appeared on the gold-selling

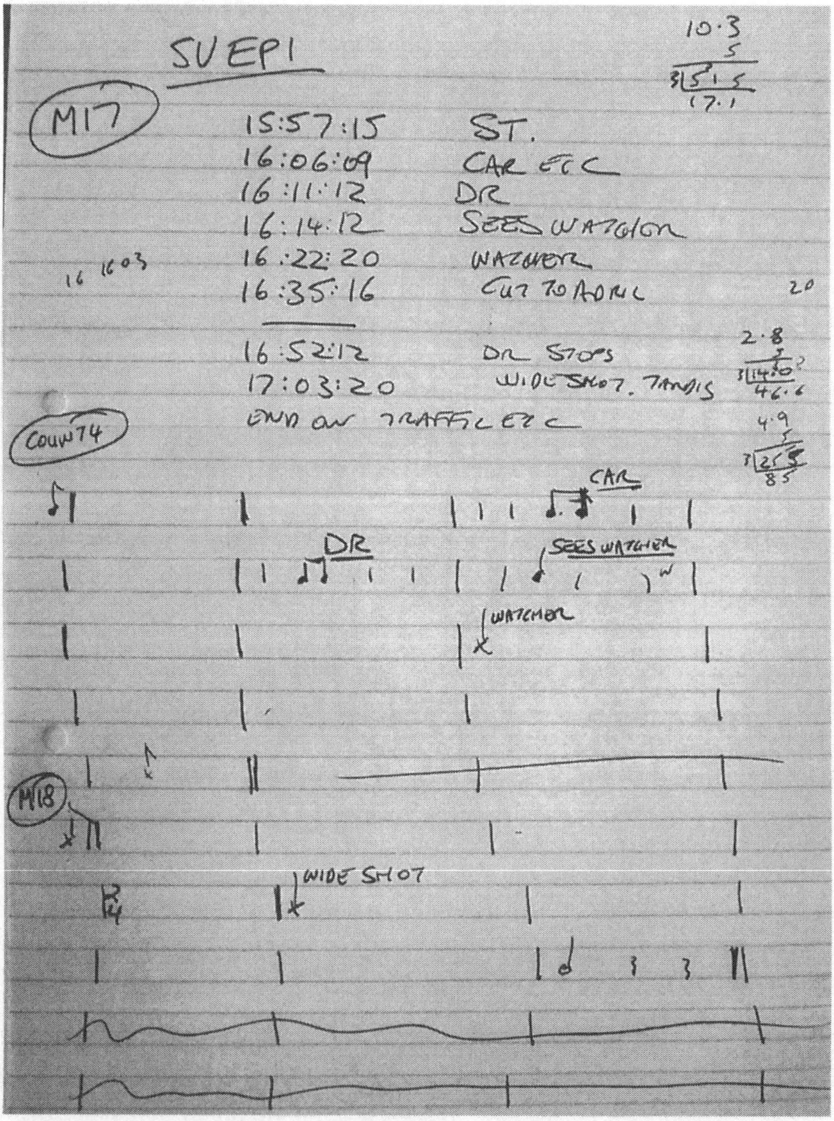

Figure 6.3. Guides for the playing-in of cues 17 and 18 from Paddy Kingsland's score for *Doctor Who*'s "Logopolis." Photograph by the author.

album. Kingsland kept his hand in the commercial game in other ways as well. In 1972 he released an arrangement for synthesizer of the recent Beatles hit "Get Back" through EMI as part of a deal with Abbey Road. While working with EMI he met Richard DaSilva in the Easy Listening Department, and they worked on some ideas for other arrangements, such as an "easy" version of the popular hit "Killing Me Softly." While this never resulted in anything, Kingsland never lost the desire to work in the more commercial side of music, and in 1980 he left the Workshop to set up an electronic music studio of his own. Unlike with Brian Hodgson's earlier attempt to do the same, by the early 1980s, technology had changed to the extent that he didn't have to design, build, or modify his own equipment—he could simply purchase them off the shelf, reducing the huge capital investment Hodgson had faced. Kingsland recalls:

I had always done freelance projects for EMI, Amphonic music etc, with permission from the BBC, but they couldn't allow me to do commercials because that was seen as working for the opposition, i.e., ITV, and I wanted to get into that area (foolishly, in hindsight), also films if possible. I enjoyed my time at the workshop and I don't think there was actual bad feeling between Desmond and Brian about my leaving, even though they knew I might be taking some work with me.

Figure 6.4. Paddy Kingsland. Copyright © BBC.

For the first two years after he left, he continued to write music for *Doctor Who*, providing his fledgling studio with a regular commission and getting his independent career off to a solid start.[29]

The Living Planet (TV, 1982–1983): Parker

When Kingsland left the Workshop, Elizabeth Parker was able to rise in the ranks. She had arrived at the Workshop in 1977, and after an initial trial period she was so highly regarded that she took over from Richard Yeoman-Clark the huge job of providing special sound for the third and fourth series of the Workshop's second biggest special sound commission, *Blake's Seven*. The composer recalls first hearing about the studio when she was doing a postgraduate degree in electronic music at the University of East Anglia in Norwich: "I thought 'Oh God, they sound fantastic, I'd really like to go there!' I joined the BBC as a studio manager after leaving university and then got a [three-month] attachment to the Workshop, which was the way to do it at that time." Her postgraduate work had come about when Parker was offered a scholarship to study at the new electroacoustic studio at Norwich, run by ex-Decca employee Trygg Tryggvason, and Workshop veteran and EMS founder Tristram Cary. Her conflicts with Cary while there working with the cumbersome EMS Synthi 100 highlight an important division between the newer and older generations of electronic music composers: the younger composers were encouraged to think spontaneously and were comfortable with technology that allows such spontaneity. "I'm not sure I got on terribly well with Tristram Cary....he was telling us how to make music...and I was thinking 'This isn't music! This isn't what I want to do!' I always had this idea that I could make electronic music sound more musical."[30]

One of her first jobs while on attachment was to realize the special sound for the 1978 *Doctor Who* story "The Stones of Blood," as series regular Dick Mills was on vacation. For this she experimented with traditional tape manipulation, slowing down and speeding up, as well as taking advantage of the Workshop's new Eventide Harmonizer. When Yeoman-Clark left the studio in November 1978, Parker took over his *Blake's Seven* duties. There was an underlying feeling at the Workshop that special sound work didn't require as much creativity, and it was therefore traditionally given to new composers or those, such as Mills or Yeoman-Clark, whose background was in engineering rather than music. In addition, Parker remembers,

There was an enormous rivalry between *Blake's Seven* and *Doctor Who*. I suppose in the Radiophonic Workshop there was a bit of rivalry between Dick and I, but it was a friendly rivalry. I always reckoned that *Blake's Seven* was treated as the underdog to *Doctor Who*. But it really was all good fun. Sometimes Dick would help me out, if I went and asked how he would set about doing something, and so I learned a lot.

However, Kingsland's departure in 1981, and his replacement in 1982 by Jonathan Gibbs, opened up key new commissions of a more "musical" nature, and that same year she was selected for the program that more than any other would define her tenure at the Workshop. David Attenborough's Emmy-winning twelve-part nature series, *The Living Planet*, was the first "prestige" nature series to be scored by the Workshop, and the process for Parker's selection was arduous, although she downplayed her own selection, once stating that commissions were given to the first person Briscoe saw in the morning![31] As postproduction began on the series, production coordinator Charles Dixon approached Brian Hodgson, who recommended Parker for the job. Dixon left her a videotape of fifteen minutes of rough-cut scenes from the series as an "audition." Parker wrote a preliminary version of the signature tune and scored the eclectic mix of scenes given to her. After visiting Parker at the Workshop for a playback, Dixon took her efforts back to the BBC's Bristol Natural History Unit, where the program was being edited, and played it for the production committee, including Attenborough and executive producer Richard Brock (with whom Parker collaborated for many years after the success of *The Living Planet*). She remembers,

> When I went down to Bristol to hear whether I had got the commission or not, I was ushered into a great room. There were innumerable grey suits and, truly, about 3 females apart from myself.... Anyway, David Attenborough got up after my 15 minute clip had been played and said, and I do quote because I remember the words so well, "Well, I don't know about anyone else but..." that was how he began and then he went on to say he definitely thought I was the right person to write the score.

Since many of the synthesizers were "assigned" to specific studios, it was a challenge to Parker as the "new girl" to lay her hands on any of the newest equipment. For example, the Jupiter 4, which Paddy Kingsland had used so effectively before his departure, was installed in Peter Howell's studio, as was the Yamaha CS80. And although the new expensive Fairlight Computer Musical Instrument (CMI) was on wheels and could be moved, it spent most of its time shuffled between Roger Limb and Peter Howell's studios. But when Parker began work on the series proper in 1982, the Workshop acquired a new synthesizer that offered a similar sampling capability to the Fairlight CMI, the PPG Wave 2.2. Although a notoriously difficult instrument to use, with frustratingly frequent crashes and a diabolically counterintuitive interface, it quickly became Parker's signature tool, enabling her to define her distinctive "organic" sound much more easily than if she had had to depend on traditional synthesizers.[32] Her approach for the series was to try to use natural sounds, via the PPG's sampling ability, to evoke the spirit of the animals depicted in the series, a blending of old-fashioned *musique concrète* and conventional harmonies. The sounds that emerged then were not simply samples of animal noises, but a sonic representation and complement to the visual image. This avant-garde approach to scoring what had traditionally been a very musically conservative genre, the nature film, gave some members of the executive committee pause. She was intending to create a very different atmosphere than that created by another popular nature series of the day, *Life on Earth*, with its large, bombastic orchestral score by Edward Williams. At one point Attenborough himself came to the Workshop to interview Parker, essentially checking up on her. She played an excerpt from an episode she was scoring, and he left satisfied that she was on to something exciting. In fact, the most disappointing musical element of the program for Parker remained the signature tune, which she had written without the PPG, primarily using the Yamaha SY2 (for the opening fanfare) and the newly acquired EMS vocoder. Indeed, it lacks the rich, natural quality that defines her incidental music for the series, but it does grab the attention of the viewer with its overtly electronic sound.

Parker worked largely alone, without much contact with the foley crew, who were trying to realistically reproduce the actual sounds of the animals. Largely because of this, Parker attended all the dubbing sessions in Bristol with the director, making sure her music was effectively integrated with the careful foley work. This didn't concern Parker too much, because "having been very sound-based, I had a pretty good idea of what they would be laying, referring natural sounds so it was not difficult to try and make sure the music worked with those foley bits." One challenge she faced, though, was the age-old problem of synchronization. As all composers at the Workshop had to do at the time, she was forced to laboriously work out each cue using a multitrack player with a click track on track 8 and a special "sync blip" track on 7. "I would just run and rerun the tape, adding extra sync points. It sounds excruciatingly hard but I got very quick at it." Indeed, when one hears how carefully Parker's music lines up with individual actions on screen, it is impossible not to admire the level of dedication such precise timings would have required. Video example 6.2, ⬤ showing a battle between a black widow spider and a scorpion, uses altered samples, not to re-create the sound of the animals but to suggest aspects of their character. The score was ultimately extremely well received, and an LP of Parker's music from the series was released in 1984.

Jonathan Gibbs and the Digital Revolution

It wasn't until Jonathan Gibbs's arrival on permanent appointment in 1983 that the problem of synchronization would be solved once and for all. He served his three-month attachment in 1982 as an extension of his current job in Features, producing the music for Michael Mason's *Tales from the South China Seas* almost entirely on the Fairlight CMI. For this, he sampled Indonesian gamelan music recorded in the Indonesian Embassy basement, pausing between takes to allow office workers to use the photocopier, which was situated right next to the ensemble! Gibbs loved the instrument, especially the quality of the samples it produced:

> The Fairlight had a built-in sequencer. It was a programming language. You literally typed in the notes: it was one up from punched cards, but not much. It was best for sharp, quick attacks, like glass breaking, which is how [Kate] Bush uses it in her song "Babooshka," but not so great at held-out.

Peter Howell noticed the same thing in his work on *Doctor Who*, having scored the story "Kinda" in the months before the Fairlight CMI's arrival. Without the benefit of the sampler, he recorded the sound of his finger moving around the rim of wineglasses, manipulating the tape on multiple tracks and adjusting the pitch through different speeds the old-fashioned way. When it came time to score that story's sequel, "Snakedance" (1983), the Fairlight had arrived and the whole process was much easier: "There were a lot of mirror themes in that story; much of the mood for that came from manipulating stuff digitally on the Fairlight."[33] Gibbs also took advantage of its ability to manipulate scales beyond basic equal temperament:

> They put it in because they could, because it was a really obscure feature, like on page 12.... I tried to research the indigenous music for *Tales of the South China Seas*, and established that the main scales are five-note and seven-note intervals.... For the purposes of experimenting you couldn't set individual differences between notes, but you could say, "OK, I want a five-note scale..."

Since Hodgson had implemented his budget in the late 1970s, all six studios had been refurbished, and they were now cycling through a constant progression of updating. Much of this was also due to the prestige the studio had acquired in the last few years; finally this department was respected and revered within the BBC as providing a completely unique service. This helped when the Workshop wanted something outside its traditional budget, such as the Fairlight. Gibbs, who had a knack for the business side of operations, discovered that within Radio the Workshop was seen very much as the jewel in the crown:

> And the fact is, comparatively, the kind of money we needed to do
> things, within television terms was nothing, absolutely nothing. It was
> possible for us to say, "Look, we really need some new synthesizers" or
> whatever. In television budget terms that could be the scraps under the
> table and out of that you would probably have the biggest collection of
> DX7s in the country.

Another helpful factor was a report prepared by Workshop organizer Brian Hodgson on the future of the studio. Called "Radiophonic Workshop: The Next Ten Years," it laid out his ambitious plans, including the purchase of new twenty-four-track recorders and state-of-the-art mixing desks and digital synthesizers for each studio at the rate of one a year.[34] He also indicated a need for more treatment devices and suggested refurbishing the old, largely unused Delaware synthesizer as a portable effects trolley. Finally, he insisted that a solution be found for the frustratingly small work spaces in Studios C, E, and H, suggesting that if nothing practical could be done the entire Workshop should be relocated. In total, he requested a more expansive equipment budget of between £190,000 and £210,000 for the next several years, with the budget decreasing after that to around £95,000 per year until 1993.[35]

As Gibbs mentioned, this new budget situation meant that the Workshop now had the money to acquire the latest technology, so that when the first digital synthesizer, the Yamaha DX7, arrived in 1983, the BBC purchased one for each studio. This shift from analog to digital happened at the same time as the arrival of MIDI (Musical Instrument Digital Interface), the standardized format for the integration of digital electronic musical instruments. For the Workshop's composers, these two developments were seen as major advances, and continued the trajectory electronic musical instruments had been traveling along since the 1970s toward greater ease of use and affordability. The DX7 was based on the principle of Frequency Modulation (FM), developed and patented by John Chowning of the Center for Computer Research in Music and Acoustics at Stanford University in 1973, and offered a cheap and powerful new method of tone generation that makes possible the synthesis of complex tones (containing both harmonic and inharmonic partials) with only two sine oscillators.[36] Like the Fairlight before it, the DX7 had some serious limitations, as Howell noted: "It [FM synthesis] does some things absolutely well, and is dire with others. With plucked sounds, bell sounds, all those sorts of sounds, but the staple diet, that people assumed, was instant glue, the square wavey string sound was awful, absolutely terrible, it was awful."

For Gibbs, however, both MIDI and FM synthesis represented a huge leap forward. The relative affordability of the technology, and its reliability, led to the purchase in 1984 of the Yamaha TX816, a rack-mounted system containing eight DX7 modules, controlled by MIDI. With it, one could overcome some of the coldness, particularly the kinds of problems with held-out notes. Using all eight channels, each making a nearly identical sound but each slightly altered, you could get a much richer timbre, for strings in particular, something Gibbs took full advantage of in his 1984 score for the *Doctor Who* episode "The Mark of the Rani": "You could still have kind of soft wafty stringy sounds, but they've got the precision and bite of FM synthesis. With 'Rani,' it was much more the pure harmonic structures. There's a bit in that straight out of Shostakovich 15, which I must have just been listening to, which was rather embarrassing."

The score itself benefited from a project he and Workshop engineer Ray White had been working on since Gibbs's arrival, a solution to the perennial problem of sound-picture synchronization. The solution, called Syncwriter, was the Workshop's greatest engineering triumph since Dave Young designed the Crystal Palace and Glowpot mixing desk in the 1960s. White constructed the hardware out of a BBC Micro computer, and Gibbs developed the software, which helped composers synchronize music to a moving picture by allowing them to insert cue points at any point along a moving ruler locked to a time-coded image. In his explanation of the device for an IBC award, Gibbs summarized its operation:

> Instead of laborious calculations to work out a click track for a music
> cue, the composer defines the synchronization points that are the
> skeleton of the piece, and then uses Syncwriter to construct a framework
> of bars and beats to fit those points. This framework is then displayed,
> and a cursor moves through the display to conduct the performance. The
> whole device is driven by SMPTE Timecode.[37]

For "The Mark of the Rani," Gibbs was able to really put the program to the test, creating a score that moves in time much more freely than those Kingsland had complained about only a few years earlier. Traditionally, with the kind of click tracks composers were forced to use to help synchronize their scores, music had a tendency to follow metrically the beat of the click, resulting in less rhythmically interesting scores. Now, composers had the image of the Syncwriter ruler to guide them rather than an audible click, and they were much less inclined to be guided by that than by the image. Gibbs described the problem he faced on "The Mark of the Rani" when trying to get image and sound lined up in a fluid, organic way. In the scene he relates, the Doctor fights with his enemy, the Master, before rolling away in a mine car: "All those points have got to be 'hit' with the music. And they are all happening at whatever is right on the picture, not what's going to be right for 4/4."[38] By laying a timecode onto track 16 of the sixteen-track recorder, Syncwriter could read the timecode and offer a display that "conducts" the music. One of the most effective things about the program was that for the first time, you could anticipate an upcoming cue by seeing the moving curser get closer and closer to it, as Gibbs notes: "You've got anticipation—you can see the thing coming up and put expression in. It does encourage much more expressive writing and expressive playing."[39] Video example 6.3 demonstrates how Gibbs ultimately realized this scene with Syncwriter.

Gibbs's schedule for "The Mark of the Rani" was unusually tight, even given the ridiculous time frame composers were used to working against in *Doctor Who*, and ultimately precipitated the Workshop's ending its relationship with this particular series, at least as far as the music was concerned. Originally, Brian Hodgson had tried to give the Workshop a bit of breathing room by hiring his music partner John Lewis to score "Rani." When Hodgson had left the Workshop in the early 1970s, Lewis had been one of the founding members of Hodgson's independent studio Electrophon. They had later collaborated successfully on two albums under the name Wavemaker, so Lewis had an established reputation with the Workshop's composers. Unfortunately, he was suffering from AIDS-related illnesses during the production, and he completed only the first episode before falling gravely ill; he died shortly thereafter. The disclosure of the nature of Lewis's illness, and the attending publicity, caused a perhaps not entirely surprising negative reaction among the production crew. This reaction stemmed from a combination of homophobia and an understandable ignorance about AIDS, as it was still mostly misunderstood in Thatcher's Britain (and Reagan's America) in 1984. AIDS remained a topic too politically sensitive to be openly discussed in a public forum by a conservative government, and most people had very little idea what the symptoms were or how the disease was transmitted. Hodgson remembers the reaction clearly:

John was very, very ill at that point. It was a terrible thing, because John died, and the next thing, I had to tell the director. Sarah Hellings [the director] was on the phone to me saying I'd endangered the life of her children and her because John had died of AIDS. It was a really bad time. Unfortunately the weekend before John died there'd been an article in the *Sun* newspaper which had given the symptoms of AIDS which were virtually the same as the common cold, and so everyone had thought they'd got it. There was utter panic, and I had newspapers ringing up, and John Dutot, head of resources said "I think you should go off on tour, and go look at all the studio centers throughout Europe, and we'll pay for that, and you'll be out of the way," but it was all over in three days, it all blew over in three days.

Jonathan Gibbs was brought in on incredibly short notice to replace Lewis, and despite the success of his score, the pressures of always working under the gun on the program led to a discontinuation of the musical relationship with *Doctor Who* when it returned after an eighteen-month hiatus in 1986. Although the Workshop would continue to supply special sound for the program, Hodgson felt there was little choice: "It was a very heavy workload. I was getting uptight that we would start a series off with loads of time and end up doing sixteen minutes of music in three days. I just felt that the quality was going. Also, I think that John Nathan-Turner thought that the show was getting a 'sound' and he wanted to break it up with freelance musicians."[40]

Given his facility with both finances and the nuts and bolts of the Workshop's operation, it wasn't surprising that when Desmond Briscoe retired in 1983 and Brian Hodgson assumed his position as director, Gibbs was tapped to replace Hodgson as organizer, beginning in January 1984. Hodgson remembers:

Jonathan hadn't been with us very long when Desmond left and I took over. And I went to Dutot and said, "Look, there's no one in the Workshop I want as my assistant except Jonathan Gibbs, 'cause I think this guy's got his head screwed on." And so we promoted Jonathan from new boy to deputy head, which caused a few shocked responses within the Workshop, but once he settled in they really appreciated him.

Gibbs's love of new digital technology in particular helped guide the Workshop through the rest of the 1980s in exciting directions, especially as the studio sought to explore the possibilities MIDI offered and the digital sequencing ability it allowed. The first experiment was with the rather frustrating Yamaha QX1 sequencer, a freestanding piece of equipment with a nontraditional key-entry system connected to equipment through a MIDI connection, and a 5.25-inch floppy disk drive to record and edit sequences. While it was a step in the right direction, Hodgson remembers how counterintuitive the device was: "The QX1 was slow and difficult to use and had only a tiny LCD display for editing the music. So the search was on for a better system, possibly computer-based.... We were achieving very sophisticated music with the hardware so whatever new gear we invested in had to take us forward."[41]

The Macintosh

While the search continued, the Workshop hired its final permanent member, Richard Attree, in 1985. A year before, Hodgson had decided that since electronic music composition was no longer exclusively in the hands of institutions like the BBC, it was in the studio's best interests to broaden the search for potential Workshop composers by advertising outside the BBC for the first time. This would also serve to potentially diversify the studio's output, and with a background in music from City University in London, Attree had a unique history, having previously written both concert and media music. He brought the same kind of youthful "pop" energy into the studio that Paddy Kingsland's arrival had fifteen years earlier, but as the most recent hire, he was put in the smallest studio, H. The decision was also made at this time to limit future hires to short-term contracts rather than hire permanent appointments.[42]

That same year, Desmond Briscoe and Brian Hodgson traveled to Los Angeles to investigate up-and-coming technology. There they met Adrian Freed, who showed them the new Macintosh computers. These computers were to have a profound effect on the operations of the studio. Within a few years, most of the old analog keyboards were gone, replaced by a single keyboard driving rack-mounted synthesizers and treatment devices, all connected through MIDI into Macs. Therefore, before moving past this point, I'd like to stop and review the contents of the old, "clunky" studio just before the Mac brought about such drastic changes. Just after Attree's hire, Gibbs wrote an essay detailing the floor and equipment layout of the studio in late 1985, offering a rare chance to peek in at a specific moment in the Workshop's history.[43]

Attree's small, slightly dilapidated studio contained the Yamaha TX816 (the rack-mounted system containing eight DX7 modules) and a DX7 keyboard, coupled with a Yamaha QX1 eight-track sequencer and RX11 Drum Machine. For Attree it was a memorable collection of aging equipment: "I spent my first year or two in Studio H with fairly basic gear and a desk that crackled and had channels and buttons that only worked intermittently." Next to this were the engineers Ray White and Ray Riley (known as "the Two Rays"), and next the film area, in Studio F, for viewing 16mm film on two Steenbeck editing machines and an in-house transfer machine, which enabled composers to check synchronization. Next to this, in Studio E, was Roger Limb, whose studio contained an ARP Odyssey, a DX7, and an Elka Synthex (an instrument he favored for its string sound). The Fairlight CMI could often be found in Limb's studio, but as it was on wheels, it could move around. Also, by 1985, it was slowly being superseded by superior equipment. Across from Limb's studio was Studio A, which belonged to Elizabeth Parker. As well as the DX7, her studio contained a PPG Wave 2.3 with a Waveterm computer, and various treatment devices, including a Roland vocoder. Next to this was Studio L (for Large), an acoustic recording space, and beside this was Studio B, Peter Howell's area. Besides a DX7, he had an Elka Synthex, a TX816, a QX1, an Eventide Harmonizer, and one of the Workshop's Syncwriters. Studio C, with its distinctive red-and-cream-colored acoustic boxes, housed Malcolm Clarke. (The front door of his studio contained a cardboard "larke" next to the C so that any visitor knew immediately whose space they were entering.) It housed a DX1 synthesizer (an early version of the DX range, with a piano-weighted keyboard) and an Emulator II, an effective if not overly versatile sampling device. These two synthesizers were also coupled with the QX1, a TX816, and a Syncwriter. Finally, Dick Mills was located in Studio D, which was laid out specifically for special sound work. It contained three different types of reverb (Lexicon, Roland Spring, and AKG plate), a small Akai sampling machine, and Roland 100M, DX7, and Oscar Mono synthesizers, and, most interestingly, the British-designed Wasp Deluxe, another early digital synthesizer.

This description captures the state of the Workshop immediately before the arrival of the Macintosh computer, which completely changed the operation of all the studios. That the computers had such an impact on operations didn't pass unnoticed by the Workshop's composers, who realized how precarious their position was. Hodgson in particular, as head, had to work hard to fight the impression that the studio was increasingly irrelevant in an environment where any independent composer could set up a MIDI studio relatively cheaply with a few pieces of equipment and a Macintosh: "As we moved on, we were using sequencers rather than tape recorders, and the minute we saw the Macs, that was it. The moment the Mac came out it transformed the whole technology."

The staff had noticed advertisements for sequencing programs for the Mac in *Computer Music Journal*, in particular Southworth's Total Music and Performer. Hodgson attempted to contact Apple directly to explore the possibility of installing a system, but "they were singularly unhelpful."[44] A year later, he contacted someone with experience using the programs and borrowed a Macintosh to try them out for himself, and he found that Total Music was really too slow for the Workshop's needs. Jonathan Gibbs was sent to a computer music conference shortly after this to investigate their options. As Hodgson remembers, "Jonathan was not convinced, but after he'd been to the conference, and realized that most of the software that worked well and was available *now* was for the Macintosh, he came back and said that he thought we should go for the Mac."⁴⁵ The studio initially purchased thirteen Macs: seven Mac IIs, each with 4MB RAM and 40MB hard drives, and six Macintosh Pluses, fairly quickly replaced by Mac SE/30s, running Mark of the Unicorn's Composer as well as Professional Performer for their sequencing, but still largely relying on Gibbs's Syncwriter. Composer was eventually replaced by Vision, and StudioVision with Digidesign's Sound Tools.

Peter Howell led the way, using the Mac to compose music for a television adaptation of the children's novel *Children of the Green Knowe* in December 1986. Shortly after this, Howell briefly left the Workshop for a three-month attachment with another department, but when he returned he brought with him an exciting new idea. Rethinking the layout of the Workshop's studios, he reasoned that with the new central position of the computer in each studio, there was no longer any need for the chaotic array of instruments, mixers, and tape recorders; instead, the studio could be configured around this one item, attached to one slave synthesizer keyboard and a series of digital Yamaha DMP7 mixers. Malcolm Clarke explains:

> One of the major decisions we made soon after MIDI came in was that really one needed a central keyboard—a proper weighted keyboard—that you could actually learn the touch of, which then controlled all the other devices in studio. It was pointless having lots of synthesizers with their own keyboards because they are expensive. Not only that, but you tend to find that on the lower-range synths the keyboard is only perhaps five octaves.⁴⁶

By 1988, with the support of Hodgson, Howell was able to begin his project, with a budget of £60,000 for each studio, beginning with his and Liz Parker's studios. He determined that the new configuration should be built around a horseshoe shape, with the middle area containing in a position of prominence the computer and keyboard, with other components arranged to the right and left. Howell recalls:

> Up until the end of 1987, most of our studios had consisted of a room dominated by a comparatively large mixing console, speakers arranged in the time-honored fashion, video monitors in-between and to one side

the master keyboard, rack-mounting synthesizer and computer. This last is used primarily for recording MIDI information, but also for such diverse tasks as word-processing and sound editing.[47]

With the new configuration came new software needs to control the streamlined function of the studio. Three kinds of custom software were created through a program called Hypercard. The first controlled the routing of analog audio, enabling the establishment of a set of connections between the devices on the matrix—the digital equivalent of a patch bay, or the pin system on the old EMS equipment. These sets of connections, however, could be saved and recovered when needed. The second program stored all the "static" information required to re-create a piece of sequenced music, such as the sounds for the synthesizers, initial mixer settings, settings for effects devices, and the analog connections between the devices. The third controlled the flow of MIDI information through the computer. Development Coordinator Mark Wilson, who wrote all this software, also wrote an umbrella application called CueCard to sync all the equipment; CueCard used HyperCard to make accessing all the other software easier. When Wilson left to develop Mac software through the BBC's Multimedia Corporation, he was replaced by Tony Morson, who shifted Wilson's programs from HyperCard to C++ and the Mac operating system.[48] Richard G. Elen described the new design of the studio in a publicity document released in 1991:

> In front of the composer on the upper level are the control systems: the "master" DMP-7s to the right; the Roland S-550 monitor to the left. And in the center, in pride of place, controlling it all, an Apple color monitor, keyboard and mouse. The Macintosh IIfx itself is in a cupboard under the work surface.... An interesting feature of the design is that virtually nothing is installed in the room itself—it's all in the circular table.[49]

By 1991, even the Syncwriter had been replaced by the central computer. This radical redesign of the Workshop achieved a notable amount of publicity, and Howell commented at the time that "there is now enormous interest elsewhere in the BBC and at Apple, about the way we have used the Macintosh II as the front-end for sophisticated music studio equipment."[50] The Workshop was now Europe's most advanced MIDI environment and, according to an internal publicity document, was "at the forefront of the rapidly developing technology. It attracts professional visitors from all over the world including Manufacturing, Research, Educational and Broadcasting organizations."[51]

Figure 6.5. Liz Parker at work in the new "horseshoe" workspaces. Copyright © BBC.

The End of the Workshop

All of this optimism and excitement, however, was hiding a disastrous reality. Although (and because) the studio was at the cutting edge of technology, it was operating at a financial loss, and producers had started to discover they could get the kind of results they wanted from cheaper independent studios outside the BBC. Hodgson had read the writing on the wall much earlier, however. Ten years before this, as the Macs were first introduced, he knew big changes were in store. "In a way that was the beginning of the end, people were seeing what we were doing, and as the computers got more sophisticated and cheaper, it was laying the seeds of its own destruction." This sentiment—that the Workshop and the huge amount of influence it exerted over other studios, amateur and professional alike, by the end of the 1980s was ironically to blame for its ultimate downfall—is echoed by Howell: "What was the final demise, of the Workshop, come 1990-ish, 1992, was when the pressure on the outside equaled the pressure on the inside. You could go down the High Street and buy things, and the reason you *could* buy things is because of the Workshop." This fear is detectable as early as June 1986 in a Workshop Situation Report, when Hodgson writes,

As prices fall and complex operations become possible on cheaper equipment, we face increasing competition from home studios and, at the other end of the spectrum, the emergence of "tax loss" electronic studios with "state of the art" technology are already making us look rather homely and tatty. It is more important that we retain our own confidence and buy only that which will enable us to do the job more efficiently and imaginatively, while maintaining the confidence of our customers, who may well be drawn to more exotic temptations outside. This is a balancing act and is acknowledged as such. Ultimately, the Workshop will stand and fall on the level of creative service it provides, rather than possession of the latest gadget or the lower cost of an ineffective and unprofessional service.[52]

Part of the problem was the very accessibility of the interface of the Mac: the Workshop composers (as well as outside musicians interested in electronic music) found the software much easier to use than dedicated hardware. It is also possible that electronic music as accompaniment for non–science fiction projects just went out of fashion. Perhaps the Workshop had been overexposed in the first years of the decade. Regardless of the reasons, commissions for television drama dropped from nineteen in 1983–84 to ten in 1984–85 before bottoming out at three in 1985–86, the last years for which figures are public.[53]

This situation was only made worse in the fall of 1991, when John Birt, the BBC's deputy director general, introduced the policy of Producer Choice, a "new way of managing resources" that essentially required each department to be self-sustaining.[54] Under Producer Choice, program producers had the right to obtain services either within the BBC or outside, where resources were potentially cheaper. According to a study of this new policy, "when the money was denied to any internal resource because of the outcome of these negotiations, the internal resource would fail to break even on its targets or resource utilization; if the situation could not be corrected within a year, plant closures and redundancies would follow."[55]

For the Radiophonic Workshop, this meant that while the studio was limited to accepting work from within the BBC, commissioning producers were allowed, and indeed encouraged, to look elsewhere for less costly options. The problem was underestimated in a document from the late 1980s, written as a sequel to the 1982 report "Radiophonic Workshop—The Next Ten Years." In this second report, entitled "Radiophonic Workshop—The Next Ten Minutes," the author (presumably Brian Hodgson) writes, "Freelance composers are becoming more organized and before long are likely to force up the relatively low level of fees paid, so demand seems likely to remain, at the worst, constant but probably to increase."[56] In an equally optimistic comparative costing analysis done in 1990 between the Workshop and several independent studios (including former Workshop employee Paddy Kingsland's studio), the Workshop was overly positive about its chances for survival in a free-market environment.[57] It reported that the Workshop was still an economical choice for program makers, and it offered three additional incentives: First, unlike most studios, the Workshop could also offer other services, such as special sound. Second, by using the Workshop, productions remove music copyright complications when attempting to sell the program abroad. Third, the new arm, BBC Music, could be used in conjunction with the Workshop to help market the final product.

While the Workshop was in fact able to stay above water for a while, the policy of Producer Choice more than anything else led to its slow, drawn-out gutting over the first half of the 1990s, and although the studio didn't officially close its doors until 1998, it was for all intents and purposes dead by 1996, the year Brian Hodgson left. The effect Producer Choice had over all segments of the BBC was controversial, to say the least. This opinion appeared in the *Guardian* on February 8, 1997: "Kenith Trodd who worked closely with Dennis Potter...said the BBC drama department is a 'total mess.'...decisions are being taken by 'uncreative people whose talent is keeping a shaky grip on stationery supplies.'"[58] Michael Attwell, a Channel 4 commissioning executive at the time, observed that "what strikes all outsiders is the BBC's confusion of objectives and responsibilities, all hallmarks of a poor management, molded by a culture which elevated program makers. This remains untouched by Birtist programs of Producer Choice, efficiency drives and new layers of accountants."[59]

At the Workshop, Hodgson knew that he couldn't offer producers the least expensive service, so he spent the first half of the 1990s promoting the studio's offerings as reliable, professional, and of a higher quality than the cheaper options on the market. He was not naive, though, and understood that under Producer Choice, the temptation would be strong for producers to take the least expensive option. When asked about the Workshop's future in 1992, he was realistic:

No one is safe. Things that you are fairly sure about one day may change the next. I think we'll survive. Maybe not in our current form, but we will survive as long as professionalism is still valued. If we go down the "lets do it the cheapest way we can" route, we will *not* survive. We will probably aim for the middle of the market, charging around 300 to 400 a minute for incidental music. That sounds like a lot of money, but that's what it costs outside as well. People know that they will get a good product from the Workshop. As long as people want quality, we will survive.[60]

One strategy the Workshop had for survival in a post–Producer Choice world was to diversify their offerings. The most prominent of these was to operate a noise-reduction service for CD remastering based on Sonic Solution's NoNoise Workstation, with the majority of the work done by Dick Mills. The NoNoise software removed clicks, pops, hums, and crackle from archive material, allowing Mills to create a cleaned-up recording. While relatively successful, this entrepreneurial enterprise was still not enough to keep the wolf at bay. Many of the things that made the Workshop such an exceptional place in the years since Hodgson had been able to implement a real budget ultimately worked against the studio as well. The final composer to remain at the Workshop was Elizabeth Parker, and she remembers how the luxury of having an engineering department at her disposal if anything went wrong, and a seemingly unlimited budget for new equipment, gradually degenerated into a situation where it was impossible to update anything: "So by the time the Workshop actually closed we had a lot of very old gear and we were definitely past our sell-by date. And the worst thing was that I was there right until the very end, and it was horrendous, it was horrible."[61]

Richard Attree also recalls the studio's last few years as particularly disturbing:

> Basically out of my eleven years, the first five or so (till maybe 1991-ish) the morale was fine and then it started to slide downhill as the Workshop was shrinking. The last year or so was very depressing. We were all basically waiting for the inevitable closure. One day about a week before Christmas the marketing lady from RPR (Radio Production Resources) came round to each studio and announced that we were being laid off/ made redundant. There was no choice in the matter.... In the end it came down to simple economics, and we just weren't "cost effective" under the Producer Choice system.

By the middle of the decade, commissions had by this time essentially dried up: from 133 in 1992, to 101 in 1993, to 72 in 1994, to half that by 1995–96, and only 8 in 1997. Peter Howell and Elizabeth Parker's music for Michael Palin's travel series *Full Circle* was the final big project completed there. The last record in the Radiophonic Workshop's archive, project number 11736, was Parker's incidental music for *Assignment*, entered on May 8, 1997.

While even toward the end, composers were writing exciting, original, and award-winning music, such as Peter Howell's setting of the book of Revelation, and Richard Attree's *Peace on Earth*, the influence of the Workshop in its final years was primarily to be felt in the excitement for electronic music it inspired in others. With a near-closed-door policy to outside composers built into the very mandate of the studio since its opening in 1958, it was very difficult to reach out and allow new, independent voices to contribute to the future of the studio. According to Howell,

We were treated as the place and the people who offered some sort of guidance. So that is the common ingredient throughout. Right through the 1970s and '80s, people were still looking to us to, if you like, be a test bed for things. I think exactly this is the same thing as the early days. We came out with innovative things that surprised people. Now, when you got to the 1970s and '80s, although in fact the element of surprise was harder to achieve, and only happened once in a while, I have to admit, it didn't alter the fact that we were still looked at as somewhere that was able to come to conclusions and show people what was possible with what was currently available. It isn't necessarily just the sounds, it's something else.

All of which makes a proposal written sometime in the late 1980s more heartbreaking and leaves the reader wondering what a Radiophonic Workshop of the future would have looked and sounded like if it been allowed to remain a working, productive place for the exploration of technology and music. Titled "The Step Beyond," it envisioned an exciting, vaguely magical place, written in a tone not unlike early press accounts of the studio, and reading it, one gets a real sense of the forward-thinking attitude that defined the studio for nearly four decades. The anonymous author imagines a relocated Workshop at Television Centre in White City:

Will a flat surface plasma display be our control surface, flanked by a musical keyboard, a vocal mouse and an Ascii keyboard? Will visual monitoring be hung or projected on the opposite wall? Will the sounds be generated on area mainframe computers and their manipulated performance data stored in another bank of the same machine ready for recorded "live" transmission? Or will the control surface house a dedicated computer in contact with the Network mainframe which calls up its contents as desired and routes the music straight to the studio handling the assembly of the final program? Indeed, will the result of a final mix even be a mix or just a set of data which mixes the contents of the Drama Computer with the outputs of the Radiophonic Computer and the Presentation Computer and routes it to the transmission device?[62]

216

We will never know what the Workshop would have evolved into, but the excitement and innovation the studio brought to the production of electronic music guides nearly every aspect of music making in the contemporary music industry. That it emerged out of Britain's peculiar position as "outsider" to the developments in academic electronic music as it evolved in France, Germany, Italy, Japan, and the United States renders its unique and influential contributions to the field of electronic music a fascinating counterpoint to these more publicized academic styles. Britain's "official" position on the subject was largely determined by one body, a crucial aspect of this project; it can be easy to forget that the BBC has served as a central cultural producer with near-monopolistic power for nearly seventy years, essentially controlling and distributing musical styles and techniques. The alternative history I have told of British music electronic music attempts to reconcile "highbrow" or "lowbrow" music and show how out of this collaborative art emerged a vibrant new sound medium: radiophonic sound. As the first studio in the world to make electronic music accessible to ordinary people, to show that electronic music didn't have to be scary (although it can be) or restricted to science fiction (although it is often at its best when it is), to make electronic music normal—ubiquitous, even—its legacy is alive every time you turn on the radio, walk onto a dance floor, watch the television, or go to the movies; it has indeed been "special sound."

Notes

Chapter 1

1. See Luigi Russolo, *Arte dei rumori*, trans. Barclay Brown, *The Art of Noises* (New York: Pendragon Press, 1986). See also Rodney J. Payton, "The Music of Futurism: Concerts and Polemics," *Musical Quarterly* 62, no. 1 (January 1976): 25–45, and Tristram Cary, introduction to *Dictionary of Musical Technology* (New York: Greenwood, 1992).

2. As Tim Taylor has shown, Henry has in many people's ears replaced Schaeffer himself as the primary figure behind the strength of *musique concrète*, primarily because Schaeffer stopped composing in the early 1960s, and also because Henry embraced the pop music world, thus directly influencing a larger number of people. Tim Taylor, *Strange Sounds: Music, Technology, and Culture* (New York: Routledge, 2001), 60.

3. Stockhausen quoted in Seppo Heikinheimo, *The Electronic Music of Karlheinz Stockhausen: Studies on the Esthetical and Formal Problems of Its First Phase*, trans. Brad Absetz (Helsinki: Suomen Musiikkitieteellinen, 1972), 14.

4. Hans Heinz Stuckenschmidt, "The Third Stage," in *Die Reihe* 1 (1955; English ed., Theodore Presser Co., 1958), 11.

5. Susan McClary, *Conventional Wisdom: The Content of Musical Form* (Berkeley: University of California Press, 2000), 136.

6. Paddy Scannell and David Cardiff, *A Social History of British Broadcasting*: Vol. 1, *1922–1939, Serving the Nation* (Oxford: Basil Blackwell, 1991), 194.

7. Asa Briggs, *The Golden Age of Wireless*, vol. 2 of *The History of Broadcasting in the United Kingdom* (Oxford: Oxford University Press, 1965), 27.

8. Humphrey Carpenter, *The Envy of the World: Fifty Years of the BBC Third Programme and Radio 3, 1946–1996* (London: Weidenfeld and Nicolson, 1996), 37.

9. "Points from the Post," *Radio Times*, May 17, 1962, 28.

10. R. D. Stanford, "Points from the Post," *Radio Times*, August 10, 1961, 59.

11. Martin Esslin, *Theatre of the Absurd*, 3rd ed. (New York: Penguin Books, 1980), 399.

12. Ibid.

13. This is by no means an exhaustive list of *Goon Show* effects. Such a project is beyond the scope of this book, but some examples include sped-up effects in the following episodes of series 5: "The Affair of the Lone Banana," "The China Sky," "The Sinking of Westminster," "The Phantom Headshaver," and "The Whistling Spy Enigma." Series 6 is filled with more elaborate effects, but most still involve manipulating the speed of either tape or gram. Highlights include the episodes "The Choking Horror" and "The House of Teeth."

14. This is referring, of course, to a standard deployment of the radio in film. Many examples could demonstrate exceptions that prove the rule, as both Lydia Goehr and Claudia Gorbman have shown with Stanley Kubrick's *Eyes Wide Shut*. Both *The Sopranos* and *Twin Peaks* also reveled in breaking the boundaries between diegetic and nondiegetic music: often diegetic music, at first seeming to emerge from a radio, is revealed to exist in a nondiegetic plane, or vice versa.

15. Michel Chion, *Audio-Vision: Sound on Screen*, trans. Claudia Gorbman (New York: Columbia University Press, 1994), 63.

16. Ibid., 224.

17. Colin Richardson, "Points from the Post," *Radio Times*, September 25, 1953, 27.

18. Donald McWhinnie, *The Art of Radio* (London: Faber and Faber, 1959), 51.

19. Louis MacNeice, "Portrait of a Would-Be Hero," *Radio Times*, November 7, 1952, 6.

20. Michael Hardwick, "More Radio Writers Than Ever Before and More Scope for Them," *Ariel* 3, no. 10 (1958): 14–15.

21. Hardwick, "Radio Writers," 14.

22. Rayner Heppenstall, "In the Steps of Laurence Sterne," *Radio Times*, January 18, 1952, 8.

23. Archie Campbell to Donald McWhinnie, Memo, n.d. but reply dated March 15, 1955, BBC Written Archives Centre (hereafter cited as WAC), Rcont 2—Cooper, Giles, Scriptwriter, file 2b, 1955–56.

24. Giles Cooper, *Mathry Beacon*, in *Giles Cooper: Six Plays for Radio* (Letchworth, Hertfordshire: BBC Books, 1966), 14.

25. "Electronic Music," *Score* (March 1955): n.p.

26. Douglas Cleverdon, Notes for Broadcast, n.d. WAC R97/34/1.

27. Ibid.

28. "Radiophony and Melodrama," *Radio Times*, July 7, 1955, 39.

29. This is true, if one doesn't count the "musical" effects used in *Journey into Space*, discussed above.

30. Tristram Cary, introduction to *Dictionary of Musical Technology* (New York: Greenwood, 1987), xv.

31. He did this by dividing his "new aesthetic" into seven main features: (1) Any sound became available for use as music using recording. (2) Using oscillators, quite new sounds would be available. (3) One was not limited to standard, fixed tuning. (4) By editing and changing speed and direction change, one could use only parts of sounds and

could combine sounds in unique ways. (5) Using "montage," an orchestra of any size could be created. (6) Elaborate cross-rhythms became possible outside real time. (7) Timbre could be altered using manipulation of sound.

32. Because of concerns that he would be seen as taking jobs from unemployed musicians, he was credited as "deviser of Special Effects" rather than composer.

33. Humphrey Searle, *Quadrille with a Raven: Memoirs by Humphrey Searle.* Available at www.musicweb.uk.net/searle/break.htm (accessed December 1, 2008).

34. Carpenter, *Envy of the World*, 159.

35. Esslin, *Theatre of the Absurd*, 406.

36. Ibid., 343.

37. Donald McWhinnie, "A Season of New Radio Plays," *Radio Times*, March 26, 1954, 8.

38. Clas Zilliacus, *Beckett and Broadcasting* (Abo, Finland: Abo Akademi, 1976), and Martin Esslin, "Samuel Beckett and the Art of Broadcasting," *Encounter* (September 1975): 38–46.

39. Donald McWhinnie, "Writing for Radio (I)," *Ariel* 2 (July 1957): 7.

40. McWhinnie, *Art of Radio*, 133.

41. Zilliacus, *Beckett*, 73.

42. McWhinnie, *Art of Radio*, 82.

43. Samuel Beckett, *All That Fall* (London: Faber and Faber, 1957), 26.

44. McWhinnie, *Art of Radio*, 146–47.

45. Desmond Briscoe and Roy Curtis-Bramwell, *The BBC Radiophonic Workshop: The First 25 Years* (London: BBC, 1983), 18.

46. Unless otherwise noted, all unfootnoted quotations are from my own interviews. See the bibliography for a complete list.

47. The term is, again, Chion's.

48. McWhinnie, *Art of Radio*, 37.

49. *Manchester Guardian,* January 15, 1957.

50. Philip Hope Wallace, *Time and Tide,* January 19, 1957.

51. Paul Ferris, *Observer,* January 20, 1957.

52. Harold Hobson, *Times* (London), January 20, 1957.

53. Giles Cooper, *The Disagreeable Oyster*, in *Giles Cooper: Six Plays for Radio.* (Letchworth, Hertfordshire: BBC Books, 1966).

54. Timothy Taylor, *Strange Sounds* (New York: Routledge, 2001).

55. Ibid., 89.

56. Briscoe, *BBC Radiophonic Workshop*, 19.

57. Mollie Greenhalgh to Barbara Bray, memo, August 31, 1956, WAC RCont 1—Cooper, Giles, Scriptwriter, file 2b, 1955–56.

58. Cooper to Bray, memo, August 25, 1956, WAC RCont 1—Cooper, Giles, Scriptwriter, file 2b, 1955–56.

59. Barbara Bray to Giles Cooper, December 19, 1956, WAC RCont 1—Cooper, Giles, Scriptwriter, file 2b, 1955–56.

60. Donald McWhinnie to M. F. C. Standing, memo, November 20, 1956, WAC RCont 1—Cooper, Giles, Scriptwriter, file 2b, 1955–56.

61. Frances Gray, "Giles Cooper: The Medium as Moralist," in *British Radio Drama*, ed. John Drakakis (Cambridge: Cambridge University Press, 1981): 140.

62. *Radio Times*, August 9, 1957, 5

63. *Radio Times*, March 15, 1957, 4.

64. Robert Robinson, *Sunday Times* (London), March 24, 1957.

65. Donald McWhinnie, "Private Dreams and Public Nightmares," *Radio Times*, October 4, 1957, 27.

66. Ibid., 27.

67. Donald McWhinnie, "A Radiophonic Poem (Third Programme, October 7, 1957)," WAC R97/7/1 Radiophonic Effects and Electronic Music (1956–63).

68. McWhinnie, *Art of Radio*.

69. Giles Wilson, "Daphne Oram, the unsung pioneer of techno," news.bbc.co.uk/2/hi/uk_news/2669735.stm(accessed December 1, 2008).

70. The Third Programme Listening Panel had been set up in the fall of 1954 to express the views of listeners. Members of the panel filled out questionnaires related to forthcoming broadcasts, and these were studied by the Audience Research Department and the results assembled into a report.

71. *Times* (London), October 8, 1957, 3.

Chapter 2

1. Alec Nesbitt, Report on *Musique Concrète* and Electronic Music, November 1956, WAC R97/7/1—Radiophonic Workshop General (1953–73, file 1).

2. The EEC was composed of Pip Porter (chairman), Dr. F. W. Alexander (senior superintendent engineer, External Broadcasting), D. Winget (superintendent engineer, Recording), Eckersley (assistant head in charge of program operations, Recording), and M. R. G. Garrard (organizer, Studio Operations).

3. Desmond Briscoe and Roy Curtis-Bramwell, *The BBC Radiophonic Workshop: The First 25 Years* (London: BBC, 1983), 27–28.

4. Timothy Eckersley to M. Garrard, memo concerning minutes of December 14, 1956, dated December 19, 1956, WAC R97/11/1 Radiophonic General (1953–73, file 1).

5. Briscoe, *Radiophonic Workshop*, 37.

6. Ibid., 3.

7. R.V.A. George to M. Garrard, memo, November 12, 1956, WAC R97/11/1.

8. A complete list of the revised committee members is as follows: Mr. E.W. S. Porter (assistant head, central program operations, Studios), chair; Dr. F. W. Alexander (senior superintendent engineer, External Broadcasting); Mr. D. Winget; Mr. T. H. Eckersley (assistant head in charge of program operations, Recording); Mr. M. R. G. Garrard (organizer, Studio Operations); Mr. L. Harvey (central services planning officer); Mr. F. O. Wade (head of light music programs, Sound); Mr. D. McWhinnie (assistant head of drama, Sound); Mr. G. R. S. Dixon (Schools Broadcasting); Mr. T. D. K Cleverdon (Features); and Mr. P. K. M. Dixon (Variety).

9. Douglas Cleverdon to multiple recipients, memo, February 13, 1957, WAC R53/483/2.

10. Douglas Cleverdon, telegram, May 2, 1957, WAC R97/11/1 Radiophonic General (1953–73, file 1).

11. Minutes of Radiophonic Effects Committee (REC), March 6, 1957, WAC R97/11/1.

12. Edward Pawley, *BBC Engineering 1922–1972* (London: BBC Publications, 1972), 198.

13. When he was informed of the new availability, George sent a memo immediately to Senior Engineering Sound Broadcasting, writing, "We had almost given up hope of finding suitable accommodation for the Radiophonic Effects Unit and the area which you are kindly making available promises to meet the needs of the unit with the minimum expenditure on wiring, acoustic treatment, etc. I am very grateful." Briscoe, *Radiophonic Workshop*, 29.

14. Minutes of the REC, March 6, 1957, WAC R97/11/1.

15. Frank Wade to H. S. B. A., memo, February 11, 1957, WAC R97/11/1.

16. Ibid.

17. Ibid.

18. Ibid.

19. The instrument was eventually premiered in an experimental concert recorded on October 3, 1959, in a program performed by William Davies that consisted of the following: 1. Belle of the Ball (Anderson), 2. Pavane (Gould), 3. Passepied (Delibes), 4. Summertime (Gershwin), 5. Midnight at Mayfair (Chase). The internal record at the BBC also lists an item, "VK 29.9.59—James Dufour," which could conceivably be a concluding "experimental" work; although listed without a publisher, it is placed in line with the other items on the program. September 29, 1959, WAC R53/483/2.

20. Douglas Cleverdon to multiple recipients, memo, February 13, 1957, WAC R97/9/1. This led to the monthly internal playing of radiophonic music, as detailed above.

21. Cleverdon was helped in his programming of these demonstrations by the electronic studios in Paris and "Dr. Stockhausen" in Cologne, who sent tapes of their music to the BBC. Douglas Winget to A. H. C. P. Ops (Recording), memo, November 5, 1957, WAC R97/11/1.

22. As English music critic Reginald Smith Brindle had labeled the composers of electronic music in an influential article read by the entire EEC committee, "The Lunatic Fringe II: Electronic Music," *Musical Times* (July 1956): 300–301.

23. These two were Francis Chagrin and Marc Wilkinson. Both Chagrin and Wilkinson were prolific composers of film and television music, and Chagrin frequently composed for BBC productions. This early advocacy of the creation of the Workshop allowed these two, especially Wilkinson, to be, along with Roberto Gerhard, among the few independent composers to use the facilities after its opening in 1958.

24. Bernard Keefe to C. Music, memo, February 13, 1957, WAC R53/483/1.

25. For more on this topic, see Jennifer Doctor, *The BBC and Ultra-Modern Music, 1922–1936: Shaping a Nation's Tastes* (New York: Cambridge University Press, 1999).

26. Frank Wade to C. Music, Memo, February 14, 1957, WAC R53/483/1.

27. Frank Wade to C. Ent, memo, March 19, 1957, WAC R97/11/1.

28. Howes was the one-time chairman of the BBC's Music Advisory Committee and as such rarely programmed contemporary music.

29. An excellent history of the Miller Organ Company and its electronic organs can be found in Ted Crampton's "A Lasting Invention," *Choir and Organ* 8, no. 3 (May–June 2000): 24–25.

30. Frank Wade to C. Ent, memo, March 19, 1957, WAC R97/11/1.

31. Ibid.

32. Head of Features, Gilliam to C. Ent (Sound), memo, April 3, 1957, WAC R97/11/1.

33. Ibid.

34. H. L. M. P. (Sound) Wade to A. H. C. P. (Ops) Porter, memo, October 29, 1959, WAC R97/11/2.

35. A. H. C. P. (Ops) Porter to H. L. M. P. (Sound) Wade, memo, October 30, 1959, WAC R97/11/2.

36. Minutes of the Third Programme Meeting, minute 108, January 27, 1958, WAC R34/11217/1-3.

37. Glock discusses his complex professional relationship with Johnstone in his always-entertaining autobiography, where he also details the obstacles he faced in trying to program more difficult music during his tenure at the BBC. For example, he was responsible for reshaping and expanding the scope of the ultra-traditional Proms concert series, including for the first time the works of Boulez, Carter, Messiaen, and Webern. William Glock, *Notes in Advance* (Oxford: Oxford University Press, 1991).

38. Briscoe, *Radiophonic Workshop*, 29. Here Briscoe states £2,000 as the amount offered, but the internal paperwork contradicts this claim.

39. As befits the bureaucratic nature of the BBC, even the acquisition of equipment has to go through its own department.

40. For the more obscure-sounding items, a few definitions will probably be useful. Jackfields were bays into which power plugs could be inserted. Disc racks were, quite simply, for the storage of recorded discs. The details of the redundant plant inventory are documented in two memos, A. E. Hawkeswood for the Head of Equipment Department, both dated January 17, 1957, WAC R97/7/1.

41. This use of the word "workshop" to describe the Radiophonic Effects Unit is the earliest such reference I can find. The name "Radiophonic Workshop" was officially adopted at the April 23, 1958, meeting of the REC.

42. The Blattnerphone was the first magnetic tape recording system used at the BBC, starting in 1930. This used steel tape 6 mm wide and .08 mm thick, and a full twenty-minute reel weighed twenty-one pounds. Several innovations in design led to the Marconi-Stille machine—which still used steel tape but was more reliable—in 1935. These were used until just after the end of the war.

43. The BBC disabled other unique functions of the original machines, including, most interestingly, their ability to record programs longer than the length of one tape. Both machines would be loaded with full reels. As the first tape recorder reached the end of its reel,

a button on the central console would be pressed, so that the second machine would start recording. At the precise moment of overlap, a small piece of editing tape would be placed on both reels at the same time—both to facilitate editing later, and for easy rebroadcasting. The first machine would then stop. When the two tapes were played back, the second player's speed would be controlled by a manual "tram-handle," enabling the engineer to adjust the position of the tape, faster or slower, synchronizing the two before switching the second machine's output on. When the machine was acquired by the Workshop, this feature was no longer functional, but still allowed for interesting interplay between the two machines.

44. Sound engineers throughout England praised this machine, including G. A. Briggs and Edward Pawley. G. A. Briggs, *Sound Reproduction*, 3rd ed. (Bradford, Yorkshire: Wharfedale Wireless Works, 1953), 232–34. Edward Pawley, *BBC Sound Engineering, 1922–1972* (London: BBC Publications, 1972), 391.

45. The BTR/2 was also manufactured in another version that could be recorded at either 30 ips or 15 ips.

46. Report on *Musique Concrète* and Electronic Music, November 1956, WAC R97/7/1—Radiophonic Workshop General (1953–73, file 1).

47. Minutes of the REC, minute 5, April 4, 1957, WAC R97/11/1.

48. No author, memo, April 9, 1957, WAC R97/7/1.

49. Minutes of the REC, minute 4, December 10, 1957, WAC R97/11/1.

50. E. W. S. Porter to H. C. P. (Ops), memo, March 5, 1958, WAC R97/9/1.

51. Briscoe, *Radiophonic Workshop*, 37.

52. The surviving material from this broadcast has been issued on the double CD *BBC Radiophonic Workshop: A Retrospective*, Grey Area of Mute Records, phonic3cd, 5099923698826 LC05834.

53. H. C. P. (Ops) from E. W. S. Porter, memo, March 5, 1958, WAC R97/9/1.

54. A few anecdotes about "Dickie" Bird related to me by his coworker Dick Mills: "He was very precise over certain things, specially his beloved cars. If it was raining, he would take his wife, Olive, to her work, then drive back home, wipe the car dry, and come to work on the train! When he went abroad to France for holidays he would have fitted duplicate important items (ignition coils, carburetors, etc) in the engine compartment ready to be switched over in event of breakdowns. . . . He had no children, 'not until they came as "boil in the bag" items and you got change with them,' he used to say. . . . He took great pride in maintaining any equipment we had (his own domain was one end of Room 13). . . . Paradoxically, he hardly ever created an original piece of equipment. . . . I think this was Dickie's way of secretly showing that he didn't really believe in any of this nonsense and was always in fear and trembling of having to find a proper job!"

55. This culture has been eloquently described in Tom Burns's sociological study *The BBC: Public Institution and Private World* (London: Macmillan, 1977).

56. To this list can be added several productions of which little is known other than that they contained some degree of radiophonic sound: the signature tune for the program *Tuesday Tune Time, Music in All Directions* (mentioned in the minutes of the Radiophonic Effects Committee meeting, April 4, 1957); *Prometheus Unbound*—"several Radiophonic Effects employed," broadcast March 25, 1957 (also mentioned at April 4 meeting), and

described in an undated list from around 1958: "Translation by Rex Warner, adapted by Helen Wood and produced by Val Gielgud. Includes Radiophonic effects devised by Daphne Oram and Madeau Stewart" (WAC R97/7/1 Radiophonic Effects and Electronic Music, 1956–63). Three productions not mentioned in later sources referred to in an undated document, likely from 1958–59 (WAC R97/1/7, Complete Programmes, BBC), are *The Quintaphone* (28:52), "with text and *musique concrète* by Jeremy Sandford, produced by David Thompson. Effects limited to those that can be obtained with a single tape machine—doubling and halving of speed, reversal and loops of tape"; *The Unexpected Country* (28.38), produced by Sasha Moorsom: "This contains obsessive background sounds of the type most easily produced by tape loops. These 'montages' are by Roberto Gerhard"; and *Death of Grass* (84:40), produced by Donald McWhinnie, "story by John Christopher, adapted by Stephen Grenfell. Existing recordings of French *Musique Concrète* have here been successfully applied to a science fiction story. These are mostly used in the first thirty minutes of the programme." These are mentioned in a letter dated February 25, 1958, from R.V.A. George to McWhinnie in his capacity as assistant director of sound drama. He also mentions that "a small amount of work has also been undertaken for Features, Light Music, and Television Drama": *Heartbreak House* (January 26, 1958), a television program with effects by Daphne Oram (noted in a letter dated February 10, 1958, from M. R. G. Gerrard to the assistant head controller of program operations). *Heartbreak House's* reception was influenced by the broadcast immediately preceding it—a news program, *Monitor*, where director Peter Brook demonstrated the techniques of *musique concrète*. None of these productions would be mentioned in later Workshop documentation. Finally, I have discovered an undated note handwritten by Daphne Oram during her work on Gibson's *Winter Journey* (December 1957) listing radiophonic projects to date. Some are familiar, while for some nothing more is known and they were never mentioned again: "1. Light Music Signature Tune 2. Attempt to provide TV News Signature Tune 3. Prometheus 4. Kraken Wakes (experimental—not broadcast) 5. The Cocktail 6. Private Dreams and Public Nightmares 7. The River Man 8. Metamorphosis 9. The Hungry Spider. Numbers 5, 7, 9 contain only minor Radiophonic treatment" (WAC R97/7/1 Radiophonic Effects and Electronic Music, 1956–63).

57. A. H. O. C. P. O. (Studios) [E. W. S. Porter] to REC, memo, April 11, 1958, WAC R97/11/1.

58. Minutes of the REC, April 23, 1958, WAC R97/11/1.

59. Press Release, n.d., WAC R53/483/1.

60. Ibid.

61. "BBC's Radiophonic Workshop," *Times* (London), May 24, 1958.

62. Madeau Stewart, "Is It Really Music," *Tablet*, April 26, 1958.

Chapter 3

1. With the exception of *Under the Loofah Tree* and *Orpheus*, all of the works or tracks discussed in this chapter have been commercially released.

2. Donald McWhinnie, "The Ocean," *Radio Times*, May 16, 1958, 6.

3. Ibid.

4. Roy Walker, "Sound Broadcasting: Drama," *Listener*, May 29, 1958, 915–16.

5. Unlabeled, undated newspaper clipping, WAC R97/9/1.

6. Margaret Marsh, *Suburban Lives* (New Brunswick, NJ: Rutgers University Press, 1990), quoted in Keir Keightley, "Turn it down!' she shrieked: Gender, Domestic Space, and High Fidelity, 1948–59," *Popular Music* 15, no. 2 (1996): 153.

7. Ibid., 157.

8. Giles Cooper, *Under the Loofah Tree*, in *Giles Cooper: Six Plays for Radio*. (Letchworth, Hertfordshire: BBC Books, 1966). There is a clear connection between these scripts and the radio plays of pioneer Lance Sieveking in the 1920s.

9. Daphne Oram, *An Individual Note: Of Music, Sound and Electronics* (London: Galliard, 1972).

10. An excellent compilation of Oram's music has been released on CD: Daphne Oram, *Oramics*, Paradigm Discs PD 21.

11. Liner notes from Daphne Oram, *Oramics*, Paradigm Discs PD 21.

12. Daphne Oram to Managing Director of BBC Radio, letter, January 17, 1983, WAC R97/12/1.

13. Ibid.

14. Ibid.

15. Ibid.

16. Desmond Briscoe to Managing Director, Radio, letter, February 8, 1983. Solicitors Department to Desmond Briscoe, letter, February 15, 1983, WAC R97/12/1.

17. Including (besides Oram) Jenyth Worsley, who became a producer in BBC Radio; Margaret Etall, a successful writer and poet who is now a prolific director in BBC Radio; Elizabeth Parker, a successful composer; Maddalena Fagandini, an important director whose works include the popular *Look and Read* story "The Boy from Space"; Clare Elstow, the current head of BBC preschool programming; and, perhaps most famously of all, Delia Derbyshire, whose reputation in the world of electronic music continues to grow.

18. Jo Hutton, "Radiophonic Ladies," published online: web.archive.org/web/ 20060 517133312/www.sonicartsnetwork.org/ARTICLES/ARTICLE2000JoHutton.html (accessed December 2, 2008).

19. "Delia Makes a Hit with 'Dr. Who,'" *Coventry Evening Telegraph*, April 28, 1965.

20. Film music scholarship's centrality is due to the simple fact that since the inception of film theory in the 1960s there have been no correlative studies of how music for radio drama works.

21. Claudia Gorbman, *Unheard Melodies: Narrative Film Music* (Bloomington: Indiana University Press, 1987), 15.

22. And, indeed, this function is precisely what defines the output of the Workshop in official documentation: "To produce sounds which convey to the listener's imagination the *mood* or *emotional idea* behind the author's theme of his radio or television drama." Quoted from F. C. Brooker, *BBC Engineering Division Monograph: Radiophonics in the BBC* (London: BBC, 1963), 5 (emphasis in the original).

23. Caryl Flinn, *Strains of Utopia: Gender, Nostalgia, and Hollywood Film Music* (Princeton, NJ: Princeton University Press, 1992), 7.

24. See chapter 1.

25. "We have chosen to number it because we feel that others might then follow." Head of Presentation, Television, Rex Moorfoot to G. G. Derrick, memo, January 2, 1961, WAC R97/11/2. E.W.S. Porter to Assistant Head of Programme Contracts F. L. Hetley, memo, January 19, 1961, WAC R97/11/2.

26. Assistant Head of Programme Contracts F. L. Hetley to Assistant (Administration), Presentation, Television, memo, July 20, 1961, WAC R97/11/2.

27. "Odd Place for a Star to Be Born," *Daily Herald*, January 26, 1962.

28. Ibid.

29. "It Ain't Human But Sounds a Treat," *Daily Mirror*, April 12, 1962.

30. E. W. S. Porter to J. C. Miles, memo, February 1, 1962.

31. "It Ain't Human But Sounds a Treat," *Daily Mirror*, April 12, 1962.

32. Unless otherwise noted, all unfootnoted quotations are from my own interviews. See the bibliography for a complete list.

33. Reginald Smith Brindle, "Broadcast Music: Radiophonics," *Musical Times* (April 1962): 244.

34. A. A. Central Programme Operations to A. C. S. A. M., memo, May 22, 1962, WAC R97/7/1.

35. Minutes of Interim Meeting of the Radiophonic Technical Sub-Committee (RTC), February 3, 1964, WAC R97/10/1.

36. Minutes of Meeting of the RTC, June 9, 1964, WAC R97/10/1.

37. Grainer was called the "Master of the Signature Tune" in an episode of the series *Tonight* broadcast May 25, 1963. Up to this point, Grainer had written incidental music for television plays, like *The Birthday Party*, and had become famous as a writer of signature tunes, beginning with *Maigret* in 1960. He continued on to write the themes for *That Was the Week That Was*, *Steptoe and Son*, *Comedy Playhouse*, and *Fanny Craddock* (one of the first BBC cooking shows).

38. Mark Ayres, at http://ourworld.compuserve.com/homepages/mark_ayres/DW Theme.htm (accessed December 1, 2008).

39. *Listener*, May 30, 1963.

40. Philip Blake, *Radio Times*, May 16, 1963, 25.

41. Paul Ferris, "Radio," *Observer*, February 10, 1963.

42. Mark Ayres's Web site contains the most thorough written description of the history of the theme and its composition: http://ourworld.compuserve.com/homepages/mark_ayres/DWTheme.htm (accessed December 1, 2008). The following articles in *Doctor Who Magazine* contain excellent discussions of the compositional process with the composers: Austin Atkinson-Broadbelt, "Soundhouse: Brian Hodgson," no. 193 (November 25, 1992); Austin Atkinson-Broadbelt, "Soundhouse: Delia Derbyshire," no. 199 (May 12, 1993); Austin Atkinson-Broadbelt, "Soundhouse: Dick Mills," no. 198 (April 14, 1993); Marcus Hearn, "The Dawn of Knowledge," no. 207 (December 22, 1993); Andrew Pixley, "Doctor Who Archive Feature: 100,000 B.C.," *Doctor Who Magazine Summer Special*

(1994). Other excellent sources include *Alchemists of Sound*, BBC4 2003 documentary, "Doctor Who—30 Years," Radio Program, BBC Radio 2, 1993; Jeremy Bentham, *Doctor Who: The Early Years* (London: W. H. Allen, 1986); John Tulloch and Manuel Alvarado, *Doctor Who: The Unfolding Text* (New York: St. Martin's Press, 1983); David J. Howe, Mark Stammers, and Stephen James Walker, *Doctor Who, the Handbook: The First Doctor* (London: Doctor Who Books, 1994).

43. Austin Atkinson-Broadbelt, "Soundhouse: Delia Derbyshire," *Doctor Who Magazine*, no. 199 (May 12, 1993): 14.

44. Bentham, *Doctor Who*, 93–94.

45. Tulloch, *Unfolding Text*, 19.

46. Howe, *First Doctor*, 202.

47. Desmond Briscoe and Roy Curtis-Bramwell, *The BBC Radiophonic Workshop: The First 25 Years* (London: BBC, 1983), 102.

48. Howe, *First Doctor*, 210.

49. Atkinson-Broadbent, "Brian Hodgson," 42.

50. They were the Arabic version of *Science and Industry*, *Time on Our Hands*, and an unused arrangement of "Get Out and Get Under" for a car maintenance program, *Know Your Car*. Brian Hodgson, introduction to brochure notes for *BBC Radiophonic Workshop—21*, BBC Records 354, phonodisc.

51. Interview at www.delia-derbyshire.org/interview_surface.php (accessed December 1, 2008), originally published in *Surface*, May 2000.

52. Briscoe, *Radiophonic Workshop*, 83.

53. Atkinson-Broadbent, "Delia Derbyshire," 14.

54. Atkinson-Broadbent, "Dick Mills," 44.

55. Brian Hodgson, "Doctor Who: Thirty Years," Radio Program, BBC Radio 2, 1993.

56. Atkinson-Broadbent, "Dick Mills," 44.

57. Atkinson-Broadbent, "Delia Derbyshire," 14–15.

58. Tulloch, *Unfolding Text*, 19–20.

59. "Verity's Tune Is Way Out—of this World!" *Daily Mirror*, December 7, 1963.

60. Hearn, "The Dawn of Knowledge," 15.

61. Desmond Briscoe to RTC, memo, November 12, 1963, WAC R97/10/1.

62. *Northern Echo* (Darlington, Durham), January 11, 1964.

63. *New Comment*, BBC radio broadcast, Bermange interviewed by H. A. L. Craig, December 30, 1964.

64. Ibid.

65. Briscoe, *Radiophonic Workshop*, 83.

66. The original recording is labeled in the script for the work as "Plain Song Antiphon, unaccompanied. Back, band 1, Lib. No. LP 27101."

67. Delia Derbyshire, undated notes. Delia Derbyshire Archive, Centre for Screen Studies, University of Manchester.

68. Ibid.

69. Minutes of the RTC, May 4, 1965, WAC R97/10/1.

70. Press memo, no author, no date, WAC R97/25/1.

71. Delia Derbyshire and Brian Hodgson to Derek Cutner, publicity memo, January 13, 1965, WAC R97/25/1.

72. "Square Wave, Hip Sound," *Observer*, March 14, 1965, WAC R97/25/1.

73. "Composers without Crochets," *Daily Express*, June 10, 1965, Manchester Edition, WAC R97/25/1.

74. Patrick Skene Catling, "Television," *Punch*, June 9, 1965.

75. An excellent summary of British regional radio stations can be found at www.geocities.com/thehotw/aircheck_UKNotts.htm (accessed December 1, 2008).

76. Baker recorded an interview for Radio Nottingham explaining the techniques behind the call-sign. This was issued alongside many other fantastic and hard-to-get radiophonic rarities by Baker in a two-CD collection, *The John Baker Tapes, Vols. 1 and 2* (John Baker, *The John Baker Tapes: Volume 1, BBC Radiophonics*, Trunk Records; John Baker, *The John Baker Tapes: Volume 2, Soundtracks, Library, Home Recordings, Electro Ads*, Trunk Records).

77. Mary Crozier, "Out of the Unknown on BBC2," *Guardian*, January 15, 1966.

Chapter 4

1. WAC R97/9/1, undated.

2. Unsigned document, May 1963, WAC R97/9/1.

3. Jo Hutton, "Radiophonic Ladies," online at web.archive.org/web/20060517133312/www.sonicartsnetwork.org/ARTICLES/ARTICLE2000JoHutton.html (accessed December 2, 2008), p. 3.

4. Unsigned document, May 1963, WAC R97/9/1.

5. Radiophonic Effects Committee Minutes, December 19, 1961, WAC R97/8/1.

6. Unsigned letter, May 1963, WAC R97/9/1.

7. Unsigned letter, May 1963, WAC R97/9/1. By 1963 the Miller Multi-colour Tone Organ, originally purchased by the Music Department as a way of eliminating the need for a Radiophonic Workshop in the first place (see chapter 2), was sitting disused by all but the Workshop staff in Maida Vale Music Studio 3 until the Workshop engineering staff rescued it and moved it to Room 32, Workshop territory, where it subsequently broke down.

8. Unsigned letter, May 1963, WAC R97/9/1.

9. F. C. Brooker, "The BBC Radiophonic Workshop," *Electronics and Power*, January 1965, 27.

10. Head of Radio Production Services, Invitation, WAC R97/25/1.

11. Minutes of the Radiophonic Technical Committee (RTC), February 4, 1969, WAC R97/25/1.

12. M. H., "BBC Radiophonic Music," *Gramophone*, September 1969.

13. Minutes of RTC, June 9, 1964. "It was agreed that Music Department should be approached." They decided not to get this and instead got a "normal" piano in 1965. WAC R97/25/1.

14. S. A. A. S. A. F. (S.) Weston to C. P. O. (S.), memo, June 21, 1963, WAC R53/483/2.

15. H. Davies (?), "The Mellotron: An Appreciation of the Present Position and Future Possibilities," May 28, 1964, WAC R53/483/2.

16. H. J. Houlgate, "Designs Department Recording Section Test Report No. 1.114: The Mellotron Multiple Tape Reproducer," May 1964, WAC R53/483/2. This report is followed up by an attempt within the Design Department to design their own Mellotron that could do all they wish. "It does not appear that the Eric Robinson Organization [makers of the Mellotron] itself disposes of the technical knowledge that would enable it to develop the sort of machine that we require, though it would undoubtedly be ready to manufacture and to market alongside the Mellotron a machine of our design which would have a very wide market in other broadcasting organizations, in film studios and so on. We, on the other hand, are in an excellent position to carry out the development of an 'effects machine' of this kind and it would appear to be entirely possible to negotiate an arrangement with the Eric Robinson Org. whereby they would manufacture and market machines of our design, paying us a royalty on each machine sold. There would appear to be very substantial advantages to the BBC in this. We should obtain the use of a valuable new facility before anyone else and then would profit by the extension of its use elsewhere." This was pursued by R. V. A. George in a memo of July 30, 1964, where he says "Mr. Davies' new proposal for the design of a machine based on the Mellotron idea is an interesting one and somewhat revolutionary. In my opinion, it would not be worthwhile unless it could provide the complete flexibility which we at present enjoy with the disk system.... There is the need (a) to have the facility to cross-fade from one sound to another (an operation which cannot be delegated to a panel operator). (b) The need for speed variation. These, as I say are just two points and I only mention them to emphasize the importance of taking into full account the *operational* requirements at the design stage." Memo from R. V. A. George, head of central program operations, to C. E. S. B. July 30, 1964, WAC R53/483/2.

17. Three documents: (1) J. K. Rickard to M. F. C. Standing, controller, Program Organization (Radio), memo, June 18, 1969; (2) M. F. C. Standing to M. D. R., memo, June 19, 1969; (3) M. F. C. Standing to M. D. R., memo, June 23, 1969, all WAC R53/483/3.

18. Clive Webster to unknown recipient, memo, January 20, 1967, WAC R97/10/1. This was the same date as the meeting of the RTC.

19. This was the first mention of the Moog in the minutes. Minutes of the RTC, June 28, 1968, WAC R97/10/1.

20. Minutes of the RTC, October 15, 1968, WAC R97/10/1.

21. Minutes of the RTC, February 4, 1969, WAC R97/25/1.

22. Tristram Cary has written what to my mind is the definitive explanation of electronic music's classic techniques and equipment in his monumental *Dictionary of Musical Technology*. My discussion of how this technology works and how it was implemented in early synthesizers owes a great deal to this book. Cary, *Dictionary of Musical Technology* (Westport, CT: Greenwood, 1992).

23. Minutes of the RTC, May 6, 1969, WAC R97/10/2.

24. Minutes of "Radiophonic Development" meeting, February 24, 1970, WAC R101/339/1.

25. Prepared by H. Prog. Ops (Radio) and S. E. R. B. (Equip), report on status of Moog, "BBC Radiophonic Workshop, Maintenance and Development," October 15, 1969, WAC R97/25/2.

26. Eddie Veale to Desmond Briscoe, letter, March 4, 1970, WAC R97/10/2.

27. Minutes of the Meeting of the RTC, April 7, 1970 ("April 17" date on document is a typo), WAC R97/25/2.

28. Veale to Briscoe, letter, July 3, 1970, WAC R97/10/2.

29. Briscoe to Robert Moog, letter, July 16, 1970, R97/10/2.

30. Veale to Briscoe, letter, July 20, 1970, R97/10/2.

31. Moog to Briscoe, letter, July 28, 1970, R97/10/2.

32. Assistant Overseas Liaison Officer Irene M. Elford to Briscoe, memo, October 14, 1964, WAC R97/10/2.

33. Peter Zinovieff to Briscoe, letter, January 30, 1970, WAC R97/10/2.

34. Briscoe to D. S. Browning, March 6, 1970, WAC R97/10/2.

35. Projects Engineer G. W. Daymond (Radio) to E. I. C. Tech. Ser. (R), memo, June 17 1970, WAC R97/10/2.

36. Dave Wagner, "BBC Producer Explores 'Radiophonics,'" *Capital Times*, June 18, 1970.

37. Although some sources say the ARP Odyssey wasn't released commercially until 1972, a letter issued by Tonus in October 1970 clearly states it was available by this time. WAC R97/10/2.

38. Meeting of the RTC, July 7, 1970, WAC R97/10/2.

39. Projects Engineer G. W. Daymond (Radio) to A. (A.), memo, November 18, 1970, WAC R97/10/2.

40. Daymond to H. S. M. Radio Studios, memo, January 29, 1971, WAC R97/10/2.

41. Minutes of the RTC, January 19, 1971, WAC R97/10/2.

42. Briscoe to Geoffrey Manuel, memo, October 6, 1971, WAC R97/11/2.

43. Minutes of the RTC, April 27, 1971, WAC R97/10/2.

44. Briscoe, *Radiophonic Workshop*, 134.

45. Desmond Briscoe, untitled discussion before "IEE 100" (Royal Albert Hall, May 19, 1971), unpublished recording.

46. Unless otherwise noted, all unfootnoted quotations are from my own interviews. See the bibliography for a complete list.

47. Christopher Ford, "Sounds of Science," *Guardian*, December 30, 1971.

48. Ibid.

49. Brian Hodgson to Desmond Briscoe, memo, June 21, 1971, WAC R97/10/2.

50. Peter Zinovieff to Hodgson, letter, September 24, 1971, WAC R97/11/2. Hodgson's comments to Briscoe are handwritten at the bottom of this letter.

51. Briscoe to S. E. R. B. (Equip), memo, September 28, 1971, WAC R97/11/2.

52. Minutes of RTC, November 2, 1971, WAC R97/10/2.

53. Briscoe to Manuel, memo, November 26, 1971, WAC R97/11/2.

54. Manuel to H. Pers. A. R., memo, September 28, 1972, WAC R53/483/2.

55. No author, undated report, 1971, WAC R97/11/2.

56. Manuel to C. E. R. B., memo, June 15, 1972, WAC R53/483/2.

57. Sally Brown, "Having a Whale of a Time Making Electronic Music," unnamed newspaper, June 1973, WAC R97/25/1.

58. Peter Fiddick, "Trevor Play," *Guardian*, November 5, 1971.

59. Trevor Pinch and Frank Trocco, "The Social Construction of the Early Electronic Music Synthesizer," in *Music and Technology in the Twentieth-Century*, ed. Hans-Joachim Braun (Baltimore: John Hopkins University Press, 2002), 73.

60. For the DVD release of this story Mark Ayres has done an excellent job restoring, in an "audio only" feature of the episodes, those cues of Clarke's cut by the director, using the composer's original master tapes. Ayres lists on his Web site the areas that have been restored. Online at ourworld.compuserve.com/homepages/mark_ayres/DWRWS002.htm#sd (accessed December 1, 2008).

61. Briscoe to Manuel, 18 April 1973, R97/10/3. The program included a stereo version of Delia Derbyshire's "Great Zoos of the World"; Richard Yeoman-Clark's "History of Seven Families of the Lake Pipple Popple," based on an Edward Lear poem; Glynis Jones's "Dylan Thomas's The Force That Through the Green Fuse Drives the Flower"; Malcolm Clarke's "La Grande Piece de la Foire de la Rue Delaware"; and several other pieces, including Kingsland's contribution, originally called "Grimm Fairy Tale."

62. David Gillard, "The Men in Front of the Machines behind the Sounds," *Radio Times*, September 27, 1973. The title of the article is telling, in that it helps to explain the omission of both Delia Derbyshire and Glynis Jones's contributions.

63. Minutes of the RTC, 11 July 1972, WAC R97/10/3.

64. No author, *Andover Advertiser*, July 7, 1973.

65. "Radiophonic," *Bournemouth Evening Echo*, July 19, 1973.

66. "In the Moog," *East London Advertiser*, July 20, 1973.

67. Briscoe to Projects Engineer, Radio, memo, January 11, 1973, WAC R53/483/2.

68. Different version of memo from Briscoe to Projects Engineer, January 11, 1973, WAC R97/10/3.

69. Action memo from meeting of RTC, June 12, 1973, WAC R97/10/3.

70. Briscoe, memo, April 18, 1973, R97/10/3.

71. Notes of the Radiophonic Workshop's midmonthly meeting, October 20, 1972, WAC R97/11/2. The full staff list of the Radiophonic Workshop at this time was Briscoe, Glynis Jones, Cain, Young (engineer), Tombs (engineering assistant), Clarke, Mills, Kingsland, and Yeoman-Clark.

72. Briscoe to Manuel, memo, November 1, 1972, WAC R53/483/2.

Chapter 5

1. Desmond Briscoe, "The BBC Radiophonic Workshop," 1973, typewritten manuscript, WAC, R97/5/1.

2. Ibid.

3. Ibid.

4. G. W. Daymond to S. E. R. B. (E), memo, October 5, 1972, WAC R97/10/3.

5. Graham Punter, "Radiophonics—BBC's Box of Tricks," *Music Week*, March 9, 1974.

6. Minutes of the Radiophonic Technical Committee (RTC), June 11, 1974, WAC R97/10/3.

7. Minutes of the RTC, February 26, 1974, WAC R97/10/3.

8. Briscoe to Acting Head of Engineering Radio Projects, memo, December 9, 1975, WAC R97/10/3.

9. Briscoe to Head of Engineering Radio projects, G. W. Daymond, memo, September 25, 1974, WAC R97/10/3.

10. Memo from H. O. E. (TV) to H. E. R. Projects and Briscoe, October 8, 1974, WAC R97/10/3.

11. Minutes of the RTC, October 15, 1974, WAC R97/10/3.

12. Peter Zinovieff to Briscoe, letter, March 25, 1975, WAC R97/10/3.

13. Briscoe to Zinovieff, letter, March 26, 1975, WAC R97/10/3.

14. Zinovieff, letter, May 21, 1975, WAC R97/10/3.

15. Briscoe to Zinovieff, letter, June 5, 1975, WAC R97/10/3.

16. Minutes of the RTC, June 10, 1975, WAC R97/10/3.

17. Unless otherwise noted, all unfootnoted quotations are from my own interviews. See the bibliography for a complete list.

18. Jeff Smith, *The Sounds of Commerce: Marketing Popular Film Music* (New York: Columbia University Press, 1990), 74.

19. Carey Blyton to Dick Mills, letter, November 18, 1974, WAC R97/10/3.

20. Minutes of the RTC, October 11, 1977, WAC R97/10/4.

21. Briscoe to H. E. Tele. Rec, memo, December 2, 1976, WAC R97/10/4.

22. Minutes of the RTC, March 9, 1976, WAC R97/10/4.

23. Minutes of the RTC, July 6, 1976, WAC R97/10/4.

24. Desmond Briscoe and Roy Curtis-Bramwell, *The BBC Radiophonic Workshop: The First 25 Years* (London: BBC, 1983), 144–45.

25. Julian Studio Instruments Rentals Limited, and Eel Pie Publishing, November 17, 1978, "Rental of Yamaha CS80, one week £160-00. To be hired from Tuesday 20th June–27th June," and another rental document dated November 17, 1978: "Instrument should be delivered to BBC studios, Delaware Rd, etc. for the attention of Peter Howell. As already discussed, the invoice should be sent to BBC "Body in Question," for the attention of Patrick Uden, with whom this arrangement has already been cleared." WAC R97/40/1—Body in Question.

26. Stephen Marshall, "The New Atlantis: The Story of the BBC Radiophonic Workshop," *Sound on Sound*, April 2008, 78–91.

27. David Gillard, "Rub Hands for a Monster," *Daily Mail*, March 11, 1978.

Chapter 6

1. Brian Hodgson to M. D. R. through Briscoe, memo, July 14, 1981.

2. Alan Woolgar (at Schott) to Richard Yeoman-Clark, letter, May 19, 1978, WAC R97/31/1: "I would just like to extend my personal thanks and those of Sir Michael

Tippett for the cooperation and advice we received from your department. Please convey our thanks to Richard Yeoman-Clark for his time and patience in solving our problems. With best wishes, Rick Wentworth. Head of Production (Schott Music Publishers)." And Rick Wentworth to Brian Hodgson, letter, May 4, 1978, R97/31/1, as well as a memo that reads, "A bit of unusual PR consultation by RYC for Sir Michael Tippett." Hodgson to H. P. Op (R), June 5, 1978, WAC R97/31/1.

3. John Nathan-Turner, "The John Nathan-Turner Memoirs: Chapter Two— Season Eighteen: Brighton Beach Memoirs," *Doctor Who Magazine*, no. 234 (January 17, 1997): 16.

4. John Tulloch and Henry Jenkins, *Science Fiction Audiences* (London: Routledge, 1995), 54.

5. John Tulloch and Manuel Alvarado, *Doctor Who: The Unfolding Text* (New York: St. Martin's, 1983), 175.

6. Tim Gebbels, "Out of the Soundhouse: Dudley Simpson," *Doctor Who Magazine*, no. 204 (September 29, 1993): 10.

7. Patrick Mulkern and Richard Marson, "King of the Tracks," *Doctor Who Magazine* Winter Special (1985): 16.

8. David J. Howe, Mark Stammers, and Stephen James Walker, *Doctor Who: The Eighties* (London: Doctor Who Books, 1996), 6.

9. Mulkern and Marson, "King of the Tracks," 16.

10. Nathan-Turner, "Brighton Beach Memoirs," 16.

11. Ibid.

12. Gary Russell, "Roger Limb," *Skaro*, no. 17 (1983): 14.

13. Desmond Briscoe and Roy Curtis-Bramwell, *The BBC Radiophonic Workshop: The First 25 Years* (London: BBC, 1983), 102.

14. Ibid., 102–3.

15. Peter Howell, undated notes for *Doctor Who* Theme remake, WAC R97/51/1.

16. Ibid.

17. Austen Atkinson-Broadbelt, "Soundhouse: Peter Howell," *Doctor Who Magazine* 194 (December 23, 1992): 49.

18. Howell, undated notes for *Doctor Who* Theme remake, WAC R97/51/1.

19. Atkinson-Broadbelt, "Peter Howell," 49.

20. Howell, undated notes for *Doctor Who* Theme remake, WAC R97/51/1.

21. Peter Howell to Sid Sutton, Head of Drama Group TV, memo, March 26, 1980, WAC R97/51/1.

22. This was certainly my first exposure to the studio as a child in the early 1980s in Kansas City, Missouri: I clearly remember sending away for this single through *Starlog Magazine*, which featured an interview with the producer as well as a brief discussion of the Radiophonic Workshop. I remember when Nathan-Turner actually visited Kansas City in 1986 with the "Doctor Who USA Tour Bus," where he led a question-and-answer session. More important, one could purchase, at the prominent "merchandise display counter," records and cassettes of not only *Doctor Who: The Music I* and *II*, the single 45s, but other Workshop-related items, such as the theme tune to *Blake's Seven, The*

Hitchhiker's Guide to the Galaxy, and other albums, showing that the Workshop did more than just *Doctor Who*. To an impressionable fourteen-year-old like myself, and thousands others like me, the influence of these records was profound, and it's impossible to overstate the importance of this international push to the growing reputation of the studio.

23. Austin Atkinson-Broadbelt, "Out of the Soundhouse: Roger Limb," *Doctor Who Magazine*, no. 196 (February 17, 1993): 39–41.

24. Austin Atkinson-Broadbelt, "Out of the Soundhouse: Paddy Kingsland," *Doctor Who Magazine*, no. 205 (October 27, 1993): 40–43.

25. Unless otherwise noted, all unfootnoted quotations are from my own interviews. See the bibliography for a complete list.

26. George Lakoff and Mark Johnson, *Metaphors We Live By* (Chicago: University of Chicago Press, 1980), 14.

27. Atkinson-Broadbelt, "Paddy Kingsland," 43.

28. Russell, "Roger Limb," 15.

29. His scores for *Doctor Who* after leaving the Workshop have much more of a "pop" sensibility, with prominent electric guitars.

30. Sam Inglis, "Flexible Working: TV Composer Elizabeth Parker," *Sound on Sound*, February 2001.

31. Ibid.

32. Parker's score for the *Doctor Who* episode "Timelash" was also realized almost entirely on the PPG 2.2. Austin Atkinson-Broadbelt, "Soundhouse: Liz Parker," *Doctor Who Magazine*, no. 203 (September 1, 1993): 44–45.

33. Atkinson-Broadbelt, "Peter Howell," 48.

34. Brian Hodgson, "Radiophonic Workshop: The Next Ten Years," October 26, 1982.

35. A much more modest annual budget of £60,000 was approved, divided evenly between the Radio and TV Departments.

36. Tristram Cary, *Dictionary of Musical Technology* (New York: Greenwood, 1992), 210.

37. Jonathan Gibbs to Simon Chute, cc John Dutot, memo, August 14, 1985, WAC R97/13/1.

38. Richard Lamont, "Syncwriter," *Studio Sound*, April 1985, 84–88.

39. Ibid., 88.

40. Austen Atkinson-Broadbelt, "Soundhouse: Brian Hodgson," *Doctor Who Magazine* no. 198 (April 14, 1993): 42–45.

41. Mike Collins and Ed Jones, "Making Music on a Macintosh," *Apple Business*, April 1986, 13–17.

42. "Radiophonic Workshop: Historical Perspective," internal publicity materials, no date (after 1988).

43. Jonathan Gibbs, "Music Made to Measure," *Broadcast Systems Engineering*, January 1986, 18–23.

44. Richard Elen, "The Computer and the Sound House," *Sound on Sound*, October 1987.

45. Ibid.

46. Duncan E. Stafford, "Report," August, year unknown.

47. Mark Wilson, unnamed document, copyright BBC 1989, WAC R97/13/1.

48. Claire Neesham, "On the Right Wavelength," *Guardian*, draft, dated January 28, 1991.

49. Richard G. Elen, "The BBC Radiophonic Workshop," e-mailed document, January 11, 1991.

50. Mike Collins and Ed Jones, "Making Music on a Macintosh," *Apple Business*, April 1986, 13–17.

51. No author (probably Brian Hodgson), "Radiophonic Workshop," undated (after 1988) four-page publicity document, 2.

52. Brian Hodgson, "Radiophonic Workshop Situation Report," June 1986.

53. Brian Hodgson, "Television: Hours per Department, 1983–1986," June 1986.

54. BBC, "Producer Choice, a New System for Managing Resources," BBC Staff Briefing Paper, 1991, 1.

55. Martin Harris and Victoria Wegg-Prosser, "The BBC and Producer Choice: A Study of Public Service Broadcasting and Managerial Change," *Wide Angle* 20, no. 2 (April 1998): 150–63.

56. No author (probably Brian Hodgson), "Radiophonic Workshop—The Next Ten Minutes," April 4, no year.

57. No author, "Comparative Costing of the Radiophonic Workshop with Outside Facilities," June 13, 1990.

58. Staff reporter, *Guardian*, February 8, 1997, quoted in Harris and Wegg-Prosser, "Producer Choice," 154.

59. Quoted in Maggie Brown, "Out of the Madhouse," *Guardian*, February 26, 1996, quoted in Harris and Wegg-Prosser, "Producer Choice," 159.

60. Atkinson-Broadbelt, "Brian Hodgson," 42–45.

61. Inglis, "Elizabeth Parker."

62. "The Step Beyond," loose page attached to "Radiophonic Workshop—The Next Ten Minutes," April 4, no year.

Selected Bibliography

Interviews

All interviews were conducted by the author unless otherwise indicated. An "interview" in this context consists of various forms of communication, including personal meetings, telephone conversations, letters, and e-mail exchanges.

Richard Attree: November 23, 2008.
Desmond Briscoe: March 25, 2002.
Maddalena Fagandini: December 10, 2002; January 8, 2004; July 20, 2007.
Jonathan Gibbs: July 5, 2007.
Brian Hodgson: January 17, 2004; July 3, 2006; July 20, 2007; March 18, 2008.
Peter Howell: July 5, 2006; April 2, 2008.
Paddy Kingsland: June 22, 2007; July 12, 2007; April 3, 2008; September 24, 2008; October 10, 2008; October 30, 2008; November 5, 2008.
Roger Limb: February 27, 2008; March 15, 2008; April 4, 2008; October 10, 2008; October 14, 2008.
Dick Mills: February 15, 2002; February 16, 2002; April 15, 2002; June 16, 2003.
Elizabeth Parker: October 19, 2008; November 3, 2008.
Richard Yeoman-Clark: October 6, 2008; October 23, 2008.

Published Sources

Adorno, Theodor W., and Hanns Eisler. *Composing for the Films*. London: Athlone, 1994.
Arnheim, Rudolf. *Radio*. Translated by Margaret Ludwig and Herbert Read. London: Faber and Faber, 1936.

Ashby, Justine, and Andrew Higson, eds. *British Cinema, Past and Present*. London: Routledge, 2000.

Ayres, Mark. *Doctor Who at the BBC Radiophonic Workshop*. Vol. 1, *The Early Years 1963–1969*. BBC CD 6023-2, 2000.

Baker, John, David Cain, and Delia Derbyshire. *BBC Radiophonic Music*. BBC Records REC 25M, 1971.

Battcock, Gregory, ed. *Breaking the Sound Barrier: A Critical Anthology of the New Music*. New York: E. P. Dutton, 1981.

Baudrillard, Jean. *Simulacra and Simulation*. Translated by Sheila Faria Glaser. Ann Arbor: University of Michigan Press, 1994.

BBC Handbook 1958. London: British Broadcasting Corporation, 1957.

BBC Handbook 1959. London: British Broadcasting Corporation, 1958.

BBC Handbook 1966. London: British Broadcasting Corporation, 1965.

BBC Handbook 1967. London: British Broadcasting Corporation, 1966.

"BBC's Radiophonic Workshop." *Times* (London), May 24, 1958.

Becker, Howard Saul. *Art Worlds*. Berkeley: University of California Press, 1982.

Beckett, Samuel. *Krapp's Last Tape and Other Dramatic Pieces*. New York: Grove, 1957.

Berman, Marshall. *All That Is Solid Melts into Air: The Experience of Modernity*. New York: Penguin, 1982.

Bridson, D. G. *Prospero and Ariel: The Rise and Fall of Radio: A Personal Recollection by D. G. Bridson*. London: Gollancz, 1971.

Briggs, Asa. *The BBC: The First Fifty Years*. London: Oxford University Press, 1985.

———. *The Birth of Broadcasting*. Vol. 1 of *The History of Broadcasting in the United Kingdom*. Oxford: Oxford University Press, 1961.

———. *The Golden Age of Wireless*. Vol. 2 of *The History of Broadcasting in the United Kingdom*. Oxford: Oxford University Press, 1965.

———. *Governing the BBC*. London: British Broadcasting Corporation, 1979.

Briggs, G. A. *Sound Reproduction, 3rd Edition*. Bradford, Yorkshire: Wharfedale Wireless Works, 1953.

Brindle, Reginald Smith. "The Lunatic Fringe." *Musical Times* 97, no. 1360 (June 1956): 300–301,

———. *The New Music: The Avant-garde since 1945*. London: Oxford University Press, 1975.

Briscoe, Desmond, and Roy Curtis-Bramwell. *BBC Radiophonic Workshop: The First 25 Years*. London: British Broadcasting Corporation, 1983.

Brooker, F. C. "The BBC Radiophonic Workshop." *Electronics and Power*, January 1965, 27.

———. *BBC Training Manuals: Engineering Division Training Manual*. London: British Broadcasting Corporation, 1942.

Burlingame, Jon. *TV's Biggest Hits: The Story of Television Themes*. New York: Schirmer Books, 1996.

Burns, Tom. *The BBC: Public Institution and Private World*. London: Macmillan, 1977.

Carpenter, Humphrey. *The Envy of the World: 50 Years of the BBC Third Programme and Radio 3, 1946–1996*. London: Weidenfeld and Nicolson, 1996.

Cary, Tristram. Introduction to *Dictionary of Musical Technology*. New York: Greenwood, 1992.

Childs, Eric. *Britain since 1945: A Political History*. 4th ed. London: Routledge, 1997.

Chion, Michel. *Audio-Vision: Sound on Screen*. Translated by Claudia Gorbman. New York: Columbia University Press, 1994.

———. *The Voice in Cinema*. Ed. and trans. Claudia Gorbman. New York: Columbia University Press, 1999.

Chissell, Joan. "A Season of Modern Composers." *Radio Times*, October 11, 1957, 6.

Collins, Mike and Ed Jones. "Making Music on a Macintosh." *Apple Business*, April 1986, 13–17.

Cooke, Deryck. "Autumn Symphony Concerts." *Radio Times*, September 25, 1953, 27.

Cooper, Giles. *Giles Cooper: Six Plays for Radio*. London: British Broadcasting Corporation, 1966.

———. "Radio Writing." *Plays and Players*, December 1965, 10–11.

Cross, Lowell M. *A Bibliography of Electronic Music*. Toronto: University of Toronto Press, 1967.

Doctor, Jennifer. *The BBC and Ultra-Modern Music, 1922–1936: Shaping a Nation's Tastes*. Cambridge: Cambridge University Press, 1999.

Dreyfus, Laurence. "Early Music Defended against Its Devotees: A Theory of Historical Performance in the Twentieth Century." *Musical Quarterly* 69, no. 3 (Summer 1983): 297–322.

Eimert, Herbert. "What Is Electronic Music?" In *Die Reihe* 1 (1955). English ed. Bryn Mawr, PA: Theodore Presser Co., 1958. 1–10.

"Electronic Music." In "Notes and Comments" section. *Score*, March 1955, n.p.

Elen, Richard G. "The BBC Radiophonic Workshop." E-mailed document. January 11, 1991.

———. "The Computer and the Sound House." *Sound on Sound*, October 1987.

Emmerson, Simon, ed. *Music, Electronic Media and Culture*. Aldershot, UK: Ashgate, 2000.

Ernst, David. *The Evolution of Electronic Music*. New York: Schirmer Books, 1977.

Esslin, Martin. "Samuel Beckett and the Art of Broadcasting." *Encounter*, September 1975, 38–46.

———. *Theatre of the Absurd*. 3d ed. New York: Penguin, 1980.

Fagandini, Maddalena. *Time Beat* b/w *Waltz in Orbit*. Parlophone 45-R 4901, 1960.

Ford, Andrew. *Composer to Composer: Conversations about Contemporary Music*. London: Quartet Books, 1993.

Geertz, Clifford. "Thick Description: Toward an Interpretive Theory of Culture." In *The Interpretation of Cultures*. New York: Basic Books, 1973.

Geraghty, Christine. *British Cinema in the Fifties: Gender, Genre and the "New Look."* London: Routledge, 2000.

Gibbs, Jonathan. "Music Made to Measure." *Broadcast Systems Engineering*. January 1986, 18–23.

Gielgud, Val. *British Radio Drama: 1922–1956*. London: George G. Harrap & Co., 1957.

———. *Years in a Mirror*. London: Bodley Head, 1965.

Gillard, David. "The Men in Front of the Machines behind the Sounds." *Radio Times*, September 27, 1973.

Glock, William. *Notes in Advance*. Oxford: Oxford University Press, 1991.

Godfrey, J. W., and S. W. Amos, with M. J. L. Pulling, K. R. Sturley, and P. J. Guy. *BBC Engineering Training Manuals: Sound Recording and Reproduction*. London: Iliffe and Sons, 1952.

Gorbman, Claudia. *Unheard Melodies: Narrative Film Music*. Bloomington: Indiana University Press, 1987.

Gray, Frances. "Giles Cooper: The Medium as Moralist." In *British Radio Drama*, ed. John Drakakis. Cambridge: Cambridge University Press, 1981.

————. "The Nature of Radio Drama." In *Radio Drama*, 58. New York: Longman Group, 1981.

Griffiths, Paul. *A Guide to Electronic Music*. Bath: Thames and Hudson, 1979.

Guthrie, Tyrone. *Squirrel's Cage and Two Other Microphone Plays*. London: Cobden-Sanderson, 1931.

Guy, Percival J. "There's Magic in Recording." *Radio Times*, November 30, 1951, 6.

Hansen, Peter S. *An Introduction to Twentieth Century Music*, 4th ed. Boston: Allyn and Bacon, 1978.

Hardwick, Michael. "More Radio Writers Than Ever Before and More Scope for Them." *Ariel* 3, no. 10 (October 1958): 14–15.

Harris, Martin, and Victoria Wegg-Prosser. "The BBC and Producer Choice: A Study of Public Service Broadcasting and Managerial Change." *Wide Angle* 20, no. 2 (April 1998): 150–63.

Heikinheimo, Seppo. *The Electronic Music of Karlheinz Stockhausen: Studies on the Esthetical and Formal Problems of Its First Phase*. Translated by Brad Absetz. Helsinki, Finland: Suomen Musiikitieteellinen Seura, 1972.

Heppenstall, Rayner. "In the Steps of Laurence Sterne." *Radio Times*, January 18, 1952, 8.

Hobsbawm, Eric. *The Age of Extremes: A History of the World, 1914–1991*. New York: Vintage, 1996.

Hodgkinson, Tim. "Pierre Schaeffer: An Interview with the Pioneer of *musique concrete*." Online at http://www.ele-mental.org/ele_ment/said&did/schaeffer_interview.html (accessed March 18, 2010).

Hodgson, Brian, ed. *BBC Radiophonic Workshop—21*. BBC Records REC 354, 1979.

Hoggart, Richard. *The Uses of Literacy: Changing Patterns in English Mass Culture*. Fair Lawn, NJ: Essential Books, 1957.

Howe, David J., Mark Stammers, and Stephen James Walker. *Doctor Who: The Eighties*. London: Doctor Who Books, 1996.

Huntley, John. *British Film Music*. London: Knapp, Drewett & Sons, n.d.

Hutchings, Arthur. "Music in Britain: 1918–1960." In *The New Oxford History of Music*, vol. 10, *The Modern Age: 1890–1960*, ed. Martin Cooper, 503–68. London: Oxford University Press, 1974.

Huyssen, Andreas. *After the Great Divide: Modernism, Mass Culture, Postmodernism*. Bloomington: Indiana University Press, 1986.

Hyde, Norman. *Four Faces of British Music.* Worthing, UK: Churchman, 1985.

Inglis, Sam. "Flexible Working: TV Composer Elizabeth Parker." *Sound on Sound.* February 2001.

Jeffrey, R. E. Introduction to *Radio Drama and How to Write It,* by Gordon Lea. London: George Allen & Unwin.

Judd, F. C. *Electronics in Music.* London: Neville Spearman, 1972.

———. "Radiophonics at the BBC." *Amateur Tape Recording* 5, no. 10 (May 1963): 8–10.

Kalinak, Katherine. *Settling the Score: Music and the Classical Hollywood Film.* Madison: University of Wisconsin Press, 1992.

Lakoff, George, and Mark Johnson. *Metaphors We Live By.* Chicago: University of Chicago Press, 1980.

Lambert, Constant. *Music Ho! A Study of Music in Decline.* London: Faber, 1966.

Lamont, Richard. "Syncwriter." *Studio Sound,* April 1985, 84–88.

Larson, Randall D. *Musique Fantastique: A Survey of Film Music in the Fantastic Cinema.* Metuchen, NJ: Scarecrow, 1985.

Linz, Rainer. "The Free Music Machines of Percy Grainger." *Experimental Musical Instruments* 12, no. 3 (June 1997): 10–12.

MacNeice, Louis. "Portrait of a Would-Be Hero." *Radio Times.* November 7, 1952, 6.

Maconie, Robin. *Stockhausen on Music.* London: Marion Boyars, 1989.

———. *The Works of Karlheinz Stockhausen.* 2nd ed. Oxford: Clarendon, 1990.

Manning, Peter. *Electronic and Computer Music.* 2nd ed. Oxford: Clarendon, 1985.

Marshall, Stephen. "The New Atlantis: The Story of the BBC Radiophonic Workshop." *Sound on Sound,* April 2008, 78–91.

McClary, Susan. *Conventional Wisdom: The Content of Musical Form.* Berkeley: University of California Press, 2000.

McWhinnie, Donald. *The Art of Radio.* London: Faber and Faber, 1959.

———. "Private Dreams and Public Nightmares." *Radio Times.* October 4, 1957, 27.

———. "A Season of New Radio Plays." *Radio Times.* March 26, 1954, 8.

———. "Writing for Radio (I)." *Ariel* 2, no. 7 (July 1957): 7.

Mendoza, Terence. "Radiophonic Workshop." *Sound and Picture Tape Recorder,* January 1973, 31–32; February 1973, 52–55.

Meyer, Leonard B. *Music, the Arts, and Ideas: Patterns and Predictions in Twentieth-Century Culture.* Chicago: University of Chicago Press, 1967.

Muir, Edward. "Introduction: Observing Trifles." In *Microhistory and the Lost Peoples of Europe,* ed. Edward Muir and Guido Ruggiero, trans. Eren Branch. Baltimore: Johns Hopkins University Press, 1991.

"Music of the Future—Science Fiction for the Piano." *Times* (London), December 19, 1956, 2.

"Musique Concrete—Noise, Sound or Music?" *Times* (London), July 1, 1954, 5.

"Musique Concrete—Tyranny over Sound." *Times* (London), July 12, 1954, 4.

Nathan-Turner, John. "The John Nathan-Turner Memoirs: Chapter Two—Season Eighteen: Brighton Beach Memoirs." *Doctor Who Magazine,* January 17, 1997, 16.

Neesham, Claire. "On the Right Wavelength." *Guardian*. Draft, dated January 28, 1991.

Nisbett, Alec. *The Technique of the Sound Studio: For Radio, Television, and Film*. 3rd ed., rev. Bungay, Suffolk: Focal Press, 1972.

Nobbs, George. *The Wireless Stars*. Norwich: Wensum Books, 1972.

Norden, Denis, Sybil Harper, and Norma Gilbert, eds. *Coming to You Live!: Behind-the-Screen Memories of Forties and Fifties Television*. London: Methuen, 1985.

Nyman, Michael. *Experimental Music: Cage and Beyond*. New York: Schirmer, 1974; reprint, Cambridge: Cambridge University Press, 1999.

O'Brian, Daniel. *SF, UK: How British Science Fiction Changed the World*. London: Reynolds and Hearne, 2000.

Palombini, Carlos. "Ideas for a Musicology of Electroacoustic Musics: Notes to a Reading of Landy." *Electronic Musicological Review* 6 (March 2001): 2.

————. "Pierre Schaeffer, 1953: Towards an Experimental Music." *Music & Letters* 74, no. 4 (November 1993): 542–57.

Paulu, Burton. *British Broadcasting: Radio and Television in the United Kingdom*. Minneapolis: University of Minnesota Press, 1956.

Pawley, Edward. *BBC Sound Engineering, 1922–1972*. London: BBC Publications, 1972.

Payton, Rodney J. "The Music of Futurism: Concerts and Polemics." *Musical Quarterly* 62, no. 1 (January 1976): 25–45.

Pinch, Trevor, and Frank Trocco. "The Social Construction of the Early Electronic Music Synthesizer." In *Music and Technology in the Twentieth-Century*, ed. Hans-Joachim Braun, 67–83. Baltimore: John Hopkins University Press, 2002.

Prendergast, Mark. *The Ambient Century: From Mahler to Trance—The Evolution of Sound in the Electronic Age*. Foreword by Brian Eno. New York: Bloomsbury, 2000.

Punter, Graham. "Radiophonics—BBC's Box of Tricks." *Music Week*, March 9, 1974.

Raaijmakers, Dick. *Cahier M: A Brief Morphology of Electric Sound*. Leuven: Leuven University Press, 2000.

"Radiophony and Melodrama." *Radio Times*, July 7, 1955, 39.

Reed, Henry. *Hilda Tablet and Others: Four Pieces for Radio*. London: British Broadcasting Corporation, 1971.

Reid, Colin. *Action Stations: A History of Broadcasting House*. London: Robson House, 1987.

Routh, Francis. *Contemporary British Music: The Twenty-Five Years from 1945 to 1970*. London: Macdonald, 1972.

Russell, Gary. "Roger Limb." *Skaro*, no. 17 (1983): 14.

Russolo, Luigi. *Arte dei rumori*. Translated by Barclay Brown. New York: Pendragon, 1986.

Scannell, Paddy, and David Cardiff. *A Social History of British Broadcasting*. Vol. 1, *1922–1939, Serving the Nation*. Oxford: Basil Blackwell, 1991.

Schaeffer, Pierre, ed. *Vers une musique expérimentale: La revue musicale*. Paris: Richard-Masse, 1957.

Schrader, Barry. *Introduction to Electro-Acoustic Music*. Englewood Cliffs, NJ: Prentice-Hall, 1982.

Sieveking, Lance. *The Stuff of Radio*. London: Cassell and Co., 1934.

Smith, Jeff. *The Sounds of Commerce: Marketing Popular Film Music.* New York: Columbia University Press, 1990.

Spratt, H. G. M. *Magnetic Tape Recording.* London: Heywood and Co., 1958.

Stewart, Madeau. "Is It Really Music." *Tablet,* April 26, 1958.

Stockhausen, Karlheinz. "Actualia." In *Die Reihe* 1 (1955): 45–51. English ed. Bryn Mawr, PA: Theodore Presser Co., 1958.

Stradling, Robert. *The English Musical Renaissance: 1860–1940.* London: Routledge, 1996.

Stuckenschmidt, Hans Heinz. "The Third Stage." In *Die Reihe* 1 (1955): 11–13. English ed. Bryn Mawr, PA: Theodore Presser Co., 1958.

Tamm, Eric. *Brian Eno: His Music and the Vertical Color of Sound.* New York: Da Capo, 1995.

Taylor, A. J. P. *English History 1914–1945.* Oxford: Oxford University Press, 1965.

Taylor, Timothy D. *Strange Sounds: Music, Technology and Culture.* New York: Routledge, 2001.

Telotte, J. P. *Replications: A Robotic History of the Science Fiction Film.* Urbana: University of Illinois Press, 1995.

Tulloch, John, and Henry Jenkins. *Science Fiction Audiences.* London: Routledge, 1995.

Tulloch, John, and Manuel Alvarado. *Doctor Who: The Unfolding Text.* New York: St. Martin's, 1983.

Ussachevsky, Vladimir. "Notes on a Piece for Tape Recorder." In *Problems of Modern Music: The Princeton Seminar in Advanced Musical Studies,* ed. Paul Henry Lang, 64–71. New York: W. W. Norton, 1962.

Vail, Mark. *Vintage Synthesizers.* San Francisco: GPI Books, 1993.

Wagner, Dave. "BBC Producer Explores 'Radiophonics.'" *Capital Times,* June 18, 1970.

Walker, Roy. "Whanged Words." *Listener,* March 6, 1958, 421–23.

Wallace, Philip Hope. *Time and Tide,* January 19, 1957.

Whitehead, Kate. *The Third Programme: A Literary History.* New York: Oxford University Press, 1989.

Williams, Raymond. *Television: Technology and Cultural Form.* Hanover, NH: Wesleyan University Press, 1992.

Wythenshawe, Lord Simon of. *The BBC from Within.* London: Victor Gollancz, 1953.

Young, Filson. *Shall I Listen: Studies in the Adventure and Technique of Broadcasting.* London: Constable and Co., 1933.

Zilliacus, Clas. *Beckett and Broadcasting.* Abo, Finland: Abo Akademi, 1976.

Index

Abbey Road Studios, 199
acousmêtre, 11–14, 16, 100, 193
   and All That Fall, 20, 23–24
   and Quatermass and the Pit, 75–78
   virtual acousmêtre, 13, 65, 70, 72
Adam Adamant Lives!, 116
Adamov, Arthur, 8, 24, 61
Adorno, Theodor, 5
Advance oscillators, 118
"Afterlife, The," 102
Aistrop, Jack, 147–148
Albiswerk variable voice frequency
   filter, 49
Alexander, F. W., 40
Alice in Wonderland, 168
All That Fall, 34–36, 39, 56, 59, 80
   and Piccadilly studios, 27, 51
   and Theatre of the Absurd, 8
   original production, 19–25
   reviews of, 34
Almuro, André, 35, 42, 59, 61
   Nadja Etoilée, 16–17, 28, 37, 42
"Amor Dei," 102–111
Amphitryon 38, 56, 59, 72
Amphonic Music, 199
Andromeda series, 65
Anouilh, Jean, 7
Antarctic Wind, 60
Arabian Nights, 60

Artbeat, 148
Artificial Reverberation Unit, 53
Ascent of Man, 140
Attenborough, David, 157, 201–2
Attree, Richard 208, 215
   Peace on Earth, 215
Attwell, Michael, 214
Audiotek, 129–30
Auric, Georges, 72, 87

Bach, Johann Sebastian, 6, 116,
   143, 174
Bacon, Francis, 4
Badings, Henk, 17
Bain, Norman 21–2, 31, 58–60, 66–67
Baker, John, 71, 96, 111, 180
   Adam Adamant Lives!, 116
   BBC Radiophonic Music, 124
   and "day of radiophonics," 110
   Dial M for Murder, 116
   frustration at Workshop
      limitations, 135, 142, 164
   "Classic Workshop" composers, 72, 96,
      102, 111, 139, 158
   jazz pianist, 115–7, 119
   Look and Read: "Joe and the Sheep
      Rustlers," 153–156, 161–162
   Out of the Unknown: "Welcome
      Home," 142–143

Baker, John (*continued*)
  "Radio Nottingham," 112–116, 142,
    147–148
  Vendetta, 116
Baker, Tom, 190
Bakewell, Michael, 23, 59
Ballad of Mari Lwyd, 61
Barry, John, 146
Bartòk, Bela, 6
Baschet, Francois, 97
Battlestar Galactica, 184
Bayerische Rundfunk, Der, 110
Beatles, The, 84, 126, 199
  "Get Back," 199
Beckett, Samuel, 7–8, 19–25, 39, 56, 80
Beethoven, Ludwig van, 6
Belshazzar's Feast, 18
Bennett, Richard Rodney, 179
Bentine, Michael, 9
Berio, Luciano, 37
Bickford, Lovett, 189
Bidmead, Christopher H., 190
Bird, Richard "Dickie," 54, 56–57, 59–62, 93
Bermange, Barry, 102–111
  "Afterlife, The," 102
  "Amor Dei," 102–111
  "Dreams, The," 102, 104–105, 110
  "Evenings of Certain Lives," 102
  Inventions for Radio, 102–104
Berry, Chuck, 149
Blades, James, 18
Blake's Seven, 170, 185, 200–201
Blair, Howard, 61
Blyton, Carey, 168–169
  Doctor Who: "Death to the Daleks," 168
  Doctor Who: "Revenge of the
    Cybermen," 168–9
Body in Question, The, 173–177
Bolero, 188
Bowen, Lawrence Gordon, 169
Bowie, David, 178
Bradnum, Frederick, 18, 29–30, 34
Brahms, Johannes, 6
Braque, Georges, 46
Bray, Barbara, 26–27
Briant, Michael, 145–146

Bridson, D. G., 20
Briscoe, Desmond, 54–56, 92–93, 95,
    199, 207–208
  All That Fall, 21–26, 56
  ARP Odyssey, 151
  and distribution of work, 147, 163,
    165, 201
  as "mad scientist," 111
  Doctor Who, 97–99, 101, 160–1, 186
  EMS synthesizer, 137–139
  and falling out with Daphne Oram, 72–73
  biography, 20
  and logbook, 60–62
  Moog synthesizer, 128–135
  and musicality of Workshop
    projects, 122–123, 158–159
  opening day, 62
  Outside, 78–81
  and popular music, 148–149, 180
  pre–Workshop projects, 59
  *Private Dreams and Public
    Nightmares*, 31–32
  Quatermass and the Pit, 74–78
  and his relationship with other
    composers, 142–143
  and the reorganization of Workshop
    staff, 152–153
  Stone Tape, The, 142
  Under the Loofah Tree, 66–67
  Wall Walks Slowly, A, 173
  and Workshop budget, 169–171
BBC
  Alexandra Palace, 170
  Ariel, 20
  Ariel Theatre Group, 168
  Audience Research Department, 33
  Bristol Natural History Unit, 201–202
  BBC 1, 166, 172
  BBC Enterprises, 124
  BBC Music, 214
  BBC Records, 147, 177
  BBC Schools, 153
  Broadcasting House, 61, 122
  and broadcast monopoly, 6
  and class hierarchy within the
    BBC, 58, 152–153

Control Room, 57–58
Design Department, 126
Drama Department, 5, 7–8, 15, 26, 37, 39–48, 56, 62, 66, 81, 93, 122, 129, 171, 185, 187, 214
Education Department, 6
Effects Library, 126
Electrophonic Effects Committee, 36–37, 55–56
Engineering Department, 38–39, 58, 93, 125, 127, 133
Equipment Department, 48
experimental fund, 27
Features Department, 5, 8, 17–18, 36–37, 40, 43–44, 46–47
Finance, 125
Further Education, 179
Home Service, 7, 9, 25, 27
Light Programme, 7, 9–10, 39, 47–48
Maida Vale, 38, 45, 58, 60, 89, 92, 122–123, 133–134, 149, 170
Micro, 205
Multimedia Corporation, 211
Music Copyright Department, 97
Music Department, 5–7, 16–17, 31, 34, 39–48, 56, 62, 123, 125, 183
Nightingale Square, 38, 45
Open University, 170
Overseas Transcription Service, 11
Piccadilly Two studio, 21, 27, 31, 51
Producer Choice, 213–215
Programme Operations, 129
Radio 1, 147
Radio 2, 167
Radio 3, 149, 157
Radio 4, 168
Radio Aberdeen, 147
Radio Nottingham, 112
Radio Production Resources, 215
Radio Sheffield, 112
Radiophonic Effects Committee, 37–40, 48, 54, 60, 62, 71, 122
Radiophonic Technical Committee, 101, 109, 127, 133, 151, 160, 170–171
Redundant Plant, 48

Research Division, 37
Savoy Hill Studios, 135
and sexism, 73–74
Sound Effects Centre, Western House, 126
Symphony Orchestra, 38, 45
Talks Department, 129
Television Centre, 216
Television Department, 84
Television Music, 97
Television Science, 172
Television Sound, 129
Third Programme, 7–8, 15–16, 18–20, 26–28, 30, 33–34, 47, 90, 106, 157
World Service, 81
BBC Radiophonic Music, 124, 151
BBC Radiophonic Workshop: A Retrospective, 78
Britten, Benjamin, 19
Brock, Richard, 201
Buchla, Don, 143
Buck Rogers, 184
Burnett, Jimmy, 71
Bush, Kate, 203
   "Babooshka," 203

C++ (computer program), 211
Cain, David, 147
   Artbeat, 148
   "Autumn and Winter," 124
   BBC Radiophonic Music, 124
   and "Classic Workshop" composers, 102
   Day of the Triffids, 138
   Foundation Trilogy, 138, 158
   History of Everyman, The, 148, 152
   Hobbit, The, 138
   Pre-Bach, 148
   RUS, 137
   War of the Worlds, 138
Cambridge University, 73, 98, 106
Campbell, Archie, 15
Canadian Broadcasting Corporation, 131
Cardiff, David, 6
Careerist, The, 14

Carlos, Walter, 143, 146, 174
  Clockwork Orange, A, 146
  Switched-On Bach, 143, 174
Cary, Tristram, 16–18, 131–132, 200
Cathn, Nesta, 60
"Cathode, Ray," 84–85
Catlin, H., 61
Changes, The, 165–167, 178
Channel 4, 214
Chase, Len, 61
Checkland, Michael, 172
Children of the Green Knowe, 210
Children's Hour, The, 61
Chilton, Charles, 10
Chion, Michel, 11–13, 23–24
Chowning, John, 204–205
City University, London, 208
Clarke, Malcolm, 197, 209–210
  2026: There Will Come Soft Rains, 173
  Doctor Who: "Earthshock," 188
  Doctor Who: "Sea Devils, The,"
    143–146, 162–163
Clayton, Harold, 59
Cleverdon, Douglas, 35, 42, 47, 60–61
  as radio pioneer, 8
  Hedge Backwards, A, 18–19
  Nadja Etoilée, 16–17
  Night Thoughts, 18, 37
  Opium, 28, 59
  Orestes, 17
  Orpheus, 63, 87–92, 93, 123
  Under Milk Wood, 24
Clockwork Orange, A, 146
Cocteau, Jean, 28, 63, 87, 91
Columbia–Princeton Studio, 3, 56
Cologne, Germany, 3–4, 35–36, 43, 56, 183
Computer Music Journal, 209
Cooper, Giles, 15, 25–28, 56, 63, 67–71
Cosmos, 173
Crawford (superintendent engineer,
  Sound Broadcasting), 61
Creation of the Animals, The, 61
Crumb, George, 145
CueCard (computer program), 211

Daily Chronicle, 120–121
Daily Mirror, 84–85, 101

Daily Telegraph, 58
daleks, 17, 131, 168, 189
  in the press, 101, 110
Darmstadt, 48
Dartington Summer School, 48
DaSilva, Richard, 199
Davies, Betty, 143
Davison, Peter, 190
Dear Sensibility, 15
Decca Records, 95, 98
Delgado, Roger, 193
Derbyshire, Delia, 117, 122, 161–162,
    164, 180
  "Afterlife, The," 102
  "Amor Dei," 102–111
  "Blue Veils and Golden Sands," 124
  BBC Radiophonic Music, 124
  and "Classic Workshop" composers, 71,
    111, 139, 158
  Daily Chronicle, 120
  and "day of radiophonics," 110
  "Delaware" synthesizer, 134–136,
    140–143
  "Delian Mode, The," 124
  Doctor Who signature tune
    ("Delaware"), 137, 140, 186
  Doctor Who signature tune (1963),
    96–102, 108, 110, 124, 133–134, 186
  "Dreams, The," 102, 104–105, 110
  "Evenings of Certain Lives," 102
  frustration at Workshop limitations, 73,
    129, 142–143, 171–172
  "IEE 100," 134–136
  Inventions for Radio, 102–104
  "Mattachin," 124
  Moog synthesizers, 130
  Play for Today: "O Fat White
    Woman," 140
  "Pot au Feu," 124
  Unit Delta Plus, 131
Dial M for Murder, 116
Dial Rix, 110
Digidesign's Sound Tools, 210
Disagreeable Oyster, The, 25–28, 56, 59,
    67, 70
Dissolution of Dominic Boot, 132
Dixon, Charles, 201

Dockstader, Tod, 122
Doctor Who, 137–138, 155, 157, 162, 180
 "Claws of Axos, The," 146
 daleks, 17, 189
 "Daleks' Masterplan, The," 131
 "Dead Planet, The," 17, 131
 "Death to the Daleks," 168
 Doctor Who: The Music, 189
 Doctor Who: The Music II, 189
 "Earthshock," 188
 "Full Circle," 190, 195
 "Horns of Nimon, The," 185–186
 "Keeper of Traken, The," 195
 "Kinda," 203
 "Leisure Hive, The," 188–189
 "Logopolis," 190–198
 "Mark of the Rani, The," 205–207
 "Mind of Evil, The," 146
 "Revelation of the Daleks," 189
 "Revenge of the Cybermen," 168–169
 "Sea Devils, The," 143–146, 162
 signature tune ("Delaware"), 137,
  140, 186
 signature tune (1963), 96–102, 108,
  110, 124, 133–134, 186
 signature tune (Howell), 186–189
 special sound, 101–102, 159, 169–170
 "Snakedance," 203
 "Stones of Blood, The," 200
 as a strain on Workshop resources, 128, 160
 "Underwater Menace, The," 117
"Dreams, The," 102, 104–105, 110
Duncan, Trevor, 75–78
Dutot, John, 172, 207

echo, 21–22, 31–32, 36, 53, 80
 echo rooms 38, 53, 61
Eckersley, T. H., 35
Edinburgh Festival, 61
Eimert, Herbert, 4–5, 37
Electronic Music Studios (EMS), 131,
 173, 180, 200
EMS vocoder 5000, 169–170, 174,
 187–188, 202
Electrophon, 139, 140, 180, 206
elektronische Musik, 4–5, 7, 16, 35
Elen, Richard G., 211

Elisabeth II, 134–135
Emery, Terry, 167, 178
EMI, 84
Eno, Brian, 117
 Discreet Music, 117
Esslin, Martin, 8, 20, 171
Etudes Übertongemische, 37
"Evenings of Certain Lives," 102
Eventide Harmonizer, 178–179, 200, 209
Exorcist, The, 145

Fagandini, Maddalena, 71, 73, 84–87,
 112, 119
 Orpheus, 63, 87–92, 93, 123
 Outside, 78–81
 Science and Industry, 81–83
 "Time Beat," 84
Fassett, Jim, 37
Fernando, John, 167
Ferris, Paul, 24
filtering, 12, 17, 23, 32, 36, 56, 67, 160
 Albis, 119
 Leevers–Rich Octave Filter, 119
 Portable Effects Unit, 52–54, 61, 70, 118
 Variable Correction Unit, 52, 118
Flynn, Caryl, 75
Foundation Trilogy, 158
Fourth Dimension, 147–151, 154, 177
Freed, Adrian, 208
frequency modulation (FM)
 synthesis, 204–205
Fricker, Peter Racine, 46
Full Circle, 215
"future," representations of, 145, 152,
 178, 186
Futurist movement, 4

Garrard, M. R. G., 42, 54–55, 60–61
Gascoyne, David, 18
Genet, Jean, 8
George, Brian, 32, 35–37, 48–49, 72
Gerhard, Roberto, 145
Giants of Steam, 93, 95–96
Gibbs, Jonathan, 201, 203–208, 210
 Doctor Who: "Mark of the Rani,
  The," 205–207
 Tales from the South China Seas, 203

Gibson, John, 23, 34, 59–60
Gielgud, Val, 8, 27
Gilliam, Lawrence, 20, 45–47
Glock, William, 47–48
Gluck, Christoph Willibald, 88
Goldsmith, Jerry, 145
Goldsmiths College, 72
The Goon Show, 9–10, 19, 23, 26–30
Gorbman, Claudia, 74
Grainer, Ron, 187
    Doctor Who signature tune, 96–102,
        108, 110, 187
    Giants of Steam, 93, 95–96
Grainger, Percy, 71
Gramophone, 124
grams, 10, 86
Gray, Frances, 27
Grey, Vera, 110
Greenhalgh, Mollie, 26
Greenslade, Wallace, 10
Grimwade, Peter, 190
Guardian, The, 117, 135, 140, 214

Hanley, James, 62, 66
Hardwick, Michael, 15
Harrison, John, 71, 93
    "day of radiophonics," 110
Heartbreak House, 56
Hebrew Section, 61
Hedge Backwards, A, 18
Hellings, Sarah, 207
Henderson, A., 60–61
Henry, Pierre, 4
Heppenstall, Rayner, 15
Heritage, The, 59–60, 62
hi-fi systems, 68
Highland Morning, 147
Hinchcliffe, Philip, 168
Hindemith, Paul, 81
History of Everyman, The, 148
Hitchhiker's Guide to the Galaxy, The, 157,
    178–180, 186
Hobbit, The, 138
Hobson, Harold, 24
Hodgson, Brian, 94, 119, 143, 161, 208
    Ascent of Man, 140
    BBC Radiophonic Music, 124

and "Classic Workshop"
    composers, 111, 139, 143, 158
and the closing of the Workshop, 213–215
and a "day of radiophonics," 110
"Delaware" synthesizer, 133–135,
    137–138
and distribution of work, 163, 201
Doctor Who incidental music 185–186,
    206–207
Doctor Who: "Sea Devils, The" 145
Doctor Who signature tune (1963),
    98–99
Doctor Who special sound, 102, 128,
    131, 133, 145, 159
Doctor Who: "Underwater Menace,
    The," 117
Electrophon, 139–140
Giants of Steam, 93, 95–96
In A Covent Garden, 140
and the multi-color tone organ, 152
on Delia Derbyshire, 142
on Desmond Briscoe, 129
on John Baker, 142
studio organizer, 171–172, 182–183,
    204, 207
Tomorrow People, The, 140
Unit Delta Plus, 131, 199
Workshop budget, 171–172, 180, 204
Holst, Gustav, 188
    Planets, The: "Mars, Bringer of
        War," 188
Honegger, Arthur, 95
    Pacific 231, 95
Hope Wallace, Philip, 24
Horizon: "The Case of the Ancient
    Astronauts," 178
Horizon: "Space for Man," 178
Hörspiele, 5
Howell, Peter, 147, 161, 205, 209–210
    Alice in Wonderland, 167–168
    and the closing of the Workshop, 212
    and the influence of the
        Workshop, 216
    Body in Question, The, 173–177
    Children of the Green Knowe, 210
    click track, 192, 197
    distribution of work, 125

Doctor Who: "Horns of Nimon, The," 185–186
Doctor Who: "Kinda," 203
Doctor Who: "Leisure Hive, The," 188–189
Doctor Who: "Revenge of the Cybermen," 168–169
Doctor Who signature tune (Howell), 186–189
Doctor Who: "Snakedance," 203
Fairlight Computer Musical Instrument, 201, 203
Full Circle, 215
Horizon: "The Case of the Ancient Astronauts," 178
Horizon: "Space for Man," 178
Mind Beyond, The: "The Daedalus Equations," 168–169
Through a Glass Darkly, 177–178
Top Gear, 168
Treasure of Abbott Thomas, 169
Wall Walks Slowly, A, 173
Howes, Frank, 45
Howgill, R. J. F., 42–44, 48
Hume, Anna, 165
Hussein, Waris, 98
Hypercard, 211

I Talk to Myself, 60
Ibsen, Henrik, 25
Innocents, The, 72
Institut de Recherche et Coordination Acoustique/Musique (IRCAM), 183
Institute of Electrical Engineers (IEE), 134–136
interval music, 66, 83–87
Invasion, 61
Inventions for Radio, 102–104
Ionesco, Eugène, 8, 24
Italia Prize, 17, 46
It's That Man Again, 9
ITV, 199
Izzard, Bryan, 61

Jack in the Box, The, 61
James, M. R., 169
Japanese Fishermen, The, 16–18

Jarre, Jean–Michel, 177, 185
Jarre, Maurice, 16, 37
Jason oscillators, 99, 118, 123
Jaws, 194
jazz, 88, 142, 166, 176
Joachim, Hans, 120
Johnson, J., 61
Johnson, Mark, 193
Johnstone, Maurice, 42, 48
Jones, Glynis, 142
  Stone Tape, The, 142
Journey into Space, 10–14, 16
Julius Caesar, 98

Keefe, Bernard, 42–44
Keightley, Keir, 68
keying units, 92, 123, 125–127
Kingsland, Paddy, 125, 171–172, 200–201, 214
  and Delia Derbyshire, 164
  and Peter Howell, 168
  and popular music, 161–162, 208
  Changes, The, 165–167, 178
  Doctor Who: "Full Circle," 190, 195
  Doctor Who: "Horns of Nimon, The," 185–186
  Doctor Who: "Logopolis," 190–198, 205
  Fourth Dimension, 147–152, 154, 177
  "Get Back," 199
  The Hitchhiker's Guide to the Galaxy, 157, 178–180, 186
  Look and Read: "Joe and the Sheep Rustlers," 153–156
  Music and Principles, 179
Kneale, Nigel, 75
Koch, Ludwig, 80
Kraftwerk, 182

Lakoff, Mark, 193
Lady Vanishes, The, 14
Lamb Lies Down on Broadway, 177
Lambert, Verity, 97–98, 100–101
Language of the Sea, The, 61
Lasry, Jacques, 97
Led Zeppelin, 178
Lenco TD/7 transcription turntables, 49, 51

Les Structures Sonores, 97
Lewell, Denis, 60
Lewis, John, 139, 206–207
Ligeti, György, 179
    Lontano, 179
Limb, Roger, 125, 172–173, 195–196,
    201, 209
    and the music factory mentality, 164, 193
    Doctor Who incidental music 186
    Doctor Who: "Keeper of Traken,
        The," 195
    Doctor Who: "Revelation of the
        Daleks," 189
    Look and Read: "Cloud Burst,"
        161–163
Listener, The, 67, 95
Littleton, Humphrey, 158
Littlewood, Joan, 20
Life on Earth, 202
Living Planet, The, 157
Lodge, Bernard, 98
Lontano, 179
Look and Read: "Cloud Burst," 161–163
Look and Read: "Joe and the Sheep
    Rustlers," 153–156
Lord of the Flies, 15, 166
Los Angeles, California, 208
Lowthor Manufacturing Company, 159
Lutyens, Elisabeth, 18–19, 43

MacDowell, Jeannie, 57, 62, 71
Macintosh Computer, 182, 208–212
MacNeice, Louis, 14, 20
Maderna, Bruno, 37
Making of the Bomb, The, 110
Manchester Guardian, 24
Manchester University, 128
Mancini, Henry, 166
Mann, Herbie, 197
Mansfield, John, 172
Manuel, Geoffrey, 138
Mark of the Unicorn's Composer,
    210
Marsh, Margaret, 68
Martin, George, 84
masculinity, 16, 25–26, 67–70

Mason, Michael, 203
Mathry Beacon, 15–16, 25, 70
McClary, Susan, 5
McWhinnie, Donald, 35–36, 48–49,
    54, 64
    All That Fall, 19–25
    as radio pioneer, 8
    Disagreeable Oyster, The, 27
    discussing radio drama, 14–15
    logbook entries, 60–61
    Mathry Beacon, 15
    Ocean, The, 66–67
    pre-Radiophonic Workshop projects, 59
    Private Dreams and Public
        Nightmares, 28–33, 64
Mellotronics, 125–126
metadiegetic music, 197
Metamorphosis, 59
metaphor, 193–4
MIDI, 156, 172, 182, 204–205, 207–211
Milan, 43, 56
Miller, Jonathan, 174–177
Miller Organ Company, 41, 122, 152
Miller Spinetta, 118, 152, 160
Milligan, Spike, 9
Mills, Dick, 71, 94, 152, 189, 200–201
    and BBC hierarchy, 58
    and Room 15, 39
    BBC Radiophonic Music 124
    "day of radiophonics," 110
    Doctor Who: "Death to the Daleks," 168
    Doctor Who signature tune (1963),
        96–102, 108, 110, 124, 133–134, 186
    Doctor Who special sound, 102, 133,
        138, 146, 159, 169–170, 185, 209
    Giants of Steam, 93, 95–96
    The Hitchhiker's Guide to the
        Galaxy, 179
    Outside, 78–81
    Quatermass and the Pit, 74–78
    Sonic Solution's NoNoise, 215
Mind Beyond, The: "The Daedalus
    Equations," 168–169
Minerva Programme, 6
Mr. Goodjohn and Mr. Badjack, 60
Mixing desks

Glen sound mixing desk, 160
"Glowpot" mixing desk, 92, 205
OBA/8, 53, 118
Yamaha DMP7 mixer, 210
modernism, 5, 65–68, 120–121
Monitor, 56, 97, 110
Moog, Robert, 127–130, 133
Morgan, Dennis, 71
Morris, John (Controller of the Third
    Programme), 20
Morris, John (discharged prisoner
    portrayed in *Outside*), 78
Morson, Tony, 211
Mozart, Wolfgang Amadeus, 6, 25
Muirhead decade oscillator, 49, 52–53,
    66, 89, 118
Muirhead squarewave shaper, 49, 53, 119
multi-colour tone organ, 118
and its location, 180, 122, 152, 160
as substitute for the Workshop, 41,
    44–45, 47
use in *Doctor Who*, 117
multi-tone piano, 125
Music and Principles, 179
Music Club, 143
"music factory" attitude, 164, 172, 189
Music, Movement, and Mime, 110
Music Now, 143
Musical Research Ltd. *see* Miller Organ
    Company
Musical Times, 91
musique concrète, 17–20, 27–30, 32–37
and the Music Department, 40, 42
and Workshop composers, 51, 56,
    62–3, 65, 96, 159–161, 202
Parisian examples, 4–5, 7, 16–17, 23,
    33, 36–37
musique concrète renforcée, 19
Mutazioni, 37

Nadja Etoilée, 16–17, 28, 37, 42
Nathan–Turner, John, 183–189, 207
National Physics Laboratory, 14
Nationwide, 173
Nesbitt, Alec, 35, 39, 55, 72
New Atlantis, 4

New Comment, 110
new wave movement, 172
Nicholson, Norman, 173
Night Thoughts, 18, 37
Notturno, 37

Observer, 24, 96, 110–111
Ocean, The, 59–60, 62, 66–67
O'Farrell, Mary, 18
One Eye Wild, 14
Operation Luna, 11
Opium: An Essay in Musique Concrète,
    28–29, 31, 34, 59
Oram, Daphne, 53–57, 59–63, 66–73,
    81, 141
Oramics, 71–72
*Private Dreams and Public
    Nightmares*, 31–32
report on electronic music, 35
Orestes, 17
Orfeo et Euridice, 88
Orphée, 87
Orpheus, 63, 87–92, 93, 123
Orwell, George, 75
Out of the Unknown
"Time in Advance," 117
"Welcome Home," 142
Outside, 78–81
Oxford Arena Theatre, 61

Paris, France, 3–4, 16, 20, 35–36, 56
Parker, Elizabeth, 172, 200–203,
    209–210, 212
Assignment, 215
Doctor Who: "Stones of Blood,
    The," 200
Full Circle, 215
*The Hitchhiker's Guide to the
    Galaxy*, 179
Living Planet, The, 157, 200–203
Parker, Harry, 179
*The Hitchhiker's Guide to the
    Galaxy*, 179
Parlophone Records, 84
Peace on Earth, 215
Pearson, Leslie, 185

Penderecki, Krzysztof, 145
Performers Rights Society, 111
Perkins, Geoffrey, 179
Picasso, Pablo, 46
"Pink Album, The" *see* BBC Radiophonic
  Music
Pink Floyd, 157
Pillaudin, Roger, 37
Pinter, Harold, 8
Planet of the Apes, 145
The Planets: "Mars, Bringer of War," 188
Play for Today: "O Fat White Woman," 140
popular music, 152, 168, 172, 177, 180
  and the use of electronic
    instruments, 95, 101, 125, 157,
    178, 197
  and Richard Attree, 208
  and John Baker, 115
  and Paddy Kingsland, 147–148,
    161, 199
  and Unit Delta Plus, 131
Popp, Andre, 122
Porter, Pip, 46–47, 56
postmodernism, 121
Potter, Dennis, 214
Pre-Bach, 148
Predator, 184
Prevost film-viewing desk, 170
Private Dreams and Public Nightmares,
    28–34, 52, 56, 59–60, 67
  introduction to, 29–30, 64
Professional Performer, 210
Prometheus Unbound, 56
Punch, 111
punk movement, 172

Quatermass and the Pit, 74–78
Quatermass series, 65, 75
Queen of Air and Darkness, The, 14

Radio Belgrade, 132
Radiodiffusion-Télévision Française, 17,
    27–28, 36
"Radio Nottingham," 112–116, 142,
    147–148
Radiophonic Workshop-21, 173

Radio Times, 17, 27, 72, 95, 149, 179
  and modern music, 7
  and Donald McWhinnie, 30, 67
Ravel, Maurice, 188
  Bolero, 188
Read, John, 94
Reagan, Ronald, 206
Red Planet Mars, 11
Reed, Henry, 18–19
Reith, John, 6
Reizenstein, Franz, 59
reverb, 11, 23, 53
Rheingold, Das, 195
Riley, Ray, 209
Riley, Terry, 179
  Rainbow in Curved Air, A, 179
Rix, Brian, 110
Robbins Music, 84
Roland vocoder, 209
Rolling Stones, The, 149
Romanticism, 5
Rose, David E., 78
Royal Academy of Music, 115
Royal Albert Hall, 48, 53, 134–135, 140, 180
Ruisselle, 37

Sagan, Carl, 173
Saint and the Sinner, The, 18
Saint–Saëns, Camille, 188
Salmon, Keith, 110
Salter, Leonard, 37, 97
Sartre, Jean–Paul, 7
Scannell, Paddy, 6
Schaeffer, Pierre, 4, 18, 21, 33, 123
Schoenberg, Arnold, 5–6
Schott Publishing, 183
Schubert, Franz, 6
Science and Industry, 81–83
science fiction, 150, 185, 217
Score, 16, 47
Scott, Raymond, 122
Searle, Humphrey, 18, 37, 43, 46
Secombe, Harry, 9–10
Sellers, Peter, 9–10
Sentimental Journey, A, 15
Shadows, The, 84, 149

Shakespeare, William, 58
Shaw, George Bernard, 56
Sholpo, Yevgeny Alexandrovitch, 71
Shostakovich, Dmitri, 205
Sieveking, Lance, 8
Simon and Garfunkel, 178
Simpson, Dudley, 133, 146–147, 162, 180,
    184–185
  Ascent of Man, 140
  Doctor Who: "The Claws of Axos," 146
  Doctor Who: "The Mind of Evil," 146
  Doctor Who: "Underwater Menace,
    The," 117
  In a Covent Garden, 140
  "Master" theme, 193
  Tomorrow People, The, 140
Smith, Jeff, 166
Smith Brindle, Reginald, 91
Smyth, Ethyl, 18
Snow, C. P., 64, 174
Society for the Promotion of New
    Music, 42, 44
Society for Radio Authors, 173
Sonic Solution's NoNoise
    Workstation, 215
sound effects, 9–11, 14–15, 23–24, 27–29,
    31, 36–37, 126
Southworth's Total Music and
    Performer, 209–10
special sound, 66, 153, 209
  and confusion with music, 75, 145–146
  and *The Changes*, 165
  and *Doctor Who*, 128, 131, 133, 159,
    169, 183, 185, 189, 200–201
  and *The Hitchhiker's Guide to the
    Galaxy*, 179
Springboard, 143
Squires, Ken, 58, 61
Standing, Michael, 27
Stanford University, 183, 204
Star Trek, 184
Star Wars, 183
Starie, Joe, 98
Steiner, Max, 195
stereo radio, 124, 137, 148, 157
Stereo Week, 149

Sterne, Laurence, 15
Stobart, J. C., 6
stock music, 124
Stockhausen, Karlheinz, 4, 21, 37,
    123, 182
  Gesang der Jünglinge, 106–107
Stone Tape, The, 142
Stoppard, Tom, 132
  Dissolution of Dominic Boot, 132
Stravinsky, Igor, 6
Stuckenschmidt, H. H., 5
Studio E, 61
Study II, 37
Sun, The, 207
Sunday Times, 28
Sutton, Sid, 187
Swann, Donald, 19
Symphonie pour un Homme Seul, 33
Symphony of the Birds, 37
Synchresis, 12–13
synchretic acousmêtre, 12, 14, 16, 75, 100
Syncwriter, 205–206, 209–211
synthesizers, 121–151, 158–159, 162,
    172–178
  ARP Odyssey, 133, 151–152, 154–155,
    159, 162, 165, 169, 176, 178,
    187, 209
  Buchla, 143
  Crystal Palace (Multi-input
    Programmable Switch), 127, 205
  Elka Synthex, 209
  EMS Synthi 100 ("Delaware"),
    132–140, 142–144, 148–150, 152,
    154, 159–161, 162, 165, 168–170,
    180, 184–185, 200, 204
  EMS VCS3 ("Putney"), 121, 131–135,
    137, 140, 142–143, 145, 148–149,
    152, 154, 159–160, 162, 167–169, 180
  Emulator II, 209
  Fairlight Computer Musical
    Instrument, 201, 203–205, 209
  Jupiter 4, 192, 201
  Mellotron, 125–127
  Minimoog, 130
  Moog, 125, 127–132, 143, 174
  Moog Synthesizer 3, 130

synthesizers (*continued*)
  Oberheim OBX, 192
  Organino, 151–152, 159
  Oscar Mono Synthesizer, 209
  PPG Wave 2.2, 202, 209
  Roland 100M, 209
  Wasp Deluxe, 209
  Yamaha CS–80, 174, 187, 201
  Yamaha DX–1, 209
  Yamaha DX–7, 204–205, 208–209
  Yamaha SY2, 167, 169, 178, 192, 194, 197, 202
  Yamaha TX816, 205, 208

Tales from the South China Seas, 203
Talking Bird, The, 61
Talking of Films, 61
Tangerine Dream, 157, 177
tape recorders
  EMI BTR/2 tape recorders, 50–51, 118
  EMI TR90 tape recorders, 50–51, 118
  Ferrograph tape recorders, 51, 118
  Leevers–Rich Mark VI tape recorders, 118, 160
  Motosacoche tape recorders, 49–51, 60, 118
  Philips tape recorders, 118, 170, 180
  Reflectograph 500 tape recorders, 49, 51
  Studer tape recorders, 137, 149, 160–161, 170
  Telefunken tape recorders, 133
Taylor, Timothy, 26
Thames Television, 140
Thatcher, Margaret, 206
Theatre of the Absurd, 8, 15, 19–20, 67
theremin, 26
This Sporting Life, 145
Thomas, Dylan, 8, 24
Thomson (producer of *The Language of the Sea*), 61
Through a Glass Darkly, 177–178
Tiller, Terence, 18
Time and Tide, 24
"Time Beat," 84
Times (London), 24, 33–34, 45, 58, 62, 135
Tin Pan Alley, 148

Tippett, Michael, 46, 183
  Symphony No. 4, 183
Tombs, T. W., 127
Tonality, 123–125
  and British modernism, 65
  and "Amor Dei," 109
  and *Doctor Who*: "Logopolis," 193–195, 197
  and *Doctor Who*: "The Sea Devils," 144–146, 162
  and *Doctor Who* signature tune, 96
  and *Look and Read*, 163
  and *The Ocean*, 66–67
  and *Private Dreams and Public Nightmares*, 32
  and "Time in Advance," 117
Towie Castle, 61
Townshend, Pete, 177
Trickster of Seville, The, 18
Trodd, Kenith, 214
Tryggvason, Trygg, 200
2001: A Space Odyssey, 184
2026: There Will Come Soft Rains, 173
Tubular Bells, 177
Tulloch, John, 184

Under Milk Wood, 8, 24
Under the Loofah Tree, 61, 63, 67–71
Unit Delta Plus, 131, 139
University of East Anglia, 200
University of Wisconsin, 132
Utrecht, Holland, 183

Vangelis, 157, 173
Veale, Eddie, 130
Vendetta, 116
Ventures, The, 149
Venus Programme, 6
virtual synchresis, 13
Vision (computer program), 210
voltage-control synthesis, 128–129, 139, 142, 157
  and move away from tape techniques, 121, 125

Wade, Frank, 40–42, 44–47
Wall Walks Slowly, A, 173

Wagner, Richard, 30, 43, 88, 195
  Das Rheingold, 195
  Tristan und Isolde, 90
Waiting for Godot, 19
Waterhouse, Matthew, 190
Wavemaker, 206
Webern, Anton, 43
Weeks, Sue, 163
White, Ray 205, 209
Wilkinson, Marc, 94
Williams, Edward, 202
  Life on Earth, 202
Williams, John, 194
  Jaws, 194
Wilson, Mark, 211
Winter Journey, A, 34, 56, 59
"Wobbulator" (beat-frequency
  oscillator), 53, 118
World in Peril, The, 11
Worsley, Jenyth, 143

Xenakis, Iannis, 124

Yamaha QX1 sequencer, 207–209
Yeoman-Clark, Richard, 133–134, 161,
  164, 171
  and composition, 138, 183, 200
  and the "Delaware" synthesizer, 137
  as "facilities organizer," 139, 151, 153,
    169–170
Young, David, 137, 164
  and "crystal palace," 127, 205
  and "day of radiophonics," 110
  and "glowpot" mixing desk,
    92, 205
  and keying units, 125
Young, Phil, 71
  Science and Industry, 81–83

Zilliacus, Clas, 20
Zinovieff, Peter, 131–132, 134, 137, 161, 173

8807209R00160

Printed in Great Britain
by Amazon.co.uk, Ltd.,
Marston Gate.